ALBERT BALMER is now retired and lives with his wife, Sylvia, in Burtonwood. He has two children and four grandchildren. Prior to his retirement he worked as a quality control technician at Triplex Safety Co, a subsidiary of Pilkington Bros PLC.

A Cyprus Journey

Memoirs of National Service

A Cyprus Journey

Memoirs of National Service

Albert Balmer

ATHENA PRESS
LONDON

ISBN 978 1 84748 335 5

First published 2008 by
ATHENA PRESS
Queen's House, 2 Holly Road
Twickenham TW1 4EG
United Kingdom

Printed for Athena Press

Acknowledgements

I would like to thank my son, Steven, his wife, Janet, and also my grandson, Ryan Dixon, for their help and patience in helping me to write this account on the computer, with which I am still not fully conversant.

Also my great friend, Dennis Baker, for his recollections of our service together, and for allowing permission for the use of the EOKA pamphlet he has in his possession.

Last but not least my wife, Sylvia, who helped to edit this memoir.

Contents

Introduction

At the outbreak of war in 1939, conscription was introduced and continued until the year the war ended in 1945. From then onwards the name conscription was dropped and compulsory time with the armed services was known by the name of national service. The only way a person could temporarily be excused from the service was to be in a reserved occupation that would give the right of deferment as long as that person stayed in the chosen occupation. An apprentice to a trade would only be deferred until his twenty-first birthday or until his apprenticeship ended. A further deferment could be obtained if the person involved was continuing in a college or university degree up to about twenty-seven years of age.

In the beginning all parts of the armed forces took national servicemen. As the years passed, however, the more elite parts of the services began to take only regular personnel. Early enlisted servicemen took over from forces scattered all over the globe and the British Empire who had witnessed years of service. From the time the war ended the Empire was starting to go into a decline as more and more countries wanted their independence. It would be a job for the national serviceman along with regular enlisted soldiers to see these transitions through. Some would be expected to serve outside the Commonwealth.

The places covered, known as combat zones, were: India, Palestine, Lebanon, Korea, Malaya, Kenya, Aden, Suez, Northern Ireland and Cyprus.

Troubles arose in these places and national servicemen took part in action in all of them. Some people will say it was a holiday. Those who can say that were the fortunate ones, because quite a number of men did not return home alive.

It could take as many as four men to keep just one soldier in the front line. Many men served in regiments that trained to be support units, not front line. However, this is not to say that an order might not send a regiment of this type into a conflict zone to do support duties.

Another false impression is that national service lasted only for the period of training. It didn't. At first, in the late 1940s, it would be eighteen months. It was later extended to a full two years. This story starts in the later years of 1957 and covers the near ending of national service a few years before the army became a regular, non-conscripted army again.

Before 1955 Cyprus was a rather quiet island where all nationalities could spend peaceful holidays with their families but, in April of that year, bombings began to happen. It wasn't very long before an organisation known as EOKA[1] commenced a campaign of bombings and shootings; the main targets would be British servicemen and their wives. However, as time passed, as with all conflicts, the problems grew until all nationalities and genders became targets.

EOKA was an organisation demanding unity with Greece and was determined to push its demands to the full extent. However, the other main body of people on the island were of Turkish descent, and this then gave a gargantuan problem to the British government.

The person who headed EOKA was an ex-British army officer named George Grivas. He had learned his skills of demolition when serving with the British army, so was more than able to use what was known as a 'ladder' system. This meant that no one outside a step of the ladder knew who was on the next step of command and as long as no Greeks were being killed things would be OK for EOKA.

The other main leader was Archbishop Makarios,[2] and in the position he was in, he was able to do most of the negotiations that had to be done.

Year after year there seemed to be no end in sight. EOKA was

---

[1] EOKA (Ethniki Organosis Kyprion Agoniston) was a Greek-Cypriot nationalist organisation that was fighting for the expulsion of British troops from the island of Cyprus, seeking self-determination and union with Greece in the mid to late 1950s.

[2] As the elected Archbishop of Cyprus, Makarios was head of the Orthodox Church in Cyprus and thus the de facto leader of the Greek-Cypriot community.

becoming so good at the disruptions that at the time of this story in 1958/59 there would be some thirty to forty thousand British troops on the island trying to keep the peace.

Pre-Army Medical and Girls

There it was: a small brown envelope. Inside was notification that I was to report to the medical centre at Fenwick Street in Liverpool. In those days, 1957, rail travel was by steam train and most appointments were made to coincide with the arrival of others coming from other locations in the area.

On reporting to the centre we were instructed to undress as required and be prepared for a complete medical inspection. There was the usual prodding at the abdomen, followed by various exercises or movements to determine mobility, such as up on your toes to check for flat feet, arm stretching, bending down to touch your toes, dropping your trousers, turning your head to the left and coughing. If all was correct at this stage it was time to move on to the next cubical for ENT (ears, nose and throat), being subjected to feeling at your throat, then checking inside the mouth with a spatula-like instrument, and looking up your nose for any kind of defect. After that would be the checking of your ears with a pointed torch. This was to check for perforated eardrums. Then, the procedure would be followed by the doctor whispering at a specified distance.

After all that next came the eye test, the normal wall chart with letters going from large to small. The last instruction from the optician was: 'What number can you see in the circle?' I hadn't got a clue what he meant. He explained that, in the circle of dots, some dots defined a numeral by being of a different colour, or not of the same shade. This was to determine whether or not you were colour blind. I passed all the checks, so at the end of the examination it was a simple statement of, 'Get dressed, you'll be notified later.'

I'd been an apprentice coach painter, but at the age of eighteen my boss, the owner of the business, died from a heart attack. On a visit to the post office, he'd pulled up and parked outside when the incident occurred. So it just shows how these things can happen without warning. There was then a period of uncertainty over whether the firm would be liquidated or sold on to another buyer or firm. The place and business were closed and eventually bought by an ex-employee some two to three years later when he returned from the army.

Still being an apprentice coach painter, and still being deferred, I needed to find another job. But this would be almost impossible, as no one would want a part-trained coach painter for two years, then be required to re-employ me after NS. However, a house-painting business close by offered to take me on until my imminent call-up. I had to make the best of a situation that was well and truly out of my control.

On the social front I had four mates all in the same age group as me. One of them, however, would marry and emigrate to Australia before his call-up for national service. His first name was Colin. My other friend, Tony, had been for his medical examination, but was unfortunately rejected because of a perforated eardrum. The third friend, Dave, worked as a painter for St Helens Council. He still had about eighteen months left before completing his apprenticeship. My fourth friend, who was called Jack or John (whichever we decided to call him), was already serving in the forces and was stationed down south in the medical corps. He would follow this career after leaving the forces. He had only a short amount of time to serve before being demobbed. Little did I realise at this stage the amount of influence he would have on my life.

There would always be girls involved. We would often meet at the top of the street to discuss all manner of things. On one Sunday afternoon at a party in the home of one of the girls, I asked one particular girl if we could go out together. I don't know if I made my intention plain enough, but she just smiled and went into a back room with the rest of her friends, where some other lads were. Knowing I would be going into the forces shortly, I did not pursue the matter any further.

Shortly after this incident I was off work due to illness. Jack came home on leave before being demobbed; finding that I was off work, he asked me to go around town with him, so that he could become more familiar with any changes that had occurred during the last two years.

Jack wasn't to know until I told him that the day we went to town was the day before I would go into the army myself. After going into places such as Woolworth, M & S, Burton's, then the covered market, the only place we hadn't seen was the main Co-op. Although I had told him that the building was being renovated, he still insisted on going inside anyway, mainly to see what alterations were being done. Eventually we came to the shoe department. It was here that Jack happened to see one of the girls who lived at the top of the street where I lived.

We stopped and began to speak to her about the changes that were being made in the store. It was during this conversation that I saw a girl walk across the back of the department. I immediately asked Janet, the girl we were talking to, who the girl was who had just walked behind her. Obviously, by the way I had asked the question, I was taken in by her looks and manner. Janet said she would get her name and address for me, if I wanted it. I explained to Janet that I would be going into the army for national service the following day, so there didn't seem to be much point in getting her address as she didn't know me at all.

That evening at around six o'clock, I was standing at the corner of the street as usual when Janet came to me and gave me the address of the girl I had seen earlier that afternoon. I looked at the slip of paper and saw that her name was Sylvia, and that she lived on the other side of town to my home. Thinking no more of it I put the note with her address on it into my wallet for safe keeping. Strangely enough though, I never mentioned the address to any of the others who were about at the time. In fact, come to think of it, only these mates knew that I was joining up the next day; the girls didn't know a thing about my call-up.

Induction, Kit Issue, Haircuts, Bulling Up and Food

The following morning, Wednesday, 10 October 1957, was the day I was to join the army at Oswestry. After finishing breakfast I took the very small travel case that had been prepared earlier, then set off to St Helens central station with my father, who would see me on to the train. My two younger brothers and sister were at school, the elder brother was in work, and my mother was a little upset, so it was down to my father to see me off. At the station were other young men, also with friends and relatives seeing them off to their respective camps and regiments. In those days the railways had a vast network and were expert at transporting military personnel to whichever army depot they had to go to. It must be remembered that this operation was happening all over the British Isles every Wednesday with both recruitment and demobilisation, a mammoth task, but everyone would reach the required destination on time.

After saying our farewells to everybody, we boarded the train to Warrington Bank Quay for the connecting train to Oswestry; I've forgotten to say that Oswestry was the Artillery recruiting depot. While we waited for the next train the number of young men waiting for connections grew steadily. The journey to the camp was uneventful. We arrived at Oswestry Station and were met by NCOs (Non-Commissioned Officers) who had seen us all with small pieces of luggage. After it had been established that we were the NIG (New Intake Group) we were told to get into the army trucks that were standing outside the station waiting for us. When a truck was full we would be taken to camp to be fed and billeted for the night.

The following morning it was up at six o'clock washed and shaved. After breakfast inside the billet, instructions were given as to what was expected of us that day, so we fell in outside the billet in three ranks, then were politely ordered to turn and march down to the QM's (quartermaster's) stores. Here we were halted and told to go inside in single file. Moving along this counter we would begin picking up the equipment that we would need for our next two years' service.

We'd all seen in the films what it would be like, first being given a kitbag, then moving along a line hearing 'Blouses two, boots two, berets two, shirts two.' With all this going on you were being asked your body measurements, then given the nearest or the appropriate kit as you passed along, all the time getting more and more kit. When all seemed OK, they decided to load you up with the big pack, small pack, bullet pouches and straps.

When you got to the end of the hut you'd be begging for an extra pair of hands, but did the sergeant care when you got outside? No not one bit! He'd seen all of this before. He just told us to fall in again and marched us in a fashion back to the billet.

After being fell out, we went inside, put all of our kit on our beds, then fell in again outside to be marched down to the canteen for dinner. It was becoming obvious that every time the unit was to move anywhere we would be fell in and marched to where ever we had to go.

After dinner it was fall in and march back to the billet. I don't remember exactly when we were given our army number, but after we had all got back inside our room we were given an indelible ink marker and told to put the last four digits of our army number on all of our kit. In some instances we would be advised where to put the number, so that it could hidden from view when worn, yet easily seen by the laundry people.

When all that had been done we had to change into the army clothes we had been issued with. I'll start inside first then work outwards. The vests were of rough white wool; the underpants were of the same material and felt like sandpaper, and itched for ages until you got used to the feeling of such clothes next to your skin. Most of us, however, kept our own underwear on underneath most of the time. The socks were of thick grey wool, and came in very handy in protecting the feet against the heavy leather boots. The shirts were also of a woollen mix but in a khaki colour. It was sometimes noticeable that not all the uniforms were the exact same shade. This was just accepted as normal, as long as blouse and trousers had the same colour tone. The braces were about two inches wide and very long (they had to be, to accommodate the tall guys who were enlisted). The underpants (long johns) had loops on them which could be placed over the buttons when fastening up your braces, but no braces could be worn when in shirt-sleeve order.

The beret looked like a dinner plate on your head. It had to be soaked in water, then wrung out and put on your head to get the required shape. Then it had to be gently removed to keep its shape and dried out. The greatcoat I got was made in 1940 (it said so on the maker's label). The lapels reached out to the ends of my shoulders; this meant that, when I put it on, all that could be seen of me stood up with the collar raised, would be a beret, a greatcoat, boots and gaiters. I don't think I could grumble too much though, because it did have the new type of what were known as 'stay-bright buttons', so I was saved the task of having to use the dreaded button-cleaning device.

The gloves I was given always gave me problems on parade. They weren't the normal woollen issue, but made of battledress material with the palms covered in horse hide. They looked out of place, because I would be the only gunner with this type of glove. During the full length of service I would have to refuse all orders to give them to the officer or NCO in charge of the parade. You see, I knew that with this type of glove I could pick up any metal objects I wanted to without the cold striking through to the palms of the hands. All officers and NCOs knew this also, so the gloves had to be kept in a very safe place at all times, so they could not be stolen.

The next item of interest was a small, rolled-up package known as a 'housewife'. In it were needles, cotton and wool to darn the socks when they got holes in them. Darning socks would be another skill to be learnt, or you took home to Mummy. Also in this pack might be buttons and other things to do running repairs with. The tie was a simple piece of woollen cloth about two inches wide all along its length.

After sorting everything out and marking the complete full kit, it was all change into the uniforms we had been given. We were then told to pack all our civilian clothes into bundles of brown paper, or pack them into the small cases we had brought with us, after which the packs would be addressed ready to be sent home the following day. The next day with ablutions done and parcels gone, nicely dressed in our new uniforms, we went from gentlemen to a f—ing shower. We were ordered to get fell in outside (and be quick about it), then sent to the barber's for 'a nice haircut'. Once again we were to fall in outside, left turn, quick march, but this time it would be 'Pick those feet up!' 'Swing those arms!' What a difference having a uniform on made!

At the barber's it was just like a production line. The barbers were very kind. They even let you keep some of your hair by letting it go down the back of your neck. This was quite easily achieved by ramming the towel as far down there as possible. The barber also asked if you would like any particular style like, say, a Tony Curtis. With a pleasant smile, up the shears went to deliver a short back and sides. 'That's not a Tony Curtis!' you'd say, but the barber replied, 'It is if he comes here.' All done, again it was fall in outside, again march back to the billet, left right, left right.

Next came the battledresses. They had to be tailored to each individual's measurements. It would take more than just a couple of visits to get everything correct – the tailors had to make alterations to nearly every blouse or trousers to some degree or another. It was often jokingly said that if a uniform fitted first time without any alterations you were deformed. The alterations had to done as soon as possible because one of the two uniforms had to be chosen for best. The second best was to be used as everyday wear. Meanwhile we were given instructions on how the beds had to be made every morning: the bottom blanket being very taut with hospital corners, well tucked in, the remaining sheets and blankets arranged into a box shape and layered like a liquorice allsort, blanket, sheet, blanket, sheet, blanket. This routine had to done every morning without fail, unless of course the bed to whom it belonged was on leave or in the sick bay. A rigid regime of how to set out your kit on the bed for general inspection also had to be adhered to.

I have left the boots until last on purpose. Again one of the two pairs had to be for best (but still had to be broken in), for guard duty or main parades. There is no easy way to bull boots, it's just shear hard slogging. All boots had dimpled surfaces both on the toe and the heel. The way I removed the dimples was to heat up the handle of a spoon over a candle, put lashings of polish on the toe and heel, then rub in the sizzling polish in order to soften and smooth out the leather. When this was achieved I got a fine duster, and a polish-tin lid with water in it. I then dipped the duster in the water to get it wet, then into the polish, and began to rub in very small circles. After a while the polish would harden, so the same procedure would be repeated alternately on the heel and toe, building up to a gradual shine. One thing to remember was not to let your boots stand in sunlight, as this would soften the polish again and take away the shine that had been built up.

The uniforms also needed to be pressed; this though was a heartbreaking job, for two reasons. First, there was only one iron available in the billet; second and worse, the uniform was very fluffy and most difficult to iron. Any pleats had to be ironed in from virtually nothing. Trying to find the correct places wasn't easy for a lad who had probably never used an iron in his life before.

Below the pockets of the blouse might be pleats. This depended on how the tailor had cut the style to the individual soldier's size or shape. To iron these pleats on a flat table for the first time was not an easy feat. The pleats would be covered with a handkerchief dipped in vinegar and water; the water was to create the steam, the vinegar would hopefully stop the cloth from becoming shiny. If for any reason the cloth did start to become shiny, a good rub with a two-shilling piece often solved the problem. The arms of the tunic (blouse) had to be pressed both front and rear of the sleeve from the shoulders right down to the cuffs. The trousers had to be creased at the back, from the join at the waistband, so as to give an inverted 'V' when one was stood to attention. The greatcoat was also difficult to iron for the first time, mainly because of its size. It had to have what were called box pleats, two at the front, two at the rear, so as to make a box appearance when the wearer was on guard.

The next major problem was the food. In all honesty it didn't seem as if anyone was at all bothered just as long as something was served up at mealtimes. The potatoes were dehydrated and mixed with only water. The outcome was a paste-like substance.

Trying to get it from the ladle on to your plate was like attempting to shovel glue. The veg more often than not would either be hardly cooked or overcooked, served with a ladleful of juices. The meat was also a mishmash of something, often only vaguely resembling its origins. That was dinner. Sweet could be anything that might look nice but tasted only average.

Breakfast was another ordeal for the stomach. Eggs could be with yolks broken and the eggs in bits, with fat of course. Bacon would be over- or underdone, and again with plenty of greasy lard. Beans could be either very runny and mashed, or as they should have been. Tea would be just as bad, depending a great deal on how long it had been brewing before being served. The evening meal wasn't much better. I often thought that if jam, bread and butter had not been available, we would have gone hungry at many a mealtime.

Even with all this new routine to contend with, walking round, strutting their importance, could be found lance bombardiers, themselves just new recruits trying to show how important they were.

Evenings in Camp, Section Photo, NAAFI and Transfer Orders

The evenings gave some kind of respite from being bawled at for what we thought was nothing at all. However, before falling out and being dismissed for the day, we received orders as to what was expected of us all for the following morning. As only one iron was available, ironing was always at the top of the list, with boots and brasses being done as we waited for the iron.

It soon became possible to go down to the NAAFI; the place was always packed out with squaddies trying to have a change from this new life we had been given. In the corner of the room, as was normal for those days, was the juke box. Time after time the song *Diana*, sung by Paul Anka, would be played. It was the top record of the day, so the song and date would stay etched in my brain for the rest of my life: October 1957.

Another thing we had drummed into us was the great importance of writing home. Letting your loved ones know that you had arrived safe and sound was an absolute must. If by any reason it was found that someone was not writing home, the person in question would be up in front of an officer to explain his reason. This may be the best place to explain that even though the average age was around nineteen, some lads could be heard crying at night due to the regime change we had experienced.

I had written to my parents and mates, but was aware that others were writing to their wives or girlfriends, and remembered that I too had an address of a girl to write to. I honestly didn't know what to expect in reply; as I explained before, I hadn't even spoken to the girl. Just seeing her from a distance was as far as I had got. So I plucked up courage and set pen to paper. What do you write to someone you haven't spoken to before? That's right, very little; all I could manage was about a dozen lines mostly about myself, where in town I lived, and the regiment I was in.

Then I asked if she would write to me as a pen friend.

Things were still rather strange, but we had been put into our training platoon so we were beginning to get used to the situation and make some friends. We had been warned about getting *too* friendly, because when training was ended we might not go to the same regiment together; this would happen much sooner than was expected. After we were assigned our platoon a photo call was arranged. I still have my photo, and when I come across it from time to time, I think we looked funny in our ill-fitting uniforms, and wonder what happened to all those men.

23 October 1957 – photograph of 20 Section

After the first week things were beginning to fall into a routine of sorts: drill, bulling, saluting correctly… Coming to the halt there was a tendency to slide about a quarter of an inch, and it was never guaranteed at any time of your service that this wouldn't happen. Depending on the ground surface and whether the studs had worn down it could be like walking on ice. It took some getting used to, but getting used to it you did.

We would go down the NAAFI as usual of an evening, but

after pay parade (something else we had to get used to), we went with our £1/11/6 which was the full week's pay. Out of this huge amount of money we were advised to send home seven shillings and six pence as an insurance so that if in service you were killed, and later became the only dependent relative of your parents, they would supposedly be able to get a government pension. After this, pay would only be to the nearest two shillings and six pence (half crown) – so it can easily be seen how little money was left to spend on things like toothpaste, razor blades, soap, Blanco, haircuts, cigarettes and matches, a cup of tea in the NAAFI, stamps and envelopes. In some cases National Insurance would be deducted if you were over twenty-one years of age and on the required amount of pay.

The next thing was to determine what job you would have during your two years in the colours. Again we had to march to a large hall, to be taken inside where there were rows of tables. After we were sat down it was explained that this was an IQ test to find out the job that the army thought we would be best suited for. It wasn't too long after this test that we were told that some of us were to be transferred to a regular regiment down south somewhere. The list was put up on orders, and needless to say my name was among the sixty or so selected to go.

The day before the transfer all our kit was packed using for the very first time every piece of equipment we'd been given. Every pack or pouch was stuffed full and bulging out because as yet we didn't have the experience of packing kitbags. That evening at tea time we stood in the queue as normal when who should come and stand directly behind us but a full bombardier, the one who would be in charge of the group to be transferred. He was as smart as they came; boots were well polished, his trousers had creases that stood out and his shirt was just as good. While looking at him two lance bombardiers walked past and straight to the front of the queue. Seeing this, the full bombardier shouted, 'Hey! To the back of the queue!' At this the lance bombardiers pointed to their tape and said, 'We are lance bombardiers.' The bombardier behind us then pointed to his tapes and said, 'What do you think this is, f—ing bird shit? Get to the f—ing back and be quick about it.' With tails between their legs they duly complied.

Those of us who witnessed this episode thought, what have we got here? This bloke will really put us through the mill if given half a chance. How wrong can you be? We were soon to find out.

At this stage I'd like to make it quite clear that it was not all of 20 Section that was to be transferred. It was done in alphabetical order, which meant that most of us going had a surname beginning with an A, B, C or D, although some did have an initial much further down the order. On the 20 Section photo only Mike Bury, third from the left, back row, and myself fourth from the right, back row, would be transferred.

New Barracks at 61st Field Regiment, Small Arms and Twenty-Five Pounder Training

The train journey to our new barracks was one of very little incident. In all honesty, the memory of crossing London on the Underground is a complete blank. I think it was mainly because we didn't have much time to take in all that was going on about us. Not only that, we'd all had this type of journey but a very short time before when going to Oswestry.

On our arrival at the station at Tidworth, we found that trucks had been laid on to pick us up and take us to our new home (so to speak). We were informed that we had joined the 61st Field Regiment RA, and that it was a regular service regiment. Being a regular regiment meant that, if it were to be sent on active service, we would have to go also, trained up or not. So we were expected to come up to 61st Field standards as soon as possible.

The regiment was stationed at Jalalabad Barracks just outside Tidworth, a town close to the Hampshire/Wiltshire border. All the buildings were of brick, not wooden like the ones we had left earlier. The interiors were as different as could be imagined: a thick type of linoleum on floor, curtains at the windows, central heating, a small bedside table, and a reading light over the head of the bed so you could read at night without disturbing anyone else. In the centre of the room was a large table, for ironing on and writing if need be.

The first thing to do was get yourself a bed and locker. All the sheets and blankets had already been installed, due only to the fact that we had arrived rather late in the day, so it was mainly a matter of unpacking and putting all your gear in its correct places. During all this activity the bombardier was still around but we now also had two sergeants to contend with. When all was finished we had our introduction to the sergeants, first by name, then through the normal ear-bashing that went with these nice, motherly chats.

Time for tea. What a difference from our former training camp. On our entering the canteen the usual remarks of 'Get some in' came across, but it sounded more like sarcastic sympathy than anything else. The ones shouting had been through everything we were going to go through, so they soon stopped and got on with their own meals. The canteen itself was also very modern, with tables laid out and neatly (at least by army standards); the counter had plates at the start of the queue, then all the different types of food on offer for that mealtime. This being our first time in the canteen we were accompanied by the NCOs in charge, just to make sure, I think, that we got treated fairly. The Duty Officer was also in attendance; he had placed himself at the very end of the counter, so he was able to see that each lad had been treated the same as the rest of the regiment.

Because our experience of army life was minimal, the following morning we were fell in, and we saw that there would be three sergeants and three bombardiers. We also had an officer with the rank of captain. This therefore would be the full intake group. Our being housed in the block meant we had very little contact with the rest of the regiment, so any extra activities we were required to do during training would not interfere with the rest of the troops in camp.

Obviously the first thing that had to be known was: What was our marching like? Well, it was a dead certainty, wasn't it, that we were all a load of blankety blank blanks. One sergeant, named Harris, didn't seem to be happy unless he was giving us the entire verbal he could muster. It would be things like, 'I'll stick my thing in your ear and knock some sense into you lad,' or, 'How tall are you?' after which he'd say, 'I've never seen rubbish piled so high in all my life.' Another was to stand behind a man and ask, 'Am I hurting you? I should be, I'm stood on your hair! Get it cut!' There were many more. Not to worry though; we survived it all in the end.

The bed-making had to be improved – well not the making actually, but the speed in which it had to be done. Everything else had to be done rapidly from now on. Washing, shaving, cleaning your brasses... every spare second had to be used to the full, otherwise failure at inspection could occur. In some cases a lad might have a problem with making his bed so someone would help him out. The thing was that if only one failed, all of us had to parade again.

One of the NCOs had shown us how to lay out our kit on the bed in the morning and make it into squares. At night it was a common sight to see all the woollen underpants, vests, socks being sewn into pre-designated sizes and shapes (mine were still sewn up the day I got demobbed). I took them home for my father to wear when working down the mines. When he undid the stitches they were white on the inside and a dirty grey colour on the outside.

Other items that needed to be boxed off would be attended to. The brasses got buffed on pieces of cardboard and Brasso, and the two brass pieces at the front of the belt often got flattened so as to make it easier to buff up on the cardboard. The boots were always a problem, and not only the bulling. For the kit inspection, under the arches of the boots had to be polished, and the heel plates had to be emery papered to remove any excess polish before thorough cleaning; this also had to be done on the toe plate. When the boots were laid on the bed for inspection they needed to be laced up. This wasn't as easy as it may first sound. The laces weren't made of cloth but square pieces of leather, which needed to be flat even when laced up and displayed for inspection. Knife, fork, spoon and mess tins also had to be meticulously cleaned.

All items on the bed had to be in exact positions. Sergeant Harris carried a stick which he would use as a gauge to measure the positions of our kit, and he seemed to delight in showing us a bed layout, then messing it all up so that we would have to memorise all the positions. In the beginning this seemed spiteful, but the result was that we could eventually put our kit out in a few minutes. Another thing was that we had to stand to attention with our boot toes in line with the foot of the bed. Nearly all kit inspections were done with us dressed in working denims, and then immediately after the inspection it was necessary to change into uniform again for parade, unless the inspection was taken by the officer, when it had to be full uniform. On one such occasion, the officer looked at all my kit and remarked that the mess tins were not clean enough. 'You have Brasso, don't you?'

'Yes, sir,' I replied.

'Well, use that and get them cleaner.'

I said, 'But Brasso can be poisonous, sir.'

'How do you know?' came back his reply.

'Because I'm a coach painter by trade, sir.'

'That's no excuse, get them cleaner for tomorrow.'

After we were back in denims, it was fall in outside for roll call, then off to our training class, be it indoors or out, raining or not. We again sat an aptitude test. This was to ensure that our IQ was known quickly, and it would not be necessary to wait for the results of the tests we had already taken to arrive.

Small Arms Lectures

THE STEN GUN

There were three memorable parts to the small arms courses. This first lecture was with Sergeant Harris. He had a table in front of him, on which he had a Sten gun. He shouted (as he nearly always seemed to do), 'This is a gun. It's made to do one thing and one thing only, and that's to kill, and by the f— it will kill. It's got no brains, only the ones of the person holding it. It will go off if dropped.' Saying this he banged the butt of the Sten on the table making the bolt action work, without his having pulled the bolt back to arm the weapon manually. His next party piece was to undo the weapon into all its individual parts, then lay them all out on the table. He told us that it cost about seven shillings and six pence (in old money – thirty-five pence in new money) while reassembling the gun. Each of us had to dismantle, then reassemble the gun in turn before Sgt Harris was happy we could handle the gun and knew what to do when we went on the ranges.

THE BREN GUN

Again we had Sgt Harris telling us how to dismantle the Bren, then put it all back together again ready for use.

Once again, each person in turn had to dismantle the weapon with others looking on. This in itself helped to familiarise you with the weapon in question. The main part of this training would come on the ranges, as you lay face down with the gun in front of you and your feet wide apart, learning how to put a magazine on and pull the bolt back ready for firing. Then you would tuck the butt into your shoulder and fire off shots, then remove and replace the magazine to continue firing. In action, a second man should be in attendance carrying extra ammunition.

THE 303 RIFLES

After the other two weapons this appeared rather straightforward, as the only part to be dismantled was the bolt action. It was at this point we were told of the danger of the pig-sticker bayonet. It looked like a twelve-inch pointed piece of metal, and when it was on the end of the rifle, as you did rifle drill and shouldered arms, if care wasn't taken the bayonet would come up under the armpit and stab into the flesh giving a very serious wound. For each of the weapons, a lesson on how to refill the magazines was given, so as to ensure the gun didn't jam when first being used.

ON THE RIFLE RANGE (BREN GUN)

The shooting of the Bren gun was rather easy, mainly because the instructor was standing over you to make certain everything was going as it should. Not only that, with a tripod fitted to it when firing, it wasn't a very easy gun to manoeuvre when you were in a lying position. In normal combat conditions a second man would be in attendance. His main job was to carry extra ammunition in two boxes and help with the reloading. However, on the ranges there was no need for this extra man.

ON THE RIFLE RANGE (303 RIFLES)

When using this rifle we also had to see if we could if possible, pass out as a marksman or a first-class shot. When my turn came, I lay down and began to shoot. After five shots I changed magazines, but couldn't reload because the rifle had jammed. I got it going again, but had lost a shot at target. I then tried to get two rounds into one target. I did it, but the rifle jammed for the second time. The officer who had been watching asked for a count back, and then decided I could have my last five shots again with another weapon. I got one from a lad named Bob Wagstaff; the target came up, I took aim, Bang! The round went without warning. I'd split my lip but, realising the problem, continued shooting until the rifle was empty. Bob said he had forgotten to tell me that his rifle had a very light trigger. This episode cost me my chance of being a marksman, but, other than a split lip, it didn't cause any problems so I wasn't too bothered about the incident at all.

While on the ranges we had to do a stint in the butts, lifting the targets up and down and recording hits. First though we were taken down the side of the range so we could listen to the bullets whizzing down the range. With the Regiment not long back from Northern Ireland it was thought that this was a way of letting us know what it sounded like when being shot at.

ON THE RIFLE RANGE (STEN GUN)

After doing the other two weapons, everybody was feeling confident with what we had to do. We'd go to the firing line in groups of about six at a time. Things were going quite well, and something like the fourth group had gone and started shooting, when all at once one of the lads turned round, pointing his Sten to the rear, shouting, 'Bombardier, the Sten gun's jammed. What should I do?' It had been very strongly emphasised in our classroom instruction that if a weapon malfunctioned, the soldier should just put up his hand, and keep the weapon pointing towards the target. This action though, caused everybody to scatter in all directions, taking evasive action as best as possible on what was open ground. While this was going on the bombardier grabbed the Sten, pointed it skyward, at the same time hitting the miscreant to get the weapon out of his grasp. The tirade of foul language was unbelievable – every person there had been well and truly shaken to the core by the experience. The only good thing was that no one had been shot.

Other Training: Twenty-Five Pounder Gun

During the same period, training on the twenty-five pounder was going on apace. As this was in a regular regiment, it was imperative that this aspect of our training was done with as much speed as possible. If the regiment had to move out on active duty, we would be expected to operate the equipment as well as the rest of the men. At this time there were six men on a gun (a twenty-five pounder). The Number One was nearly always either a sergeant or a bombardier; Number Two the layer; Number Three fed the shell and cartridge into the breech; the rammer I think was Four, who rammed home the shell, then closed the breech after the Number Three had put in the cartridge; Number Five had the job of ensuring the correct charge was in the cartridge, and seeing to any other settings that might be on the shells, i.e. airburst or smoke. The Number Six, who could be the driver acting as the limber gunner, had the job of unloading the limber.

This type of training was first done on what was known as the gun park. No matter what the weather, training still went ahead most of the time. We had been taught most of the rudimentary workings in the classroom, but the manhandling of the guns was something else. A gradual increase in workload began with the gun and limber stationary on the gun park, as you learnt how to drop the platform making sure that your feet were well out of the way, otherwise your toes would be cut off. The driver would pull forward lifting the gun on to the platform, after applying the brakes on the gun, then unhitch the gun and limber. The quad would then move the limber into the required position. While all this was being done with the limber, the rest of the gun crew would be pulling the gun so as to point in roughly the right direction, and the layer would be locking his gunsights into place.

Each gun carried a pick, a spade and a hand spike, the last was used by the Number One when changing the gun's direction of fire. The pick and handle were strapped inside the A-frame, as well as a rammer, which as the name suggests was used to ram the shell into the breech. Strapped on the outside of the shield would be four long rods with a plate at one end. Also on the shield would be strapped the spade and drag ropes. Each rod was numbered one to four. If the terrain was barren with little or no trees, a gunner would run out about fifty yards to the rear of the gun, with a rod corresponding to the numbered position of the gun in the troop. He would stick it into the ground, setting it up for the gun layer to use as an aiming point when in action. Another gunner at the same time would be taking the canvas cover off the gun muzzle, and attending to any other job that might need doing. The drivers of the quads were regular drivers in the regiment, so they knew what to do at any given time. Arm waving from a distance was an easy type of signalling; this was mainly picked up by one and all by watching the Number One as you went along. Training was done until things became second nature, and all knew what to do.

One piece of equipment that cannot be found mentioned in any books at all is a lanyard for recocking the gun after a misfire. Whether this piece of equipment was issue or just made by the Number One, I don't know. It would look something like the sketch drawn from memory. A misfire was the dread of all gun crews, because not only was there a likelihood of the gun still firing, the shell in the breech would be getting hotter and hotter as time passed. If after a third attempt it still failed to fire, the cartridge would have to be removed and replaced by a fresh one, and the shell fired off ASAP. As we were in a regular field unit and could be dispatched to a conflict zone at short notice, this drill was rehearsed until everyone could do it no matter what his position was on the gun – what's more, at this stage it wasn't certain which job you might end up with.

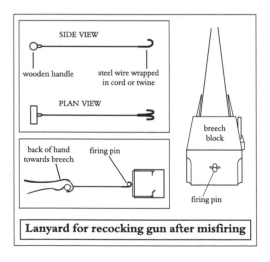

Lanyard for recocking gun after misfiring

It is not known if this lanyard was an issued item or not

The commonly known lanyard is the white rope that can be seen on the right shoulder of the uniform. Although this would have been adequate on old guns it most certainly was of no use on the twenty-five pounder.

As time went by and our knowledge increased, speed was beginning to improve, so the inevitable rivalry began to creep in, as to which gun team could set up fastest. This training went on for quite some time. Those of us who would be doing other trades – say signalling, driving or TARA work (Technical Assistant Royal Artillery) could muster only basic enthusiasm, but we still had to do it all. To clarify a point: the TARA would work in the command post assisting the officer to do the corrections on the gun after receiving orders from the OP as to fall of shot.

Early Morning Runs, Injections and Rifle Drill

Each morning at 5 a.m. the billet lights came on and the instructor's voice bellowed out, 'Hands off cocks, on to socks, come on you lazy bastards, out of bed.' The routine was wash, shave, and clean your teeth. It was pandemonium every morning getting a washbasin, then hurrying to make up the beds, change into PT kit and be outside and fell in by 5.30 a.m. A count would be done to make certain we were all there, then off we went on a nice little run, one eye open, one eye shut.

There were no exceptions, all had to go on these runs. One lad in the group was of rather heavier build than most of us. He'd done all the other tasks of marching, gun drill, small arms maintenance, with no problems at all, but when lining up on the first morning's run, this lad was adamant that he couldn't do any sustained running owing to a medical abnormality. Try as this chap might, the bombardier was having none of it and made him fall in with the rest of us.

So off we all went, but after about two- to three-hundred yards, this particular lad began to lag behind. Eventually he staggered over to the side of the road collapsing on to a grass verge. The group was halted; the bombardier went back to him, shouting all the time for him to get on to his feet. No amount of abuse took effect. Everyone went back to see what was wrong. The lad looked as if he had just run a marathon, not just three-hundred yards. Sweat was oozing out of him, his face was bright red, and his spectacles were steamed up. The instructor ordered two lads to take him back to the billets then rejoin us on the run. This scenario took place every morning for a week, after which the lad had to see the MO (Medical Officer) to verify that his problem was genuine. Even so, while waiting for a transfer to another regiment such as the pay corps or the like, he had to do the ablutions while we were on our runs.

These runs went on for quite some time during training. I'd

become friendly with a lad from the Wirral near Liverpool, whose name was Ashworth. We thought we'd have some fun on these runs, so on some mornings we'd set off and gradually start falling behind. When we were about thirty yards behind, the bombardier slowed down to us and said something like, 'Come on, speed up and get in front, you pair of lazy bastards!' So being dutiful soldiers we sped up, caught up the rest of the troop and slowly began to get ahead of the rest. When we were about forty yards in front, a voice boomed out, 'Hey, you pair of awkward bastards, slow down and get in with the rest of the troop.' The following morning we were taken to one side and told to stay in the middle of the group, otherwise we were for it. The bombardier taking us on these runs was the one who had been with us when transferring from Oswestry. He'd been a boy soldier so he knew all the tricks of army life.

There was also the gymnasium to contend with. The set-up was the same in every unit I suppose, but put to different uses. The main thing that it was used for in this regiment wouldn't be readily understood by civilians, because in the long term it seemed that the NCOs were looking for boxers first of all, and then working through other sports. This, however, didn't mean that it was easy going in the gym if you weren't a sporty person – far from it. All the equipment got used eventually. I fell foul of the wall bars. The PTI (Physical Training Instructor) didn't think that I was trying hard enough, so I was given an extra dose of the wall bars, hanging from them, lifting up the knees and moving side to side, also trying to put my legs outstretched in front while hanging by the arms. Not nice at all, but making a comment of any kind only doubled the dosage, so it was gob shut, knees up and suffer.

With all this exercise, a regular check of feet would take place. It would also be asked if any other problems had arisen like sore nipples from the vest rubbing, or soreness under the arms, and last but not least any chaffing around the buttocks or groin area. Regular use of the talcum powder issued could help to stop any rubbing. The talc was very silky in texture; had it been scented it would have cost a fortune on the high street! Nearly everybody had a tin in his locker at sometime during his service.

Another lesson to go through would be the hygiene course. This consisted of a verbal explanation of venereal diseases, followed by a short film show illustrating the problems you might experience. At this juncture it was made quite clear that if any of these diseases were caught, it would be considered a self-inflicted wound, which is a chargeable offence. Some of the graphics could put you off sex for life, especially when you saw the treatment. Happy to say though, I don't think it did us any harm in the long term to see the film.

Injections and Rifle Drill

Next came injections in case we were posted overseas. 'TAB' was printed in your pay book. Three injections were needed if you happened to go abroad, the first two given during training, the third and last when being posted. Injections were always given on a Friday afternoon. Booster jabs of smallpox and chickenpox were also given out at this time of week. Please do not think that this meant we had all weekend to get over the jabs – not by any means.

The TAB had the effect of making the left arm very sore as well as making you feel unwell. If this feeling didn't happen on the first jab, it almost certainly would on the second. On the Saturday morning after the first jab, all went for breakfast as usual. After breakfast though, it was fall in for parade again, but this time we went down to the armoury for rifles, then on to the parade ground for rifle drill. Yes, rifle drill. We could hardly pick the pissing things up with our left arms, never mind march with them, but it was rifle drill we did, like it or not. For over an hour we were drilled, doing every movement in the book – slope arms, for inspection port arms, officer salute, general salute, about turn on the march, ground arms, pick up arms. All the time the sergeant and bombardier were shouting, 'Keep those rifles up! Don't drop those left arms, keep them up!' Then came the order to trail the rifle in the right hand and march along swinging the left, to a tirade of abuse: 'Swing that left arm, it won't f—ing come loose and fall off.' There was no sympathy whatsoever; in fact we all thought that this was one drill the NCOs really liked to do.

The following morning, Sunday, the lad in the next bed to me was rather ill, so we were allowed to bring him some milk, toast, butter and jam from the canteen. That particular morning, the captain in charge of training (Captain Pettifer) came into the billet to see what the problem was. The gunner in question had to lie to attention when the officer came into the room, and discuss how ill he might be, and whether he might be hospitalised. When it had been determined that the TAB was the probable cause, it was decided to wait until Monday morning for further assessment.

On Monday he was OK, and was on parade with the rest of us. It was never allowed for anyone to tip a person out of bed, simply because the person in question could be genuinely ill. It was always left to the medical officer at sick parade to make any diagnosis. Verbal abuse was dished out every chance they got, but physical abuse was rare. Maybe this was because we were in a regular regiment for training, and one might eventually be in the NCO's troop, and didn't want any bad feelings from the outset. This cautious approach proved to be a wise thing in months to come.

On Parade, Cinema Trip, Classroom and Field Work and Radio Training

Some things stand out more than others when looking back. One such time was with Ashworth, the lad I'd palled up with in training at this part of army service. We were stood outside the barrack-room window, which was on ground-floor level, taking our usual last puff on a fag, dressed in full uniform waiting for Officer's Parade, not talking about anything in particular, when the order to fall in in three ranks was given.

All was going well except for the normal comments of what needed to be done to improve the standard of dress. It soon became my turn for inspection. I could tell that the inspecting officer was looking for any faults that he could find. He zoned in on my lanyard; looking at it he said, 'No blancoing of lanyards.'

'It's not blancoed, sir,' I replied. At this he hit my shoulder and lanyard with his stick, which he always had with him when on parade. No white powder or dust came off, so he hit the lanyard again; still no dust or powder came off. At this he came very close and began to examine the article, turning it round with his fingers.

'How did you get it so white?' he asked.

'By using toothpaste, sir,' I replied, which was met with a 'Hmmm.' He continued the inspection. This episode he did not forget.

We were duly fell out and began to make our way to our room, when Ashworth put his hand up behind his right ear, and took down a dog end and lit it. On doing so, he realised he had been on parade with fag end behind his ear without being seen and got away with it.

The Cinema Trip

Because we often had to wait for the iron every evening, Ashworth and I decided to fill in time with a trip to the local cinema. The bombardier got to know of our intentions – some stooge had told him, but it didn't matter. He gave us a lecture on why we shouldn't go, and how if we did go he'd go over us both with a fine toothcomb to see if anything was wrong. So what? Off we went, entering the cinema with lots of others in uniform. Sat down, we just blended in and watched the film without any trouble.

The show finished and we began to file out with everyone else, but just outside were two military policemen (MPs). They saw us two coming out, and started to give us a long look. At this point, as if on cue from a director, some others in uniform came out and, quickly seeing the situation, began to make a noise. This drew the attention of the two MPs. As this was happening, another soldier came up to us and politely said, 'Go on, piss off while you can.' We didn't need a second telling. Away we both went as fast as we could. Looking back, we must have stood out like a sore thumb, the way we were dressed. The MP didn't know that there was a training intake at Jalalabad Barracks. That, I think, was the only thing that got us both off the hook.

It was not too long after the cinema episode that Ashworth and I asked the bombardier if we could apply for the Airborne Division. The application went in, but came back with a negative answer, saying that only regulars were now being taken – but if we still wanted to go in the Airborne Division, we'd have to sign on for three years. It wasn't long after this, that Ashy began saying that he was having problems with arthritis. He persisted with this until eventually, a short while after he'd been posted to 120 Battery (Bty), he was duly discharged and I lost complete track of him.

Going back to the bulling of kit: irons in those days had a length of flex attached. One evening a lad named Pete Barlow was the last to use the iron. Very late at night, feeling very tired, Pete put the iron down on the floor and began to fold all of his ironing up, but completely forgot about the iron. He was on the first floor. He went to bed and the following morning the iron had burnt a hole in the floor/ceiling and was still switched on and red hot. Why nothing caught fire will never be known. I have often told this story to my wife, and it was only some forty years later when we met Pete in Warrington that he confirmed it was true.

Other classroom lessons included orienteering: telling the difference on a map between A-roads and B-roads, cart tracks, boundary lines, contour lines and spot heights, and knowing where a steep hill or cliff might be. We also had to be able to tell whether a road had gradients up or down depending on which way one might be travelling, identify a river or a canal, swampy ground or marshy land. We learnt how to recognise whether railway lines were going into tunnels or over bridges, if a beach was sandy or pebbly, how to take back readings on a compass, then follow a line across country, or if a church has a spire or tower. (There is a church in Ormskirk near Liverpool that has both a spire and a tower; we never found the symbol for that type of church though.) The easiest way to find a pub for a drink is to find a church on the map – there's nearly always a pub within fifty yards. One pub for each religion – this tradition dates back centuries to when England was having religious disputes.

After the classroom we would go on the ranges near Larkhill to put the learning into practice. Those of us who had applied to be radio operators began to be taught the phonetic alphabet. We learnt which call sign belonged to which vehicle or officer, how to send, receive, relay and organise a shout, how to set up and use a 10-line exchange, then set up a remote control unit. Obviously we were taught to learn how to operate and tune in the various kinds of radio we would get to use. Then we had to know how to mix the acid in order to make electrolyte for the batteries, and how to work out the length of time it should take to charge up either the twelve-volt or six-volt batteries. We learnt what charge to set on the little charging engine, then how to run that small engine without it being heard beyond a radius of about fifteen feet.

At first it seemed easy, in a classroom where it was nice and warm. But line-laying was another aspect we needed to learn, outside in the elements, using a telephone with a ten-line exchange system. Then we had to lay a cable line across a track which tanks would use, putting tiebacks on each side of the track. To bury and conceal the cable, either overhead or underground, was harder than you may think. If a tank commander saw the wire, or suspected the ground had been disturbed, he would give an order to the driver to swivel the tank, so as to rip up all the cable that had been laid down. They probably thought it very funny, but the line would have to be done again.

To help us we had self-soldering joints. This process involved a small tube with solder inside and a lump of brimstone at the centre on the outside. Putting each end of the wire in the tube, then striking the brimstone like a match, would heat up the solder enough to make a quick join. It was advisable to carry self-solder joints at all times if on manoeuvres.

Because we had been called up in October, it wasn't long before Remembrance Sunday came around. Leading up to it all, every one had to have a poppy, which was worn behind the cap badge. All trainees had to attend. Having been fell in for church parade we were all marched off to the local army church. Upon our arrival other detachments could be seen there, as well as civilians and female army personnel entering church.

The familiar service seemed to take on a completely different meaning this time. Maybe it was because of the predominance of khaki-coloured uniforms, or the sound of a largely male voice congregation. This is not taking anything away from the women who were there; far from it, the nurses and doctors play a much more vital role than they are given credit for in army welfare. Even to this day, a Remembrance Day service has a special feeling for me. I didn't know it at the time, but the next church service for Remembrance Day I would have in camp would be even more significant, and would deepen my understanding of the one I'd just taken part in.

As time passed each section would get more training in the trade that they had been assigned. Even so, early morning runs combined with regular kit inspections went ahead as usual. Bulling boots, ironing uniforms and polishing brasses still had to be done at night after being dismissed for the day. A gradual improvement in everything we did was becoming obvious. Without a great deal of shouting from the NCOs, tasks were beginning to get done automatically. Passing out would be virtually at Christmas time. From now on our instruction was to be more hands-on.

Radio Training

The regular drivers liked the radio exercises best. We'd drive to some isolated location, then tune in to control, lock on to the frequency and ask for a signal strength reading. Then we would begin to send and receive messages. The 19 set had a variometer designed to bring in the signal better. This piece of equipment was a cylinder-shaped device bolted to the top of the set, and it had to be adjusted to find a better signal strength. While all this was going on, with each signaller taking turns at tuning in, the drivers would just sit in their warm cabs reading a daily paper or a book. It was only when the cab became cold that the driver started to moan and groan.

Another type of set was a 62 or 72. This kind had two dials for tuning in, and was often used as an air OP plane set, as it was smaller, lighter and easier to handle than the 19 set. There were other sets to operate, but these two were the main ones we would be using. Most of them, I might add, were ex-Second World War sets, so you can see how readily the British Government splashed out money on modern equipment for its fighting forces!

The most difficult part of instruction was writing down messages. Did we not know the type of message to expect? No we didn't. With the weather being cold, I had my thick leather gloves on, so using a pencil, and getting the correct paperwork done was rather clumsy to say the least. With cold winds blowing it was nice to have the headsets on, if only to keep the ears warm.

After all our tests we had all passed the exam, so the next and final trial was the gunnery test.

This took us back to the gun park. For the test, the gun was already deployed. Number One was in charge of the gun, making sure it was manoeuvred into firing position. If it needed to be realigned he would normally put his hand out and, using hand and finger widths to gauge the degrees of movement needed, move the gun to an approximate position.

The Number Two had to line his sights on to two solid, unmoveable objects. If the first was destroyed, he would move to the secondary aiming point in order to continue the shoot. At each correction the Number One would go to the sights and make certain the settings were right. I used moveable objects in order to fail, but Sgt Clay passed me out anyhow. Then he later said he would get me two stripes if I went on his gun as the layer. I told him I had my heart set on being a signaller. Some might think this was a stupid decision, but who could tell what the future held?

Christmas Pass Home and Passing Out Parade

Passing out would be after Christmas, so we all thought we'd be in camp over the holiday period. It turned out, however, that nobody wanted to be arsed with a load of NIGs, especially when all other officers and NCOs would be on leave, leaving just a skeleton staff behind. The staff were made up mainly of Scottish personnel who wanted to be home for Hogmanay. That is their most important and enjoyable time.

After our Christmas leave was confirmed, it was all hands on pen and paper as we frantically wrote home to our loved ones telling them our good news. I wrote to my mother to tell her I would be home. My eldest brother, who had already been in the forces, had told her that by rights we should not be on leave until after passing out parade, which would have been after Christmas.

I then wrote to Dave and Tony telling them the good news and asking if they could get an extra ticket for any events that they might be going to so that I could go too. I had begun to write more often to Sylvia, so I wrote and told her also that I would be home for Christmas. Could she make some arrangements for us to meet up and get to know each other better?

Her reply was only to be expected: she had already made plans with her friends as to where they were going. We would therefore have to meet up in between the main party nights. This was a strange time for me really, because I had not had a girlfriend at all before going into the forces. I had mostly been interested in football. To be juggling my time between home, my mates and a girlfriend was something quite new to me. I had to show my mother my pass in order to convince her that I wasn't AWOL.

Holiday over, I returned to camp for preparation of passing out. The spit and polishing still continued along with bumping and polishing floors, the inspections of kit lay-out in the mornings, and personal hygiene checks with final medical jabs if required. Passing out parade had to be done with rifle drill, probably because it helped when having to go on guard mounting for the very first time. Each morning as the day approached, on to the parade ground we would go, drilling for hours through the same routine until it was almost second nature.

The bombardier in charge had come from the Paratroop Regiment. He was a Scouser, and as hard as they come. The reason he had been posted to another regiment was that he had broken a leg in a jump. He knew that I came from St Helens near Liverpool, so for the last fortnight before passing out he would come along the ranks, stand in front of me, do his inspection and say, 'Balmer you're a f—ing big tart, what are you?' I would reply each time with, 'I'm a nice boy, me, Bombardier.' He would then carry on inspecting as if nothing had happened.

Day after day I put up with this verbal abuse until the final day of the passing out. On this morning he did his usual routine, until, that is, he came and stood in front of me. Looking up and down, then all round, he said, 'Now Balmer, you're a nice boy today, aren't you?' To which I replied, 'No, Bombardier, I'm a f—ing big tart.' At this he looked at me again and bellowed out, 'You f—ing awkward bastard!' I think he got the message that all his bawling and shouting and foul-mouthed tirades hadn't had a great effect on me.

During the parade could be seen the RSM (Regimental Sergeant Major) and other officers watching. It was a great satisfaction and relief to have finished basic training, and to join the rest of the regiment properly. On returning our rifles and going back to our bunks, we were given our new battery and troop assignments. Mine was to Charlie Troop, 170 Imjin Battery. Many might think that after passing out things would be much easier. Wrong, because training with the full regiment, followed by divisional training, was to come, as well as getting to know new guys in the billet.

Joining Charlie Troop, 170 Battery, Manoeuvres on Bodmin Moor and at Sennybridge

With kit all packed up, off we all went to our designated troops. Charlie Troop, 170 Imjin Battery was my destination. I was one of only two going to 170, the other being a lad named Bob Bailey. I think he went into Delta Troop as a driver, but later got the job of driving Captain Pettifer, who was in C Troop.

An end room on the second floor was where I had to go. As it was just across the barracks from where we already were, I had an easy task to lug my kit there. From the doorway of the room I'd been told to go to, it seemed to me that every bed was taken. But when I stepped into the room I saw a space immediately to the left, hidden behind a large locker. That was to be my bed for the next nine months.

The room was well laid out, much the same as the one I'd just left, with a small bedside cabinet, a reading lamp over the head of the bed, and curtained windows. In the centre was a table with a chair, which could be used for letter writing or pressing our kit on; a radio was also visible on the table. A payment of sixpence per person each week was required to hire it.

Putting my stuff on the bed I began to unpack and place all my gear in the locker as usual, putting my boots on top. One of the lads, who was a Jock (a Scot), came over, picked up my boots, looked at them, then threw them to the other end of the room saying, 'We're not bulling to that f—ing standard for a f—ing start off.' Just think: all that hard work gone in two seconds. He'd spoiled a pair of pristine bulled boots that any guardsman would have been justly proud of. What could I do? Absolutely sod all. I was just one in a room of six. I picked my boots up and put them back where they'd come from. That was my welcome to true army life.

The NCO had a room of his own adjacent to ours. Most of

the time though he seemed to be quite happy to leave us to get on
with our normal duties. We knew quite well a room inspection by
an officer might come at any moment. So bumping the floor and
dusting down lockers was an additional task to attending to our
normal uniform and civilian clothes.

The corridor had other rooms leading off, but at the head of
the stairs was a drying room. This was for drying out webbing
after it had be blancoed, and any other article that may need
drying out. It was not unusual at the end of a day's duties to see
civilian clobber hanging up to dry as well.

Most of the lads had packs with either cardboard or plywood
inside, to keep them square and free of finger marks – otherwise
they'd need cleaning more often, which is what we didn't want to
do. Denims were the normal everyday wear. They were made
from a lighter type of material than the denim of today. They
were worn, buttoned up to the neck, and except for cap badge and
NCO stripes, no distinguishing signs would be seen. Denims
were for work purposes only. If by chance someone had a
uniform on it was because they would be on an assignment of
some kind – sick, escort duty or something similar. An NCO gave
out mail and issued the duties for the day. Only on the odd
occasion would we see an officer when more important orders
had to be given. The NCO took nearly all morning parades.

Captain Pettifer was now the Troop Captain, and I was asked
to be his batman. I thought I would give it a try and see if I liked
the duty. Every morning I was off to his rooms to sort out his kit,
iron and polish and clean up the room. He had a small dog named
Spot. It was little swine, barking and nipping at first, but after a
while it got used to me and settled down OK. Getting to know
Spot like this became an advantage of tremendous value, although
I didn't know it at the time. One thing I learnt how to do was to
prepare his dress uniform for a regimental dinner. It consisted of
white shirt and dicky bow tie, a waistcoat-size jacket with medals,
and a pair of narrow drainpipe trousers with loops at the very
bottom of each leg that fitted under ankle-length riding boots
with spurs inserted in the heels.

Not being backward in coming forward, I had to ask Captain
Pettifer how on earth one got the boots inside the trousers. The

answer was simple: put the boots on the floor in front of a chair; roll down the trouser legs and place the boots inside from the bottom up, making certain that the pants are facing forward; put the loops under the insteps of the boots, then insert the spurs into the heels. After putting on the boots it was an easy matter to draw the pants up to waist level, then fit a black cummerbund, and all was ready for dinner.

Being a man of leisure he also had riding attire: calf-length riding boots with spurs, a black hat, whip and gloves. I mention his red riding coat last, because to say I was amazed at it is an understatement. It was so thick that I tried (and all but succeeded) to stand it up without any other support. It was only after a few seconds that the coat began to collapse in on itself.

After a couple of weeks of these tasks, I was becoming bored, so I asked if I could be relieved of this duty. Without any fuss at all I went back into the troop.

There it was general duties as normal. Then for some reason or other, I had to go down to the guardroom with the BSM (Battery Sergeant Major). He entered first with myself close behind. Inside, I was directly behind the BSM with my right shoulder close up to a wall on my right side. He immediately threw up a salute – an officer was directly in front. Being so close to the wall and caught unawares I just stood rigidly to attention. I received an instant ear-bashing from the sergeant on duty, who asked why I had not saluted also. My brain was in a whirl, so I replied that I'd just come out of training and had been instructed to go the longest way up and the shortest way down when saluting an officer, but with the wall being so close I couldn't do this. So I had stood to attention instead. The reply is not hard to imagine, and the TSM (Troop Sergeant Major) was told to take me back to barracks and give me what for.

Off we went round the camp and down the side of the quadrangle. Again the building and the TSM were on my right side. I was looking right talking to him, when once again he made a salute. I looked left only to see another officer, to whom I saluted forthwith. I then got another bawling out, and was told to 'keep your f—ing eyes wide open at all times, otherwise you're going to get your arse right in it!' I don't know how, but I survived both incidents without getting any extra duties of any kind. However, it was an experience never to be forgotten.

Further training had now begun. I was to be with Captain Pettifer at the OP (Observation Post) as his signaller. This time it was for real with a full battery, becoming more used to using our call signs and getting to know the voices with any slight accent that might be there. Now, being January going into February, with the weather always very cold, I was even more thankful for the horsehide gloves and huge greatcoat that I had. Moving in troop formation on public highways was another challenge. I say this because drivers of quads needed to move their steering wheels only slightly and the gun would sway from side to side. If you were close behind when this happened you'd get a horrible feeling that the gun was coming loose.

Next, orders came for us to stay out on a scheme for two days; being winter we knew it wasn't going to be easy. Rubbing salt into the wound, we could see the lights of our camp about three miles away. This position was chosen so that the officers could go back to camp where it was nice and warm. We therefore had to find a nice cosy place to bed down. The group I was with had a load of hessian and camouflage nets, so we began the task of making a bed of sorts. Knowing that the temperature could be as low as minus seven degrees, we used everything we could. Then we bedded down together under this heap we'd made. Early next morning, as we were getting up, a sergeant appeared only to see two of us coming from under the camouflage. He pointed out right away that it was not accepted in the army to have two people in one bed. The answer he got was, 'That's OK then, Sarge, there's four of us that's been under here.' He just laughed and went away, smiling and shaking his head.

Another thing of interest was that Spot, Captain Pettifer's dog, would sometimes get loose during guard mounting time. About 5.30 p.m., all spruced up, the guard marched on to the square and lined up ready for inspection; as if by magic the dog would appear. The command to order or port arms seemed only to prompt the dog into jumping up and biting hands or uniform, so it became a common sight to see someone kick the dog if ever the chance came along. Upon hearing a yap-yap-yap the guard commander glanced around, only to see the dog rolling away and the soldier who had kicked it shuffling back into line. It was that or having a person going to hospital for dog bites. Once it was established whose dog it was, steps were later taken to have it kept in when guard mounting was due.

It wasn't very long before it was my turn for guard duty. Notification was always on Part One Orders. It was a must to read them because no excuse whatever would be taken for non-compliance of orders. As normal the guard was assembled just off the regimental square. A quick once-over was done, then we were marched on to the square. This particular evening we saw the RSM standing in the very far corner of the parade ground. I think word had got around about the dog, so he was looking to see what happened. All correct, we were given open order march,[1] and inspection began. The one considered best turned-out would be what was called stickman, and his job would be to fetch and carry food and drink, and perform any errands that needed doing; but he got a good night's sleep, so it was a sought-after job.

All was going well until the dog appeared and jumped up to bite someone's hand. Then it ran in between ranks causing havoc, and at every chance it was kicked. It never seemed to bother with me, though – I think in the short time I had been batman the dog had come to know who I was. There was no interference from the RSM at this time because no one but the officer is in charge when guard mounting.

A 'stag' was a two-hour patrol of duty. The one I got was down near the nurses' quarters. I went around as usual with little or nothing to do, but on the next stag it was dark and it wasn't easy to see if a nurse was an officer or not. I saluted anyone I thought was an officer and just said goodnight to those I was unsure of, but I never received a reply except from one nurse. Back in the guardroom, I remarked about this. Then one lad began to tell me that another bloke in our troop had been going out with a nurse, had had a fall-out and been accused of rape or something like that. It was now quite clear that when the citation I was wearing was seen it told them to be stand-offish. Being a

---

[1] The front rank would take two paces forward to allow the officer to walk between ranks. If in three ranks, the back rank would take two paces to the rear.

new lad I got the worst stag without knowing it, and here's me thinking other things.

Captain Pettifer was Charlie Troop's captain, which meant he was also the OP Officer – and guess who was to be his permanent flaggy. Yes, that's right, me. So from training, to batman, then OP flaggy – I still couldn't get away from him. As time passed though, I found him good to be with, and had some enjoyable experiences with him at the OP schemes, with the exception of the all-night ones. Up to that time, however, most had been of one-day duration. The practice of picking up, loading and signing for everything we were taking with us became mundane. Yet signing made sure that you began to know which headsets, mouthpieces, batteries and connections, telephones, remote controls, drums of wire and carriers and other radio equipment we would be taking out on any given scheme. Signing for everything also ensured that items had to be paid for if damaged due to neglect or loss. I soon cottoned on to this system, and took every chance I had of picking up broken or discarded materials. I'd bring them back and make out a recce note for the article in question. At first the sergeant thought I was being rather reckless with my kit, until he noticed my kit was still coming back in good order. At this rate it didn't take long for others to cotton on and also bring in excess kit. Doing this meant little or no problem if anyone lost any kit.

It was the driver's job to fill up with petrol. Then, in a trailer, he would pick up rations from the cookhouse, before making his way to the Signals store where I would load all of the radio equipment, fixing it into specified locations in the champ. A champ was a vehicle not unlike a Land Rover; it was about the same size but with more rounded features. The most singular and important feature was that the engine was completely encased in a waterproof shell, giving it the ability to go under water and continue to operate by way of a snorkel device. The vehicle was made by Rolls-Royce and was a very good piece of equipment. Its only downfall, was that, if for any reason it needed to be repaired, having to take the engine out of its shell made for a very lengthy job.

Putting any surplus into the trailer, last but by no means least, together we'd go and pick up our officer, who was nearly always

Captain Pettifer. On most occasions I would get the opportunity to help the driver, which I did whenever possible, because if you were seen to be hanging around for any reason you'd be given an additional job to do. This made it hard to complete your own tasks, and get to the gun park in readiness for deployment out on to the ranges.

Training on Bodmin Moor

Our first major scheme was to be at Oakhampton, on Bodmin Moor. However, it took place only after 120 or 180 Bty had been before us. When they came back we heard of the awful weather they'd faced. On one occasion they had used drag ropes to haul the guns up a hill because the quads couldn't get any wheel grip on the icy roads.

The day came when it was 170 Bty's turn to deploy for our Bodmin scheme. As we had a radio on board, the responsibility of keeping all vehicles in contact with each other fell upon both OP champ and the BC (Battery Captain) champ, running up and down the convoy line to make certain there were no stragglers left behind. My memory of this base camp is rather vague, so I don't think it could have been too bad.

On day two it was off on to the moors for our first shoot. The guns went to their location and we, the OP, went to ours. With visibility at something like two- to three-hundred yards it was a relief when the shoot was handed over to Delta Troop, who I suppose were in a better location for seeing things. Being stood down allowed us an opportunity to go to the gun positions to see how things were turning out. At the bottom of a slight hill we found what we were looking for, but the weather was still closing in. We stopped near to the CP (Command Post) and heard a commotion because the CP was starting to sink, both sideways and backwards. A decision had to be made whether or not to abandon the position and relocate; the choice was to abandon. Guns were also sinking slowly down into the bog. The nearest one to us was twisting round because of the weight of its barrel and its position. Every one of the gun crew was trying his best to stop any further movement but was failing miserably. At seeing us three from the OP just standing there watching, the bombardier in charge let forth a tirade of f—ing and blinding. All three of us were ordered to get our shoulders to the gun and help to get it off its platform. This was eventually achieved, then the gun had to be lifted up to be secured for turning, then turned so that the quad could retrieve it from its position. In the Artillery the gun is more important than anything or anyone, hence the tirade to us three, who included the captain from the Number One. Without guns you are no longer a unit.

Later in the week, with the weather getting better and Delta Troop OP doing the ranging, we again found ourselves at our own gun positions. A previous target had been fired on and the lads were having their packed lunches. They were sprawled about on limbers and guns, happily eating away, when the tannoy boomed out: Take post target… At this everyone dashed to their positions, loaded up and began to fire. The first recoil sent the food and mugs of tea all over everywhere. Firing still went ahead; nobody took any notice of what had happened to the food. It was only on the order of 'stand down' that gunners started to look for what was left. Some lads had had the presence of mind to wrap up their lunches and take them to the gun – obviously old sweats who had done this before.

The week seemed to be a hit-or-miss affair, but some good was coming out of all these exercises we were doing. It was only on further exercises that you could see improvement on deployment, and an automatic understanding of who had what to do. We returned to Tidworth later that week to await our next big scheme.

Sennybridge Scheme

After a few weeks, up on orders came news that our next scheme was to be on the Brecon Beacons, at a place called Sennybridge. All the gear was packed and the regiment set out on what was to be a rather long trek. This saw all the regiment on the move, with the same problem of keeping things together in convoy, but this time on a much grander scale.

Camp at Sennybridge was nothing to write home about; to all

intents and purposes it looked more like an old, disused prisoner of war camp. Huts were an all-wooden structure and had a musty smell as if they hadn't been occupied for some time. From what I can remember, the so-called parade ground was a basic tarmac area. The wagon lines and guns were furthest away from our hut. The cookhouse had huge cauldrons heated by steam coming from a central boiler house. All of the camp seemed to be in a kind of semi-readiness. Because national service would be coming to an end in 1960, this meant there would be fewer personnel to contend with. Maybe, however, the run-down impression was because the weather wasn't very good. The entrance to camp from off the ranges was by way of a bridge, which had a ford running alongside; this stream would become very useful indeed. After settling in and securing everything for the night we prepared whatever kit we might need for the following day's exercise, and then turned in for the night.

Early next morning after vehicle inspection, all having been found correct, we were given an order for deployment, and away we all went on to the ranges. At this exercise, gun crews were being reduced from six to five men. This meant doing away with the limber and limber gunner (the Number Six), also the quads, and using three-ton trucks to do the job of both pieces of equipment. Nothing of note happened on the shoots and it was decided to leave guns and equipment out all night with a one-man guard. 'You should never volunteer for anything in the army' is the motto, but after weighing up the situation and location I offered to stay behind for the night.

Nearby was an old drystone wall, which over time had become covered with soil and grass. With help from other lads I obtained a huge tarpaulin and built a lean-to against the wall, then transferred what kit I thought would be needed for the night. The radio was put inside with headsets and batteries, and a storm lantern which would not only give light but heat as well. Having already taken water, food, a small kettle and shaving and washing kit from the trailer, I settled down for a lonely night all on my little Jack Jones. When everyone had departed I checked all around just to make sure thing were OK, then went inside the lean-to. I switched the radio over to Radio Luxembourg and settled down for a hard night of spine-bashing, instead of listening to NCOs giving their orders.

Next day, up nice and early, having cooked my own breakfast, washed and shaved, and checked around to make certain all seemed OK, I began to put everything back in the trailer to save time for when the troop turned up. Just after nine o'clock they all arrived. I could then get help to put the radio and batteries back into the champ ready for the off.

A gun position on clear, open ground had been chosen the previous day. It soon became apparent when we reached it that, over night, heavy rain had caused the gun to become stuck in soft ground. Therefore a new site had to be picked before we could carry on shooting. Three ton trucks appeared on site, coming over a small but rather steep bank. The first truck was driven by a lad named Eddy Spinks, who many thought was one of our better three-ton Bedford drivers. On his coming to the banking it became more obvious than ever that things weren't going to turn out as easy as was expected. In very low gear, slipping and sliding, the wagon eventually got on to more suitable ground, but it soon became clear that the three-tonners were not well enough equipped at this time to pull the guns out. Therefore the job was given back to quads.

First, a quad raced to a rope's length from a gun. After the rope had been connected winching began, but it was the quad that was moving towards the gun, so towing stopped. With arm-waving signals, a second quad approached the first in single file, hooked up with a hawser, and began to winch in, still getting the same results as the first. Finally a Matador was sent for. This vehicle transported tanks, and normally had a four-ton block of concrete on its drive wheels to enable it to get road grip. Its huge wheels seemed to be three or four feet high and a foot wide.

Placed in line at a rope's distance it anchored itself down, hooking up to the nearest quad. With hawser ropes slowly drawing ever more taut, the retrieval began; first gun to quad, then quad to quad, then quad to Matador. Each time slack rope was given out in order to continue the withdrawal until all vehicles had been got out. This action took quite some time, leaving all who took part with clinging mud on boots and gaiters, as well as having very cold and muddy hands.

The weather began to close in again so we returned to camp. Coming upon the bridge, the drivers decided to go through the ford instead, telling all inside the vehicle what they intended. Down into a swollen, fast-running river plunged quad, gun and limber. Mud and muck came off everything below axle height as if the vehicle were being hosed down with high-powered jets of water. Upon seeing how clean things came out the other side, every driver diverted into the ford instead of using the bridge. The champ I was in had the encased engine with a snorkel device that enabled it to travel in water with the engine submerged. As we were only axle deep, across everyone went without hesitation.

On the gun park it was all hands to the pumps, so to speak, getting all vehicles cleaned before anyone could go for tea. Having cleaned up and had tea it was back to the billets to clean our own kit. We'd been at it about an hour when in came an officer followed by a sergeant carrying two rather large jugs. As normal all stood to attention wondering what was to come. To everyone's surprise we were told to stand easy and get our mugs – we were to have a rum ration in respect of the extreme weather and the effort that had been put in on the day's exercise. Of all the stories I'd heard about army life in national service, getting a rum ration was definitely not one. I've often told this story to others after demob, only to be disbelieved in army tones and language. It can only be presumed that the other batteries also received the same rum ration.

An improvement in the weather was needed; other than snow or blizzards, things couldn't get much worse. Improvement is what we got, so exercises continued as usual. A night off was welcomed. The only place to go, however, was into Sennybridge. A dance would be the obvious place to go, so off we went, but getting in was a nightmare. To say it was crowded is an understatement. When we all got inside it looked more like a sit-in in a sardine can. All chairs had been taken. It was hard to tell where the dance floor started or finished.

Having the American citation on my uniform let it be known to other RA bods that I was in 61 Field Regiment Charlie Troop, 170 Battery. It didn't take long for the usual jibes to start, along with pushing and jostling. We put up with this for some time, when out of the blue Bob Wagstaff pushed his way to the stage, got on to it, grabbed the mike, and said: 'I'll flatten the next bastard that treads on my boots again. I'm sick of being trod on.' These may not be the exact words spoken but I think it's close enough. For the most part all the snide remarks seemed to come from a group we later found to be 25 Field Regiment.

It wasn't long after this that MPs appeared on the door, so it was decided to see if we could find another place to go. A small café a few yards down the road seemed to be the only option open to us. In we went and ordered whatever drinks we wanted, but it soon became outstandingly obvious that we weren't really wanted in that place either. Slowly we let time pass until our transport came to take us back to camp.

As we were in mid Wales, one lad named Krisher, who had a German father and a Welsh mother, did manage to hitch home and back over the weekend off. He kept the secret as to the best place to hitch from to himself. I think being able to speak the Welsh language helped a great deal.

After the weekend it was back to training. On writing this episode I now realise that, with a tank transporter available, and meeting 25 Field lads, this must have been a divisional scheme, and maybe some of the others in that dance hall I described could have been from an infantry unit. Something like another week went by, with us still doing trial exercises before returning to our base camp at Tidworth, Andover.

Schemes came with monotonous regularity, and to try to remember each one in turn is nigh on impossible. One or two, however, stand out quite plainly. On one such scheme on Salisbury plains, an officer either asked off his own bat for a night patrol, or an order was received from HQ to do a recce of the area by night. Anyhow, a signaller was needed to go out as well in order to keep in contact if need be. Captain Pettifer very kind-heartedly volunteered my services, because once again my OP had been stood down for the night. Duly volunteered, I equipped myself with what I think was a 38 set. It went the full length of my back and was fitted with an eight-foot aerial. A longer aerial could be attached but could prove too dangerous in the dark if any low pylons were overhead. The other problem was that a twelve-foot aerial swayed a great deal when one was walking, so the smaller one was the better option. A rifle was also given to me to carry, in order to simulate a genuine infantry patrol.

Being the radio man, my position was directly behind the officer, travelling in single file with the rest of the group stretched out behind. When all was ready, off we set along what appeared to be a type of farm track. We'd gone about a mile when we veered to the right down a steep embankment which dropped about thirty feet. Slipping and sliding we reached the bottom and proceeded in the same direction as the road for something like another hundred yards or so, then did a right turn away from the roadway. Still in silence and in Indian file we continued with just the sound of calf-length grass brushing our legs. When about thirty minutes had gone by a voice at the rear shouted, 'Freeze, Freeze!' The officer asked what was wrong, only to be told that we had wandered into a minefield. We had no option other than to turn around and retrace our steps, hoping that we would all be OK. It came to light that the wire fence had been broken down somehow, and the third-from-last man had trodden on a triangle, turning it over, to reveal the danger sign. The last man saw it; how he saw it in the dark I don't know, but thank goodness he did.

Skirting round the field's perimeter we continued as before, but soon came to an extent of uneven ground. Up and down we bobbed along when, all at once, whoosh! Down I went into an old infantry foxhole. The officer had stepped over it, not saying a word of warning and giving no indication at all; I just walked straight into it. My left leg was up against the far side of the hole, with my right foot tucked in under my left knee, and the right knee also jammed firmly against the far side of the hole. The rifle had twisted underneath me, going between my back and radio. With the rifle strap trapping my right arm at the elbow, my back was arched backwards, making it impossible for me to move forward, because of the shoulder straps on the radio holding me down. The only thing I could move was my left arm. Even so, the straps were restricting me in such a manner, that I was still unable to reach any other parts of my body that were trapped.

The next instant the officer said, 'Don't just lie there, get up man!' to which I replied, 'Get up? I can't bloody move.'

'Don't swear when you're talking to me,' he replied.

'Sorry, sir,' I said, 'but I still can't move.' At this he told two men to lift me up so that I could disentangle myself. They got me to a sitting position which then gave me the chance to release my legs and climb out of the foxhole. Without asking if I was OK, or if the radio was still working, he set off as if nothing had happened. I thought, what an officer! No kiss my arse, no nothing, nearly been blown up in a minefield, nearly lost his radio op and he didn't give a monkey's. Thank goodness nothing else happened on the remainder of the patrol, because with what had happened I'll swear he had his map upside down. I never came into contact with this officer again, thank goodness. The rest of the scheme must have gone OK as that's all I can remember of this one.

Life in Camp

Life in camp wasn't the same day after day with boring duties; sometimes a good laugh could come from someone else's downfall, if that's the correct way to put it. The incident I always remember was a day when a Scottish lad was on duty as battery runner. All he needed to do was deliver messages by bicycle to other parts of the camp. Well, he was sent on an errand to the sergeants' quarters which were at the top of a long slope or slight hill. After delivering his message, down the hill he came, free-wheeling all the way, steadily gathering speed.

Now, to get back to BHQ (Battery Headquarters) he needed to turn left at the end of our billet, then take a sharp right to bring himself back in front of our office. Down he came at speed, turning in at the end of our billet – but at that moment saw an officer. At this he threw up a salute, turning his head to the left, to look at the officer. Within seconds he lost control of the bike. He and the bike went headlong into a whitewashed brick surround, which had a small chain-link fence about a foot high around a small flower bed. Hitting the chain, he and the bike went flying over into a geranium flowerbed, with the bike at one side and him spreadeagled on his back. Out came the BSM, who remarked, 'If I'd have wanted a bloody gardener I'd have asked for one. Now get out of there before I put you on a charge for destroying government property.' So once again, no sympathy at all being given, no question as to whether or not he was hurt; just 'get up, I have another job for you'.

It would be around this time that I was standing on the veranda opposite 120 Bty when a voice shouted out, 'What are you doing here?' Looking to my right I saw a lad named Archie Bedford. He was about twelve months older than me, and a very good athlete. Lo and behold, stood with him was another lad named Bob Sumner. He was twelve months younger than me. Both lived on the next estate back home; all three of us had gone to the same school and played in our respective form group's rugby teams.

We'd been exchanging general info as to when and where we had joined up when a 2nd lieutenant came on the scene and began to talk to Archie. When the conversation was over, Archie pointed out to the officer that I could play rugby quite well. At this he enquired where I came from. 'St Helens, sir,' I replied. 'Oh, sorry, we want rugby players,' he answered, and began to walk away. Archie and Bob tried to convince him he was wrong but he took no notice. As I already played football for the battery team but couldn't get a game in the troop team, I wasn't too upset with his attitude at all.

'General duties' covered a great range of tasks. One duty was to go to a place we called Fargo. This was the local ammunition depot. Although our regiment was a field regiment it was often our task to unload 3.7 heavy ack-ack ammo; just one of these shells weighed about the same as two boxes of twenty-five pounder shells. The weight was so great that only six to eight were ever loaded on to a three-ton truck at any one time. Having nothing but the shell to get hold of when transferring from wagon to trucks you had to watch you didn't trap your fingers. This was especially hazardous if they were wet. We'd slide them along the railway wagons and kick them into the trucks, lifting them as little as possible. If we had our own twenty-five pounder ammo to do, we'd just slide the boxes of four shells per box to the end of the wagons, then two lads would lift the boxes by rope handles into the trucks. This chore I did about four times in all, so once every six weeks or so on average wasn't too bad really.

Other jobs such as latrines and cookhouse, painting and equipment maintenance, were designated after parade each morning, along with the handing out of any mail that might have arrived. In national service days very few people had a telephone in their homes, and mobile phones were still only in Dick Tracy comic books, so writing a letter home was one of the few ways to keep in touch with loved ones. No matter how good you were at spelling or writing, those few lines were all it took to reassure them you were still OK. Writing to your mother or girlfriend would I think be the most important. I'd got well into the habit of writing to my then girlfriend, so I was quite happy on that score.

If on latrine duty you would always have an NCO in charge of the detachment, inspecting every now and then to see if the place was clean enough or whether something had been overlooked. Floors had to be mopped, handbasins and taps cleaned, toilet bowls scrubbed and toilet rolls replaced if need be. Some latrines had mirrors – these also had to be spotlessly clean. Most of the time, any job was pushed to its limit with regard to the time it would take to complete. After all, the faster a job was finished, the faster you were found another job to do, so skiving soon became a regimental pastime. The one big problem with latrine duties was that you couldn't skive off and sit on the toilet for half an hour, having a sly drag while the others were still working.

No matter what duty you were given, none was ever so bad that you couldn't get the good old NAAFI break. It was great to go for a cuppa, but getting towards Tuesday or Wednesday it was common to hear somebody trying to bum a copper or two off one of their mates in order to get a drink and a bun.

Cookhouse duties at 61 Field were not as bad as portrayed in the films that were later made. Civilians were beginning to be employed to do most of the cleaning and such; however, this did not in any way stop the cookhouse from being made a tool of punishment in certain circumstances. In some of the more modern camps canteens had a more up-to-date layout and design to allow easier cleaning of floors and crockery. Potatoes and vegetables were prepared by an automatic peeler, with most of the large pots and pans being done by the civilians employed there, or maybe someone on jankers, who for some reason or other had done wrong.

What we would call a prisoner would be a person who had committed a serious breach of army regulations. Absent without leave is an obvious one, but other misdemeanours could result in the miscreant being brought in, if seen fit by an officer issuing a charge. One day I had an opportunity to get my hair cut; it was just after lunch so I had ample time to spare. I sat down to wait my turn, but after a short while an RMP (Regimental Military Police) walked in with a prisoner. Prisoners always took precedence, so he sat down in the barber's chair immediately it became vacant. The barber was told to give the prisoner a very short back and sides. When this was finished, up the prisoner got and left; ten minutes later, back came the same prisoner. The barber was told to cut his hair shorter, which he proceeded to do. Off the man went again; ten minutes later he was back, but this time the provost sergeant was with him. It was he who told the barber to cut the prisoner's hair even shorter still. The barber looked in amazement and said, 'I can't cut it much shorter.' Then the provost replied, 'If you don't do as I say, you'll be looking for another camp to cut hair in.' With a nod the barber obliged, but you could tell he didn't like doing what he had to do. The prisoner left the shop virtually bald, but the provost sergeant had won the day and walked out happy. It's worth noting here that the prisoner had to pay for each visit. This would be another way of getting at him while he was in prison.

Hitchhiking and C Troop

As we were short on money most of the time, the best way to get home would be to hitchhike. Writing was all well and good but to get home for just forty-eight hours was welcomed at every opportunity. A major problem was to find out in advance if you were to be on duty over the weekend. If I could, it would be easier to get a coach or a flyer down to the A338, and then thumb a lift north towards Swindon, then on to Kidderminster, bypassing Birmingham, still going north to Newcastle-under-Lyme, then St Helens.

At my first try at thumbing things were working out OK. When you were dressed in khaki, most drivers gave lifts, because they'd been in the forces and knew what money was like in those days. I got my first pick-up and went along quite well until the wagon was turning off. Giving me advice as to my next best pick-up, the driver stopped, dropped me off, then carried on his way. Soon I picked up another wagon going north. The normal procedure when the wagon stopped was to tell the driver your destination. If he was going in that direction he would tell you to jump in.

I got in and away we went. Then I realised how slowly we were travelling. After a short while we began to talk. It was only then that the driver told me that the engine was governed to a maximum speed of thirty miles per hour. Still, trundling along at thirty was better than nothing, so feeling quite happy and warm, I was content to sit and be driven. Some time had gone by when the driver remarked about liking the next bit of run we'd come to. He said that by his knocking the engine out of gear the vehicle would coast along saving petrol as it went. Well, by this time we were at the top of a very long, slow descending hill which seemed to go on for ever. With the engine in neutral the wagon began to pick up speed. Faster and faster we travelled, cab beginning to shake and bounce, rattling side to side. How fast we went I'll never know, but to say our speed reached something like sixty to seventy wouldn't be far from the mark. The wagon began to slow down gradually to its governed speed. The driver was used to doing it so often he simply eased the engine into gear, and carried on as if nothing had happened.

Having made it home, getting back to camp was dead easy. Every Sunday night a feeder coach would leave Liverpool and other major towns or cities, taking squaddies back to their respective regiments. The Liverpool coach was driven most times by a guy named Vic Bromlings, a bloke we'd all get to know very well. He'd call at Prescot, Warrington, Sandbach, always ending up at Newcastle-under-Lyme, where all other coaches met to transfer personnel as need be, to get them back to camp. With transfers completed all coaches set off for their designated dropping points. We arrived at Tidworth on average around four or five o'clock in the morning.

On one occasion when I arrived back, there was a sand and water fight going on. First sand from the fire buckets had been thrown over the balcony at lads below, who in turn grabbed the water buckets and pumps, then began squirting water on to people on the upper level. Fighting continued and the lads on the ground floor eventually got upstairs and into the rooms. After an hour or so had passed, the orderly officer appeared on the scene asking what the hell was going on. Seeing and finding out that it was just a boisterous and non-violent knock about with sand and water, he declared that no action would be taken if all rooms were spick and span for an inspection at 9 a.m. in full uniform with no defaulters of any kind. Needless to say everybody knuckled under to get the task done. That we got it all finished, as well as having breakfast and changing into full uniform by 9 a.m. was no mean feat.

On another hitchhike, I got a lift with a promise of going north towards Swindon. Just after leaving there, however, the driver turned on to the A361. Still trusting his judgement that I was going in the right direction, I sat back and chatted to the driver about this and that. Eventually he pulled in at a café. We both jumped out and went in. Doing so I pulled my comb out and began to tidy my hair, at which the proprietress or waitress told me not to comb my hair near the counter. With everyone looking on I said nothing; but the driver, pointing to a table, told me to go and sit down as he would get the drinks in. I still don't know if it was what she said or my being in uniform that caused the other drivers to go a little quiet. Tea finished, off we set again and continued north, going through Coventry, followed by Nuneaton. I knew I was on the wrong side of Birmingham.

Making conversation again I found out that the driver was going through Derby and on to Sheffield. Avoiding major cities was a must when hitching. Once inside a city it was impossible to hitch a lift – it would be thought that you should be catching a taxi. Anyhow, nearing Derby the driver dropped me off just before a large roundabout and told me to take the first road left, which I think was the A52. Out I got, walked to the roundabout, went something like fifty to a hundred yards, and began again thumbing a lift. I'd been at it for a while when a car came off the roundabout towards me. Looking at it I immediately thought, no chance, and turned away; but to my astonishment the car pulled over and the window was wound down. The passenger in the car asked where was I headed. I told him towards Liverpool. He said a word to the driver, turned back again to me asking if I had boots on. I replied 'No' to this and he said, 'Please remove your belt and get in.' With the greatest of pleasure I obeyed. You see, this car was none other than a Rolls-Royce. Sitting back I sank into the all-leather seats.

The two gentlemen were dressed in black overcoats with brushed collars, white silk scarves, bow ties and dinner suits. On the seat beside me were two homburg hats. Although I was a coach painter by trade this was the first time I'd been anywhere near a Rolls, never mind sitting in one being driven by someone in a dinner suit. The rest of the journey was heaven, I felt like a king. As can be imagined, the rest of the trip home was quite mundane, but it's been a tale to tell ever since I was demobbed. After being dropped off near Macclesfield, I made my way over towards Knutsford, and then on to Warrington and into St Helens.

It was on this forty-eight-hour leave that it was decided that due to the good weather and that Dave, my mate, was soon to be going into the forces, we should have our photos taken together he was due to be called up any time after his birthday in July. While the opportunity was available, I also had a photograph taken with Sylvia at the front door of my mother's house.

I again caught the coach back on Sunday night.

Myself and Sylvia outside my mother's house

Myself and my good friend Dave in Taylor Park

Presidential Citation and Training Schemes on Salisbury Plain

Time was passing and was mainly divided between schemes, general duties and leave. One afternoon the full troop was told to muster in a large room on the ground floor. We were to receive a lecture on how Charlie Troop won the American citation that we wore on the shoulder with the other divisional signs.

Being one of the last to arrive I had to go to the back of the room to find a seat. Looking around, on the walls I saw photographs of the troop after capture and the terrain on which they fought the battle. All the sergeants were at the front, including Sergeant Ron Clay, who had been there at the time of the battle. In came Captain Pettifer. All stood to attention, then we were told to sit down again. As all were settling down a commotion broke out at the front. All the sergeants gathered round Sergeant Clay, who seemed very upset at what was going on. It was what had been said that was causing the problem. Apparently the captain had made a remark to Ron concerning why he hadn't been captured like the rest of the troop. Sergeant Clay would not be appeased, so the only solution was to send for the colonel of the regiment. He duly arrived and was informed of what had transpired. The officer was instructed to apologise for what he had said in front of all ranks. At this Ron was satisfied and the lecture began.

Presidential Citation

Charlie Troop at the time of the battle was a mortar battery with the 1st Battalion of the Gloucestershire Regiment, while Delta Troop I believe was with the 2nd Bty Glosters. The Glosters were also awarded this citation for their gallant actions during the Battle of the Imjin River. The battle started with the troop firing with a full complement of ammunition at maximum range, being

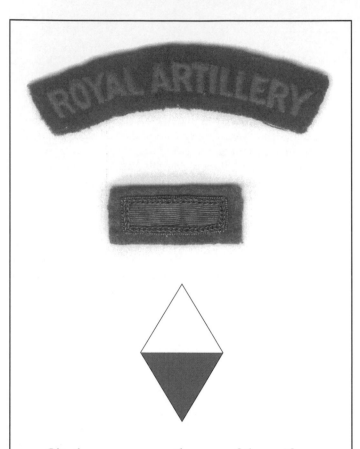

Citation as worn on the arm of the uniform

Top: Original citation, 1957/9.

Middle: Original citation, January 1958–September 1958.

Bottom: Recreation of the Southern Division insignia, 1958/9.
Original colours: white and red.

able to see the Chinese on the opposite bank advancing on to and up the hill the British troops were on. When ammunition was running very low, Ron Clay with one other was sent back to get more ammo, but while they were gone the Americans made a withdrawal, leaving the 1st Bty Glosters and Charlie Troop cut off, making their eventual capture inevitable. We were told that only four men had not been captured, two who had gone for ammunition, one who was on leave and the other who had been in hospital.

During the rest of our service with Sergeant Clay we would be able to get little snippets of what went on out there, and what conditions were like, especially during the very cold winter they had. The Yanks laughed at the long johns at first, but soon realised how important they had become to the British troops. It was so cold that, at night, a can of burning petrol needed to be put under the engines of the vehicles – it was only this that stopped them from freezing solid. Huge praise was given to the Americans for the way they allowed the British to get petrol so easily. It should be remembered that national servicemen served in this and other conflicts to follow alongside regular soldiers. Knowing that we were the soldiers wearing this citation made us only more aware how we could be picked out in a crowd.

Training on Salisbury Plain became more and more regular. It would be almost guaranteed to occur at least once a week. It's only with hindsight that it became apparent that the schemes we were involved in grew larger and harder as weeks went by. One outing involved having to get equipment into some type of hideout, the champ being left under camouflage in the rear; off I'd go with a remote control, a reel of cable, plus headset and writing pads. With the reel of wire already connected to the radio it was a matter of finding a suitable spot to observe from. More and more the officer would disagree with my choice of location. If I dared to say anything he'd say, 'If I can do it, you can do it,' then off he'd set with just one piece of gear, leaving me to struggle with everything else.

Well, it had to come sometime, and this instruction was it: 'Get it up that tree,' he said. So with remote control, cable wire, hand- and headset, I managed to get to what I thought was a good position. I climbed down and waited. 'Where is it?' he said, pointing up the tree. 'Up there, sir,' I replied. 'F— f— f— f— f—, I can't get up there!' he said. 'Well, sir, you keep telling me, if you can do it, I can do it. Well I've done it, now it's your turn,' I said. 'Don't be so impertinent,' he replied, 'get the f—ing thing down and put it somewhere else.' This was done and we continued from there to a new position.

Our next location was to be inside a concrete bunker. The concrete would have been something like three feet thick and covered by a mound of earth making it blend in better with the surroundings. Inside, halfway along, it had a dividing wall, by which I set up the op radio. We'd left the champ and driver once again in a rear area, so it was now just myself and the officer. With binoculars we had a full panoramic view of the range. All types of vehicle were dotted about the landscape, to simulate some kind of a battleground. From time to time during the next two or three shoots I was given the binoculars and asked my opinion of targets, distances and range corrections.

At about the third shoot a heavy rumbling noise overhead could be heard along with small specks of dust falling. I turned and must have had a quizzical look on my face, because I was told it was a tank on top of the bunker messing about trying to unnerve us. The tank then came in from the right to the front of where we were. At about twenty yards away in front of us it swivelled, pointed the exhaust at us then the driver revved his engine as loud as he could. Even with both hands over the ears it was still deafening. The tank belonged to the squadron next to our camp. I know this because of the names they had painted on their sides, which were all of Yorkshire towns: Hull, Halifax and Huddersfield.

Later that evening, back at the gun lines, shouts of 'Tank alert!' could be heard; this had gunners running to their guns levelling sights, then trying to track any tank that might appear by traversing guns left or right. When a tank is moving at its full speed it is nigh on impossible to track its course and anticipate when exactly to shoot. Even so the sound of breeches opening and closing, the clicking of the firing pins as simulated shots were being fired, made it all-too vividly like actual action. Tanks came and went on a few more occasions before things settled down for the night.

Later on that night each troop made up raiding parties with the idea of attempting to infiltrate each other's gun positions. I had returned to my vehicle and had started eating my supper when a voice out of the darkness said, 'The Sergeant Major wants to see you right away.' With the usual foot-in-mouth disease, I replied, 'Oh tell him to wait, I'm having my supper.' Like a shot from a rifle, another voice from behind me in the dark said, 'Well when you've finished come to my truck – you're on my radio tonight for this operation.' I was up most of the night with the TSM (Troop Sergeant Major), who was keeping checks on the raiding parties' progress; therefore I was away from the action in a safe place. From time to time all kinds of noises were coming out of the darkness. Some were very close and some sounds were far away – how the TSM knew where each detachment was I can't rightly say, but he seemed to know all locations and identifications of troops in the area around us. After a few hours at playing silly buggers we simply returned to our vehicles for the night.

The following day and night went just the same way, except that in the evening I was back at my own op job. At night in the champ with the radio working, the only light you had was from a small red bulb the size of an ordinary torch light. It may not seem a great deal of light, but after a while your eyes got used to the conditions. I'd been operating the radio from first thing the previous morning; it was now late evening of the following day. Being so tired I fell asleep, still sat operating my radio. I was awakened by being pushed and shoved and told that I was going to be put on a charge for swearing.

I knew nothing of what happened but apparently while asleep I'd started swearing for some reason.

The Bty Captain had heard me and therefore I was on a charge for it. Someone, however, told him I'd been on the set for over eighteen hours and was fast asleep sat in the back of the champ. He obviously didn't believe this statement, so to prove the point my call sign was used, to which (I was later told) I answered, wrote down the message, then carried on sleeping. It was then that I'd been woken up with violent pushing and shoving.

Because of this incident I was told I would get an operator driver for relief purposes. I did get another driver, but it didn't make much difference.

As yet I haven't spoken about a lad named Pat Woods. He was halfway through his service when I got to know him. He came from Charlton in London and would tell stories of city life and some of the celebrities he had encountered on his travels. For obvious reasons I will not relate the tales he told. Pat was the operator at the Command Post (CP), and the following are the most memorable incidents concerning him.

He was chosen to do a special parade. Each morning for about a week, he'd go to do the practices as required. One morning, however, returning from the parade ground, he slipped coming up the metal treads of the stairs. He still had his rifle in his hand. He fell trapping his fingers on a tread of the stairs, shattering the end of his fingers. After this he was hospitalised, having the tips of the fingers removed. He had visits from us in the evenings. Again I should point out that we had the Charlie Troop citation on our battledress and therefore had little if any contact with nurses, other than asking where his bed was. He seemed to have an endless supply of fags, which we always tried to bum off him when we went to see him. He wasn't in there very long and was soon back with the rest of us, but on light duties for a while.

The other memory is of a time on the ranges. We'd got used to each other's voices on radio and were also confident of each other's ability. On this shoot everything would be put to the utmost test. As usual we'd set up in one of the solid concrete bunkers right beside a dividing wall. The orders were flowing to and fro on a nice steady basis, when Captain Pettifer began to set up another target. He'd ranged only one shot when he shouted, 'I'm dead – carry on!' taking me by complete surprise. I picked up the binoculars and looked at our intended target. He muttered, 'Come on, come on!'

After what seemed like hours, I said, 'Go left three hundred.' The officer shouted, 'No, no, no, go right three hundred.' Listening to Pat reply to my message and loving every second of what I was doing I just said, 'Shut up, sir, you're supposed to be dead, aren't you?' At my remark, a burst of raucous laughter could be heard coming from the other side of the dividing wall. Ignoring all, I sent back the message, 'Wrong, go right three hundred, over,' then saying to my officer, 'Don't panic, sir, Pat'll get it right.' Pat replied, and we continued, but this time on each correction the officer would check my adjustments.

We did more shoots during the afternoon, then began to pack up to return to camp. On leaving the bunker we were confronted with a general. He was the one who had burst out laughing when I told Captain Pettifer to shut up. The general congratulated us on a very memorable day on the ranges, and remarked on the way I had been taught to cope in an emergency. This proves that in many cases, if your reply is said in jocular manner, as well as always using the word 'sir', no offence would be taken by the officer.

Back at camp, Pat told me what had happened when I had given the wrong correction to go left three hundred. He said that all the officers including the safety officer ran as fast as they could towards the command post. On hearing the correction coming over the radio then stopped, yet still began asking how such an error had been made. I suppose in the mess that night a few choice words were said about the panic that took place. On later exercises, however, Captain Pettifer would still give his binoculars to me and ask what my judgement of a target might be.

On the odd target we'd range to fifty yards from an object then record all settings for a later date. As it had been left intact it wouldn't appear that the target had been identified. This tactic was often used by the Germans during the Second World War. A building would be occupied, and then without any warning at all would receive a pounding that seemed to come from nowhere. A film was made which showed how it was done by the German artillery. The film, I believe, was called *The Steel Bayonet*, and showed how the OP officer had been cut off by the advancing German army unit, yet was in a position to observe what was going on. He was able to watch the German OP range to within some fifty to a hundred yards of the building, then stop firing. It was only later when British forces retook the building that the officer understood what he had witnessed and realised how the German artillery could fire on a target so quickly without seeming to range on to it.

What to Expect in the Event of a Nuclear War, the RAF Camp, Salisbury, Dog Trouble

As time went by other duties had to be done. One such was to go to a camp at Winterbourne Gunner not far from the city of Salisbury. We were there to conduct trials of what troops might be expected to meet in the event of a nuclear war, and find out the problems that might arise when checking in dugouts for radioactive contamination. This, we realised, was the reason for having a section of about thirty men of all shapes and sizes.

One of our first tests was to determine how to eliminate radiation burns by covering up when a bomb went off. This began by having a group in a darkened room all standing up. At the flash of a light, everyone had to drop to the floor and cover up as much flesh as possible, after which a person would come among us and mark off any area of skin that could still be seen. This was repeated several times, then again with different personnel in order to get a good average of what might be expected in civilian casualties.

To find out if a soldier had become contaminated by radiation, one of the group would have an energy battery pinned inside his clothing. The others would be given a device which could detect the battery through cloth. After being given strict orders not to touch the partners we had been paired with for that section, we had to get into a dugout. Then it was up to your designated buddy to go through a set routine to find out which of us had the battery. If by chance you touched your partner at all with the simulated Geiger counter, it had to be reported, because this would result in the counter being deemed dirty, and could affect whether the procedure was of any use. All of these operations had to be done in a confined space. At the end of each day a discussion took place to determine if anything had been overlooked. One or two things were pointed out and were gratefully accepted by the officer in charge.

It was during these lessons that we found out how many different ways an atom bomb could kill you: the explosion itself; by percussion; the blast of rushing air depressurising the area where you are, collapsing the lungs and causing suffocation. Dying from radiation would be the worst scenario, or through blindness after looking at the blast, leaving you unable to find food or water for yourself. It was also thought that if some despotic regime got hold of an atomic bomb and let it off in a random location, there could be no guarantee that the radiation would not still travel around the world and kill people later on. On top of all this, it was not possible to wash off any contamination from the skin. Direct burns gave a terrible agonising existence until finally death occurs. To wash it out of clothes would only put it into the water supply, and to try to burn clothing would only send it up into the atmosphere as dust and ash and recontaminate other areas in the outlying districts. Then we learnt about any long-lasting effects on the population i.e. cancer or disfigurement of the body. The last information imparted was that a nuclear reactor would make more fuel than it could burn. This stuff is better known as nuclear waste.

Getting to and from the compound was by the usual method of marching in squad. Each morning Sgt Clay would fall us all in and take the roll. He'd then head us off in the direction of our compound, but instead of marching alongside us he'd take a short cut with the lance jack[4] between the huts, leaving the rest of the squad to make their own way there around the huts. Marching to the compound and back like this had some onlookers baffled as to how we knew when to right or left wheel, perform eyes right if passing an officer, arrive at the compound halting and turning right and standing at ease, then easy, to wait for the sergeant. No one seemed to cotton on that the squad always had a blank file at the rear, and it was the man behind the blank file who gave the orders while on the march (simple really when you come to think of it).

The camp was I believe mainly an RAF place, but many foreign personnel were being trained up there, what for we never knew and didn't care either. However, their officers made a complaint that we were not saluting them as we should. We tried to explain that with all the different insignias on show we were uncertain as to their actual rank.

---

[4] Army slang for a Lance Bombardier or Lance Corporal, i.e. one stripe.

As ordered, saluting began, but it had gone unnoticed that at the time we went to tea they would be coming away from their lessons or whatever. So it began – up down, up down, all the way to the mess. We may have had about six to eight pairs to contend with, whereas they had thirty going for tea at random intervals, so it wasn't long before we were told to ignore the order.

The mess was a nice compact place if I remember rightly; even so, it wasn't long before the RAF lads were complaining that we were eating all the bread, butter and jam that was left on the tables. All these problems were resolved and it wasn't very long before our presence was accepted. If no one liked the situation it was hard lines; we were to be there something like two weeks no matter what happened.

Being so close to Salisbury we took the opportunity to visit the city to see what it was like. Not having much money left us with very little chances of buying anything, other than a cup of tea. One of the most vivid memories I have of the city, other than the cathedral, was looking over a low wall watching fish in the river. I wonder if the water is still so clean as to allow one to see fish swimming about in it. In most cases transport to and from the city was provided for us via army trucks, but sometimes we'd take the local red buses. If you travelled during the daytime, as you went through a village, the local women could be seen in the distance standing on their front doorsteps waiting for the bus to arrive. As it got close they would come to the kerbside where the bus would stop and pick them up; then, moving only maybe thirty or forty yards, it would stop again to pick up others. This went on all the way through the villages. It is a practice that I don't think would be tolerated in years to come, once health and safety boffins had poked their noses in.

It wasn't long before we were packing up to go back to our base camp at Tidworth and pick up where we'd left off from our normal duties.

The Captain's Dog

The following episode was very unusual to say the least. It happened on a scheme. The land champ was packed full of radio equipment, and in the back, where I was, was Captain Pettifer's little dog, Spot. The day was going quite well as we moved from location to location, when on one move we turned up an old tank track. Moving at quite a speed we hit a couple of potholes in quick succession, causing a six-volt battery to come loose and fall on to the dog. Immediately the dog mucked itself. The stench was unbearable and dog muck was all over everywhere.

Stopping the champ, the officer came around the back and began to ask about his dog. It didn't seem to matter about me. I suppose he thought he could get another operator easily enough, but he couldn't get another Spot. We dropped the tailgate, and out jumped Spot revealing all the equipment in the back full of dog muck. The inevitable order was to clean up the champ, and look at the dog to see if it was OK. As best as I could I explained to the officer that the dog was in such a state of fright that if either the driver or I tried to go anywhere near it, we might get badly bitten.

No matter how we tried it was difficult to remove all the smell from the champ. I knew that I would get the worst of it because it had happened in the compartment I was in, at the back of the vehicle, and when on the move the draught came from the front of the vehicle. I gave off a nice smell of dog muck for the rest of the scheme.

My whingeing about the smell soon got the officer to say that if it were in wartime I would have to put up with it. To this I replied that if it were warfare I'd shoot the bugger, because every time we stopped and tried to camouflage up, the dog would go off ferreting. This immediately gave away our position, and that's why we were having trouble trying to stay hidden. Obviously being the officer he was always right no matter what was said. The point went home though, because this was the last time the dog ever came on a scheme with us. Things quickly got cleaned up well enough for us to carry on, so away we went to our next location, with the lingering smell a reminder for the rest of the scheme of what had happened.

Back at Camp

Life in camp had its usual duties, but now and then something completely out of the ordinary would occur. One such instance proved what would or what would not be tolerated by others in a troop. This happened in another battery, so the tale is second-hand from Dennis.

One lad was always being told to get a bath because he was beginning to smell. In the end all his roommates got fed up with the situation and decided to take matters into their own hands. With military precision he was taken into the showers, stripped, then scrubbed with scrubbing brushes and stiff yard brushes until the lads involved thought he was clean enough – or that he had taken notice of what had been done to him. No one ever reported the incident, and, as it had the desired effect, no one seemed to care either.

Back in my own troop, one lad had got into trouble of some kind, had been AWOL, and was in jail at the guardhouse. One evening after the guard had changed, he escaped and went AWOL again. The tragedy of this was that the sergeant in charge of the guard had only three weeks or so to serve. Without a blemish on his record, he would then be in line for a good conduct medal.

Having a prisoner in his care escape meant he would have to forfeit the medal. In the days to follow it became obvious that he was more upset at losing the medal than losing the prisoner. He was a good bloke, well liked by the troops under him, and always fair when giving out any duties. To say he was heartbroken would be an understatement. The gunner was eventually caught and returned to the unit. It would be putting it mildly to say that this person received terrible threats from others in the billet. It was felt that the sergeant should not be blamed for his escape. A great deal of connivance began, looking for any way in which the sergeant could be exonerated of responsibility. The solution was to put most of the blame (if that's the correct word) onto a national service bombardier who had been in charge of the guardhouse during the daytime. The ruse worked; the sergeant came out of the preliminary inquiry blameless of any wrongdoing, and at the court martial the soldier was sentenced to serve his time at Colchester detention barracks. At a later date the sergeant would get his medal presented to him on a full regimental parade.

Before that parade I got a pass to go on leave. Getting home I got asked the usual question, 'When do you go back?' Anyone would think that you were not wanted at all. Well, my leave went OK, and it soon became time to return to camp. Going down to the local station I found out that the only train to Lime Street Station would get me there four hours before my train for London was due to leave. Knowing time was precious, my eldest brother said we could go by car to Lime Street, and have more time at home. This we did, but when I offered my ticket to the collector he looked at it and said it was invalid because I should have got the train in the first instance at my local station of Thatto Heath. I protested that I was due back to my unit by the following morning. Getting no joy from him I decided to got to the station master's office. I was still getting nowhere when my brother said, 'Well, let's go down to the police station then, and tell them of the trouble you're having and see if they can help.' Like a shot from a gun someone said, 'For God's sake give him his ticket, because if you don't, and he goes to the police, they'll be all over this station like a rash for the next few weeks checking up on everything.' Needless to say, I got my ticket without any further problem.

However, I was then told that the train I needed to get to London had been taken off (or had the ticket collector made me miss my train on purpose? I will never know). The train I eventually caught got me back to camp around ten o'clock the following morning. Having arrived, I was told to find BSM Wootley, and report to him because I was late for parade. I found him sure enough and his first words were entirely predictable. Seeing me he shouted, 'Where the f—ing hell have you been?'

'I've been coming,' I replied.

'That's bloody obvious,' he said. 'What I meant was, how come you're so late for parade?'

'Oh, they took the train off I was going to get, so I had to get on the next available train, and I travelled overnight to get here as soon as I could.'

He looked and said, 'Follow me, I'll sort you out.' This, re-member, was the BSM who was in the guardroom when I could not salute an officer because I was too close to the wall.

Having gone some thirty yards he looked at me and said, 'Don't forget to keep your eyes open, and if you see an officer for f— sake salute him, all right?'

'Yes, sir,' I answered. With me expecting the worst, we marched on until we came to the QM stores. Entering and going to the counter, the sergeant major began saying to the sergeant in charge, 'Give this bloke his full bedding, and let him carry it to his room himself. That will teach him a lesson not to be late for f—ing parade in future.' With that he turned and left, leaving me with one mattress, four blankets, two sheets, two pillows and cases, to lug some seventy yards and up a flight of stairs to my bed space. Once I had done all this I had to change for lunch and report for duty later. Nothing more was said about my being late back to camp. I was happy that nothing came of it.

When a medal is presented to a person in the forces they can make a choice of either an office presentation, with just a few people involved, or a parade ground presentation with the full regiment in attendance. An officer had been awarded a military medal for action in Korea. Apparently he had directed gunfire on to his own position to try to stop the enemy advance (at least, that's what we were told). With two medals being presented it was a complete regimental turn out, with all the trimmings to go with such an occasion. All bulled up and with best battledresses on, each battery marched on to the parade ground in turn under the scrutiny of the dreaded RSM. After all the citations had been read out, and medals issued, I found out that an OP person's life had an expectancy of about four minutes when he was in action, I thought, now they tell me! Well, I thought, I've made my bed so now I have to lie in it.

The last major scheme I can remember from this time, in-volved my having to sign four sheets of A4 paper, which listed all the equipment needed for our week on the ranges. The list mainly consisted of five radios and all the accessories to go with them, drums of cable and a back carrier (a metal thing shaped like a rucksack), six twelve-volt and six six-volt batteries along with a battery charging machine and a petrol can. With all this kit on board, the trailer needed to be packed in such a way as to allow access to most things, without the need to take everything out of the trailer.

Things went the same way as most schemes until very early one morning we were going through a village somewhere on Salisbury Plain. Halfway down the main street, we were ordered to stop, get out and have a wash and shave. We tried to tell the officer that we were very low on water, but he would not take any notice of our pleading, and insisted we did as instructed. So there we were in the middle of the high street, stripped to the waist cleaning our teeth, having a wash and shave in cold water. While we were in this state many young girls would walk past laughing and giggling at us. Where was our officer? What was our officer doing? Well, he had gone into what we thought was a pub the back way, and came out all trim and shipshape, having done his ablutions inside in private, and no doubt having a cuppa or the like.

We still had a full day ahead of us, so we filled up our canteens in readiness for what had to come. It wasn't long before a halt was made and we were told to brew up. At this point we told our officer that all our water had been used up having our wash and shave. I think after quite a few hours he knew that we weren't thirsty, so we must have had a supply of our own and taken a drink whenever he wasn't around. Nevertheless, we never did another wash and brush up in a main street again.

Later on into the scheme, having been out for so long, I had to charge up the batteries being used. After working out how long it should take to fully recharge them I dug a small trench about four feet long and wide enough to take the little charging engine. Digging down about a foot deep, I came upon some seashells in the soil. This happened on many schemes when digging holes to bury our rubbish, which only goes to prove that, many thousands of years ago, Salisbury plains must have been under the sea.

On this scheme I began to realise why I had to sign for so much kit. Besides doing ordinary shoots, the 62 set was used to do an air OP relay to the guns. After this, probably the next day, doing what seemed to be an ordinary shoot I realised that the voice on the other end of the radio was not Pat Woods. (He came from Charlton and had a slight London accent. I was almost always in touch with him on the radio because the OP was the main battle link to the CP.) After all was done and dusted, we were stood down to let the other OP have a go. The next outing was with the guards using either a 31 or 42 set. All I can remember is that the radio set needed an extra person, one to carry the radio, the other to carry a twelve-volt battery. Both would be joined together by the power supply cable. Being with infantry meant running and keeping up with them and jumping into what can only be described as shell holes. I was carrying the battery, which in turn allowed me to operate the radio and change frequencies when the need arose. When we dived into a shell hole together the battery would slam into my back knocking all the wind out of me. The same happened to my partner.

Giving orders then running while thunderflashes were being thrown as well as flour bags didn't make us two happy little bunnies at all.

The following exercise was with the tanks, finding and identifying targets for them to shoot at, each time using a different radio set. I think it was also on this scheme that I did a half-hour stint on the 10-line exchange. This was a box about the size of a small travel case with a number of holes in it like a switchboard (which is what it was really). Land lines came into it from places like RHQ, BHQ, infantry HQ and so on, in case the enemy was jamming the radio signals. So it's obvious now why I had to take out all the gear I had with me.

It later dawned on me that I'd done five different types of OP on this trip. On quick stops a kettle shaped like a milk churn would be dug out of the champ. This kettle had a funnel right up the centre of it, giving more of a surface to heat up the water. Just putting bits of paper or twigs or dried grass soon brought the water to the boil. The kettle was used many times over.

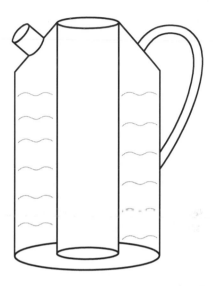

Diagram of a cylinder kettle used at the OP. Burning only grass, twigs or paper this kettle would boil a pint of water in only minutes

With all this activity going on it soon became necessary to recharge the batteries. On our second night's stop, this need became paramount, so I dug a hole and got everything ready inside the trench. I started up the engine, checked all was OK, then covered the trench with the trailer cover to keep the noise down. I was more than amazed that from three feet away from the hole, or there abouts, I could not hear the engine running.

This kind of work, for the next four or five days, was the culmination of all that had been learnt during the schemes that had gone before, and it was after this scheme that life in camp really seemed to settle down. There were football matches between batteries or troops, and trips to Fargo on ammunition detail. Everyday tasks would include sessions in the Signals store checking equipment, or instruction lessons given by an officer. This I think was simply to let all and sundry get to know who did what job when orders were flying about on the radios during action on the ranges.

We'd heard on the grapevine that Captain Pettifer would

shortly be getting married, so during one of these talk-ins we'd got Sergeant Clay ask him if it were true. Oh yes, was the reply. Because no one had ever seen her, the sergeant then enquired, 'And what is she like, sir?' 'Oh, she's got two beautiful horses,' was his reply. At this we all looked at each other, waiting for a description of some kind, but that was the only information he would give. I don't think he understood that we were interested in what she looked like.

On another occasion a GOC's, (General Officer Commanding) inspection was due, and the next thing we knew was that most of us were being sent on a day's outing so as to get us out of the way. The exact name of the place we were taken to I can't remember, but it was something-on-sea, down on the Solent. With typical army efficiency we all had a packed lunch each, and were then bundled into wagons and taken to the seaside for a nice day out. As we had little money to speak of, it was mainly a case of ambling around in search of a place of interest. Needless to say, no such attractions were found. All in all it was a waste of a good day, which meant we could not get back to camp quickly enough.

Recruiting Drive at Bristol

The next duty to get involved in was a recruiting drive in Bristol. Our camp base was Horsfield Barracks. The building, if I remember rightly, was like a small castle, with high walls all around and an arched entrance, all built of large sandstone blocks. It had the usual parade ground and other buildings. As it was just a place to eat and sleep, I can't remember much about the layout.

Our first task was to set up a display. This included a newsreel of a V2 rocket being fired at London, demonstrating how it went into orbit before descending on its target of London. The layout was a map of France and England indicating the launch site and the intended target. On a very slender metal arm about two yards long was a small model of a V2 rocket. The hissing of liquid oxygen simulated the blast off, then rising in an anticlockwise direction with sound effects this model would move in an arc towards its target. Photographs of the devastation the bomb caused were on display around the tent to complete the effect.

Other regiments had their equipment on display, such as 25 Field showing off its twenty-five pounder guns and limber. To us, being in a field regiment, this display was old hat. A light ack-ack regiment was there with its L10 guns and command truck – that's the one that gives the gun its power to operate. This was one gun we all had a go at, first sitting in the seat turning the gun in all directions, then standing in the loader's position simulating loading while someone else operated the gun. Then we whirled it round and round as if firing at an aircraft.

The Signals Regiment was there, but because that was my job in the Artillery I gave this display a miss for a time. But later I went back just to see how they did things. It was said that the Signal Regiment personnel didn't like a posting to an Artillery mob; why I don't know, but I presume it was because of the amount of damage that could be done to the sets when on schemes.

The Infantry were also present, showing off small arms of all types as well as anti-tank weapons. Thinking we would never be needing any more to do with such small arms we gave this display only a once-over so to speak. Little did we know what the fickle finger of fate had in store for us.

The presentation I made a beeline for was the parachute display. This consisted of a tower about forty feet high with a gantry at the top where the chute would be released. After having been strapped in the harness you would be swung over the edge and then, with the chute still fastened by a rope from above, you would be released to the ground when the person in charge was satisfied that all the equipment was properly fixed. Having applied for the Airborne Division and been turned down, I was very interested to discover what I had missed. The best time to have a go at the drops was just before all the displays opened in the afternoon about 1 p.m. when all the equipment was being tested, so those in charge didn't mind giving the rest of us a chance to try each unit's display.

The detachment I was with consisted of eleven men: one officer, one sergeant, one bombardier and eight other ranks. We were to be split into two groups of five, with one group working 2 p.m. until 6 p.m., and the other group from 6 p.m. until 10 p.m., each with an NCO in charge and the officer floating in between each section. For a few days things were going quite well. Then we heard our officer pouring his heart out to the sergeant that he'd been invited to a party in London, and because of this commitment he would be unable to attend, and would miss all the entertainment. Hearing all this set me thinking: if he could get his fun and games, would he agree if we could get ours? Like Baldrick in *Blackadder* we began to devise a cunning plan. At first Mr Bagshot Matte said no to the suggestion, as it was against the rules, but we explained that the plan was for half of the detail to work as if we were in industry, i.e., 2 p.m. until 10 p.m. with the NCO in complete charge at all times while he was away. Then, finding out that we'd already asked the lads in 25 Field to bring us packed lunches for dinner, and a container with tea if possible, he realised we'd given the problem a great deal of thought. Also, having very little to do in the mornings, we would be out of sight out of mind. Finally he agreed, so all that was left to do was to pair off with our opposite number, and off we could go.

The main road out of Bristol going north went right past the barracks so it was not hard to thumb a lift. The only question was where up north would you be going. As usual you'd tell the driver where you were headed for; if he was going your way it was all well and good. I got a lift quite easily and was able to get through Worcester without any problems and continue towards Nantwich, having informed the driver I was going towards Liverpool. He never said anything to me when he took the A51 then the A41 into Birkenhead to get to the Liverpool Docks. By the time I realised what had happened it was too late to get out of the cab, so there I was until we reached the docks near the East Lancashire Road side of Liverpool.

As I said before, trying to hitchhike out of a major city is one hell of a nightmare. No one will pick you up because of security fears. Anyhow, I did eventually manage to get a lift up to what is known locally as Windle Island. Debussing from the wagon I began to make my way towards St Helens. I'd gone only a short distance when a police patrol car pulled up and asked where I was headed. I told them Thatto Heath, which meant a walk of about four miles to the opposite side of town to where I was, and it would now be around eleven thirty. Being satisfied they drove off and left me to continue on foot.

Another half hour or so saw me walking past the Saints rugby ground when the same cop car pulled up and asked if I was still OK. After a brief dialogue they once again left me all on my own to continue walking home. I trudged up Dunriding Lane towards home but made a turning to go along the dimly lit avenues behind Taylor Park. As I passed one of the entrances a lad and a girl were coming out of the park. This girl had always pretended to be prim and proper when you spoke to her, but it being now near to 1 a.m. I don't think they were being prim and proper. It being dark, and myself in uniform, I don't think they ever knew they had been rumbled.

Smiling to myself I carried on until I reached a place called Toll Bar. It derived its name from a toll gate being on this site in years gone by. As I was crossing the road the same police car appeared again and stopped me to see if I was still OK. Having satisfied themselves that I was, they left me to walk the remaining distance to my home in Southey Road. I have often wondered why they had not given me a lift in the first place instead of tailing me. I can only presume that it gave them something to do and make a report on, or they were making certain I reached home safely. In years to come this type of thing would be called police harassment; yet even so, a four-mile walk didn't seem all that bad when I had a police escort.

The rest of the leave went well except for one afternoon. With my girlfriend working I had nothing at all to do but waste time in town. I was still in full uniform and had been inside Woolworth's browsing. Sometimes when indoors it would be normal to take off the beret and put it under the left shoulder epaulette for easy retrieval when needed. Having finished looking round, I came out of the shop, turned right, and who should I see just a short distance ahead, coming towards me outside Marks and Spencer, but a redcap (a Military Policeman). There was I, no beret on and him looking right at me. After doing a quick turn back into Woollies again, fumbling about putting the beret on, I had no option but to come outside again and see what would happen. Lo and behold, he had disappeared – he'd gone into Marks & Sparks. Who in their right mind would expect to see, a redcap in the middle of St Helens on a day of the week like that? Well I didn't, for one, and I'm only too glad that he ducked back into the shop to avoid any problems. Little would he have known that I didn't have a pass, and if I'd been picked up the rest of the detachment would have probably been found out. How lucky was I?

After that incident I became more cautious when out and about. The strange thing is, no matter how I try, I still can't remember how I actually got back to Bristol. Hitch I must have done, but what route I took I can't recall. With a full detachment now reported in it was time for the second half to go on leave. I reported as I should to the display unit we were doing, and no one seemed any the wiser. It wasn't long before the lad I had teamed with for leave purposes turned up. Seeing him I asked why he hadn't gone home yet. His reply was that because he lived such a far distance away he'd decided to stay. We settled down to our duties. One afternoon, however, who should come into our display tent but a general, red collars and crossed swords. Standing smartly to attention I threw one up. I don't think I've ever been as rigid as I was then. Returning the salute he asked, 'Is Mr Bagshot Matte here?'

'No, sir,' I replied, 'I think he may be over on one of the other displays.'

'Are you sure?' he said, 'because everyone I ask always tells me he is somewhere else.'

'Well, he is here, sir. He may have gone into town for something, I don't know.'

'I'll find him,' he said, at which we saluted and he left.

One of the lads began to get concerned that the general might find out our officer was missing. I pointed out that the general almost certainly knew that he was missing. How did I know, I was asked? 'Well,' I said, 'he isn't at breakfast, he isn't at lunch, and he isn't at dinner and to cap it all he is not in the mess at night for any drinks, so the general has got to be blind not to see that he is missing. But as long as we keep our traps shut and always say that our officer is in the vicinity somewhere we are all safe.' We kept this charade up for another two days and then our officer returned, all happy and smiling like a Cheshire cat, which proved to us that everything had gone off well.

The rest of our time would be taken up exploring around the immediate area. One attraction was the Clifton Suspension Bridge. I cannot say if it is still possible to walk across, but we certainly could then. To lean over the rail and see all the traffic below looking like Dinky toys was quite a sight. The traffic wasn't as heavy in those days so it was quite easy to cross the road from one side of the bridge to the other and see the River Avon go into the distance. Killing time was one of the worst parts of this assignment, mainly because we only started our recruiting duties in the afternoon. One day in particular three or four of us decided to explore more of the area around Clifton and it wasn't long before we found a small grocery shop. Feeling hungry we went inside to see what was on offer. Looking round we saw some individually packed fruit pies. Having found the price we decided to buy one each but when the third lad opened his, an earwig came out of the package. When he pointed this out to the shopkeeper he replied that it was only a silverfish, and wouldn't do any harm at all. After a little further discussion it was obvious that the shopkeeper would not exchange the pie.

The last lad bought something else I think; anyhow, when this lad was given his change, he looked at it and said to the shop-keeper, 'This is no good,' pointing to a very old, dark-coloured penny in his hand. At this, we all took a look at what he was holding in his hand. It was twice as thick as an ordinary penny, and about two and a half times as heavy. After the exchange about the earwig, the proprietor was quite adamant that he wouldn't change the coin either. A few seconds passed and one of the other lads asked to have look at it. Picking it up and turning it over a couple of times he said, 'Do you know what this is? It's a King Charles the First penny. Keep it, it'll be worth a fortune to a coin collector!' At this, I think the shopkeeper knew that it was he who had made a terrible mistake in handing out the coin in the first place. I've often wondered what became of that lad and his King Charles penny.

With our having some unscheduled leave to break up the recruitment drive, time just shot along and it was soon a case of packing up and returning to Jalalabad Barracks. On reaching camp we began to unpack and noticed that there seemed to be a lack of bodies knocking about. Unconcerned, we carried on unloading when all at once Mr Bagshot Matte appeared. Looking into the truck he said, 'Here's your leave passes. When you've finished, pack up all your personal belongings and report to the camp indicated on the rail warrant after you've had your leave.' With hindsight I think he wanted to get us off camp as fast as possible, without being able to say anything about our little piece of unscheduled leave.

Little did I know then that I was not to see much of many of these lads again, except for Mike Bury that is, and even then it would only be for short spaces of time. It's amazing how quickly all the gear could be packed when you tried. That evening I was catching the Red Rose Express from Euston to Wigan trying to get as much extra time on leave as possible.

Ripon Camp, Fishing and Guard Commander

Four days leave soon passed, so now I had to find my own way to Ripon. The best thing to do was to find out the train times for Leeds and which, if any, was the best connection to take me on to Ripon. I've often pondered on how I travelled on trains like thousands of other soldiers up and down the country. I point this out because there always seemed to be a duty driver waiting at a station to take somebody to camp no matter what time of day or night.

The camp at Ripon was just a stone's throw from the River Ure and wasn't a very nice place at all. There were other lads from the unit already there and settled in. One of them was an old pal from training named Dennis Baker, who came from Stockton-on-Tees. It was only a short scutch up the road for him to get home, so he was happy to be posted here for a while. Anyhow, from now on Den and I were destined to become great mates. You were told in training not to get too friendly with anyone, just in case something went wrong, but we two always seemed to end up together.

I was directed to the billet I was to be in, and on my entering, the smell of damp and must was overwhelming. I took up my bed space and was told to report to the officers' mess after I'd put all my gear away. By asking the others I soon found my way around camp.

Reporting to the mess I was confronted by a sergeant of about five foot two in height; he was the one in charge. He told me my duties were to be a waiter, waiting on territorial officers. I was to be trained first in how to lay a table, the order in which knives, forks and spoons had to be arranged, where the side plates, cups and saucers had to be, and where the wine glasses and tureen dishes should be placed for dinner. Another skill to learn was to carry more than just one plate in each hand at each trip to the table. Then came instruction on which side to serve from and which side to take away, and how to determine whether someone had finished eating so one could remove the plates. The worst thing about this assignment was having to be up so early, but having the chance of a few possible hours off during the day more than made up for the inconvenience. Not only that, there was the chance of a bite to eat. The whole operation was overseen by a head waiter; he was the one who would keep an eye on our every move, just to ensure things were going OK.

I rather enjoyed the change until one day, when serving coffee, I was asked for a white coffee. As I never drank the stuff I didn't, have a clue what the man wanted, therefore I asked him to explain. A reply of, 'Just pour it out, man,' was all I got, so still none the wiser I turned away and approached the head waiter to get an idea of what was wanted. After an explanation that all he wanted was coffee with more milk than normal, off I went again and continued serving. Afterwards the head man remarked how he was surprised that I did not know what white coffee was. It was only when the other lads said that even when coffee was available I never drank the stuff that he understood that I wasn't joking.

This particular officer always gave us problems when we served him. He would be sat talking to his fellow officers and swaying all over the place, emphasising with hand or body movements. It was only after a few days that I realised that, being the new kid on the block, I'd been given this officer's table because of this problem. Undeterred I stuck to the task and thought I was doing quite well. One day, however, I think he'd had a little too much to drink before dinner. He really was at his best this time, first going one way, then the other, at the same time putting out the opposite arm to make a point.

Other diners would warn him that I was behind him trying to serve, but it made not the slightest difference. Biding my time, in I went as he moved away, but as if on purpose he came straight back at me and the inevitable happened: all the drink I had was knocked out of my hand and all over the table. All was sorted out without any blame being attached to me, and you can be quite sure that after this he became less animated at mealtimes.

It was in the cookhouse that I first experienced how a Baked

Alaska was made. First the chef mixed up a large amount of meringue using caster sugar, eggs and double cream, whipping it up into a fluffy mixture. He then put a layer of cake on a tray, which he covered with blocks of ice cream; then, covering everything all over with the meringue mix, he put the finished lot into a red-hot oven. It'll melt the ice cream, we thought, but within a few minutes he took the whole thing out to reveal a hard-crusted, well-baked Alaska. We had fully expected to see a runny mess, but it was perfect – and as they say, the proof of the pudding is in the eating.

The sergeant in charge of the kitchen, small in stature, was thorough in his work and very fair. If a job was well done he'd say so; if not we got the obvious. As we sat down one day the subject got around to service and where he'd been. One of his remarks was about national servicemen and the role they played in Korea. He said how sad it was to see young lads being killed out there on such low money, not wanting to be in the army anyway, yet obeying orders when told to, just like regulars who would be stood alongside them. This comment made a lasting impression on all who heard it.

Recreation in camp was non-existent – because, we were told, it had been a Second World War POW camp. So like those prisoners we made our own entertainment. Going swimming in the river was one pastime; another was to teach some of the lads about Rugby League football, mostly the difference in rules from Union. League was a Lancashire/Yorkshire game and frowned upon because the players got paid.

The billets were built of prefabricated slabs of concrete. Going outside and round the back of the hut you'd find a barbed wire fence three rows deep with a ten-foot gap between each row. That was just about it. Oh yeah, the usual central heating had been installed: one pot-bellied stove in the centre of the billet. That's all we had.

Leisure time in Ripon turned out to be about average. Although a cathedral city it wasn't a very large place at all. That did not stop us from going into town at every chance we had. The obvious place to visit was the interior of the cathedral. In there you could see the usual statues of a religious nature but the objects we always looked and marvelled at were the old battle flags. How old they were I don't know, but they were so thin one could see through some of them. It was nigh on impossible to make out what was actually on them.

As always we found a nice little café in the main square, which to us lot seemed cheap. (I went through Ripon around 1988 and the café was still there. Having a tea, I heard one of the waiters speak and knew at once he was from Cyprus. In conversation I told him I'd been stationed out there but couldn't get back to see how things had changed in Yialoussa. He told me all I wanted to know and, in 1990, I went back to see the old place again and explain some things to Sylvia.) Being so close to home, most of the time I saved my money to go home by train or get a train pass. I had no way of knowing, but this decision proved to be the correct one. Going by train to Ripon was an experience in itself. Arriving at Leeds a train would already be in at the platform ready to go to Ripon, and it was known as the milk train. A porter would tell you which one it was, and along the train you'd go looking for an empty compartment. Finding one, in you'd get, then you would stretch out on the long seats and go to sleep. The banging and bumping of the train being loaded could be ignored, because when you got to Ripon another porter walked all along the train banging on every door to make certain everyone got off.

Fishing

Because life was boring in camp, one enterprising lad decided to bring his fishing rod from home. A river ran past the camp, and seemed to provide a good place for some nice relaxing fishing on time off. We'd go and watch him from time to time, and saw he was getting on quite well. One day he stood, as usual rod in hand, in uniform with blouse wide open, no tie on, no beret on, when a man approached him, and began to talk. The man asked if the fishing was good and the lad said, 'Yes, this side of the bridge is great, but on the other side past that netting it's very poor.'

'What are you doing with the ones you catch?' the man asked.

'Just throwing them back,' the lad replied.

'Well this is a private stretch of river,' the man said, 'and I'd be most happy if you would not fish here any more, on this side of the bridge, but you could help me if you wish to.' Turning and pointing to a small eddy just off the river he said, 'In there is a large pike which takes quite a few of the fish. I'd be most grateful if you could try and catch that one.'

With an offer like that everyone was happy. From then on he'd go to the pool and try his luck whenever he had time off. To everyone's amazement one day he walked in the billet with a pike about fifteen to twenty pounds in weight. 'What the f— are you going to do with that?' we asked. 'I'll show you all,' he said. At this he got two nails and a hammer, got up on a chair and began to knock the nails in the cracks between the concrete slabs over the doorway. He then got two pieces of string, tied them around the head and tail of the pike, then hung it up over the door as a trophy. If the smell wasn't bad enough before, this made things even worse.

The next couple of days passed as normal. Then, on about the third day at mid-morning as we were sorting ourselves out, the door of the billet opened and a voice shouted, 'Attention, stand by your beds. Room inspection!' A sergeant and an officer came in. All who were in the room came to the bottom of their beds and stood to attention. On entering the billet, the officer remarked to the sergeant about the musty, dank smell, saying that to him it even smelt a little of fish. All of us knew we had to stand ramrod still and get the inspection over as quickly as possible, not giving the officer any excuse to look up over the door as he left the room to see the trophy hanging up there. How he missed it we'll never know, but he did. Even the eagle-eyed sergeant missed it too. Within minutes of them leaving, the fish was cut down and buried outside. What a let off.

Guard Commander

By now it was nearing the end of August and the weather was very good, with hot days and warm evenings. One late afternoon, one of the lads came in the billet and said to me, 'You're on guard tonight, loft.'

'Oh no,' I said, 'just my bloody luck.'

'If you think that's bad, think again, because you're down as guard commander.'

'Go get stuffed, now you really are pulling my pisser,' I said.

'Well, go and have a look,' he replied.

This is serious, I thought, so off I went to look at Part One Orders. There was my name, Guard Commander Gunner Balmer A. A buckshee gunner as a guard commander – this really did highlight the shortage of NCOs on camp. Seeing my name up there I dashed back and began to get ready for the guard mounting. It wasn't the usual bull, mainly because the duty officer was from a Signals unit just down the road from us; again this showed officer shortage.

Mounting completed, a list of who was on which stag was made out and we all settled down. As it was a nice warm evening I was asked if it would be OK to have our tunics off for a while. Seeing that we'd just come on guard I couldn't see the duty officer returning for quite some time, so I gave permission for shirt sleeve order until it began to cool down a little. Everything went well until about seven o'clock, when who should be coming out of camp but the sergeant from the mess. Seeing us he shouted, 'Get your tunics on!'

'It's still warm yet, sarge,' I answered. This began a bit of a banter about our dress. In the end the sergeant asked to see the guard commander. 'It's me,' I replied; then, without the slightest hesitation, the sergeant turned and made a swift exit through the camp gates.

As the night cooled off, we all put our tunics on and got down to our task. It was getting very late when the lad on duty shouted that the sergeant was staggering through the gate. I was sent for and asked what he should do with the drunken man. I decided to get two of the lads to see him safely to his quarters. They came back job done, and it was now time for some kip. We started bedding down, except me. After a while one lad said he would stay awake so that I could get some shuteye. I got my head down but knew nothing any more until I was awakened at six o'clock the following morning. I hadn't been awake more that fifteen minutes before the Signals officer appeared making his final round of the night. I had made it just in time.

Later that day I was talking to the sergeant in some spare time after setting out the tables. The conversation eventually got round to the guard we did the previous night. It was at this stage I asked him why he had left so quickly when he found out that it was me who was guard commander. 'Well,' he said, 'you don't interfere with the man in charge of the guard. But when you told two men to make certain I could get back to my billet OK I knew no offence had been taken, thank God.' He still insisted that we should have had our tunics on. The rest of the talk went on about mess duties and other general aspects of what we were doing around camp.

Orders for Transfer and Journey to 25 Field Regiment

From now on life became rather routine, as all camp duties became predictable. We would go into Ripon for a night out and the odd trip home at weekends when things got quiet, waiting for the TA groups to change over. Getting on into September, one evening a buzz began to go around camp. One of the lads came in the billet and shouted, 'Guess what, we're all being transferred to 25 Field Regiment and going overseas to Cyprus!'

Having learnt not to trust what this lad said, I did the obvious thing and went to read Part One Orders. Sure enough, there it was for all to see. The main thing now was to wait for a relief squad to come and take over our duties. Knowing we were on the move within hours or days, we made packing our gear top priority, leaving just bare essentials to hand.

Dennis was on leave at this time, so I thought that was it between us, but unbeknown to me he'd received a telegram ordering him to make his own way back, and report directly to 25 Field at Bulford Camp. In fact he was coming to the end of sick leave, so how he got all his kit together I don't know.

It wasn't long before our relief came and we were loading into trucks all kitted out in FSMO (Full Service Marching Order) for the transfer to Ripon Station, then on to Leeds Central for the journey down to King's Cross. Arriving at Leeds, we had to wait for a special train which had two or maybe three extra reserved carriages attached, with corridors, and labelled for army personnel only. After a head count came the order to board and find a compartment for just six squaddies at a time. All settled in, and after another check by the sergeant, off we started on our journey. Having all the kit with us made things a bit cramped, but being able to walk along the corridor gave us the chance to stretch the legs and get to the toilet when need be. Also collecting packed lunches and drinks would be easier in a corridor train.

The train had been going only a short while when it was noticed that six or eight girls were sat on suitcases just inside our carriage in front of the toilets. So it wasn't long before some lads got into conversation with them and found out that they were going back to college. Talking to the girls made it even more crowded around the toilet compartments. So somebody then suggested that if only six of us vacated a compartment, the girls would have somewhere proper to sit instead of blocking the aisles of the train.

This we did, but after a short time the sergeant in charge turned up and pointed out that these carriages were for our use only, and not civilians. After a short discussion it was agreed that, if we didn't mind, the point would be overlooked and the girls could stay until they reached Peterborough. On reaching Peterborough the girls got off the train as they had said they would, and all went back to normal. At King's Cross Station, all fell in on the platform and another head count was done. Before going on the Underground we were warned by the sergeant not to put our kitbags lengthways across the big pack,[5] causing it to hit commuters on the head and shoulders when on escalators or platforms. This in the past had given rise to many complaints from the general public.

At Waterloo we'd been told to let the passengers go first, but this time get fell in into squad beside the train platform. We were then marched through the large platform gates (open of course) to an area that would normally be used by GPO vans and trolleys. On reaching this place we were instructed to down kitbags, undo our belts and let all the packs drop to the ground. We were then told that if we wanted a cup of tea or something to drink there was a tea stand around the corner we'd just passed (we'd already seen it). After falling us out, the sergeant went off, leaving us on our own to find out which platform and what time train we needed to catch. Over we all went to see what was on offer and began to give in our orders. We'd been there about twenty minutes, congregated round the van, when two MPs came into

---

[5] A piece of equipment about 18" x 18" x 6" that would contain most of the kit needed when on the move. The helmet was cross-strapped onto it for easy carriage and under it would be fastened the small pack, used when on patrol.

sight. Even though we were all improperly dressed, it didn't seem to register with one of them that we were in transit. He walked right up to the lad named Eddy Spinks, who was standing at the counter.

He shouting, at Eddy, 'You, you have your hand in your pocket.'

Looking at the MP in a nonchalant manner, Eddy replied in a broad Brummie accent (at the same time taking his hand from his pocket), 'I have to put my hand in my pocket so I can get my handkerchief out.'

Knowing his colleague had been surrounded and seeing how things were beginning to develop, the second MP shouted for his friend to come out of the crowd. On doing so he was told that all of us were in transit to go to Cyprus, and it would be very hard to have all sixty of us on charges when going on active service. At this statement they both left to let us carry on with our drinks.

In a very short space of time the NCO returned and had us fall in again. Then we took the train to Andover, and the usual truck transfer to 25 Field at Bulford Camp.

Preparations for Going Overseas and Final Leave

On arrival at 25 Field we were detailed to our rooms which, being mainly used for transport purposes before soldiers went abroad, were really quite crowded. Things being as they were, we just had to put up with it. After only a few hours here, some lads came in wringing wet. They had been out on infantry training. I missed this, but Dennis had done some before we got there. It was now a case of sorting us all out for embarkation leave, and getting rid of all our civvies by taking them all home when going on leave.

We were first given the third and final TAB jab. Going on leave would allow some time for it to take effect if it was to become sore. It was quite a sight seeing a continuous line of men going into the MO's hut, rolling up their left sleeves, then coming out at the other end a few minutes later rolling the same sleeve down, having been all done and dusted, and putting tunics back on.

Going home on leave I teamed up with Bob Sumner, the lad I knew from school days. We both shot down to Euston as quickly as possible to get the Red Rose Express north. We had settled in a compartment, just the two of us, when a young lady came along. She was all alone. Looking up and down the train she eventually came into the compartment Bob and I were in. She put her case on the rack and sat down in a corner nearest to the corridor. After about half an hour I asked the young lady why she had chosen a compartment with two British soldiers in it. (You see, most girls didn't bother with uniformed soldiers because they knew we didn't have a great deal of money to spend.) She answered by saying that she was married to an army sergeant and knew that for some reason or other we weren't trusted as we should be. Not only that, she pointed out that she'd noticed the citation on my uniform, and knew what it meant, so if anything was to go wrong she knew who to look for. We continued to talk awhile, mainly about going overseas, and it didn't seem long before we were at

Rugby. She wished us both lots of luck before getting off the train.

Our next stop was at Crewe. It was here that four girls got on the train. Two American airmen had boarded earlier and gone into the next compartment to ours; the girls looked at Bob and me then into the next compartment, and decided to go in with the Yanks. I shouted out, 'Aren't us English lads good enough for you to talk to?' After the train had moved off, one of the Yanks came past and gazed at us. He had a long look then went away, whereupon Bob remarked that we were going to have trouble with them. I tried to assure Bob to the contrary. However, Bob was even more agitated when shortly afterwards the other airman came past and also stopped and had a long hard look at us both. I told Bob that in all probability it was the American citation on my tunic they had seen, and they were trying to fathom out how a person as young as me was wearing one of their war decorations. Nothing more happened after this until we reached Warrington. As the airmen were getting out I asked them if they had any atom bombs in their cases. With a wry smile, off they got. We carried on to Wigan to catch the connection for St Helens and enjoy as much as we could of our embarkation leave.

It always amazed me how the news of my posting to Cyprus got around as quickly as it did, and how so many different people stopped me and wished me good luck on the tour of duty to come. The first encounter was with a lady who lived directly opposite from us. Her family name was Whitfield, and our families had not spoken to each other for as long as my memory serves me. Returning from my mate's house I was coming over Thatto Heath railway bridge, when who should be coming the other way but Mrs Whitfield. She came straight at me, stopped in front of me and began to ask if it was true that I was indeed going overseas. After I had confirmed that I was, she began to wish me all good luck and good fortune, and assured me that she would pray for my safe return to England. All this, from a person who didn't speak to the family, made me feel rather humble and special – even proud that she would go out of her way and make it her business to wish me well on my tour of duty.

The next person to wish me luck was a little old lady from

next-door-but-one, named O'Rourke. In those days women often stood at their gate fronts watching what was going on in the street. On this day I was in uniform, standing talking with my mother, when up came little Mrs O'Rourke. She had come to ask the same questions, and wish me luck, and say how well I looked in uniform and how tall I was. The conversation soon turned to when I was little, and played ball games in the street, and how I would run into her garden and retrieve the ball, though if she caught us she would give us a slap and tell us off. Then without any warning, she reached up and gave me a slap, at the same time saying: 'And I can still do it yet.' She would have been in the region of eighty years of age, about four foot ten tall and seven stone wringing wet through. I've often thought that if that were today, she'd be the one getting thumped and mugged by a twenty-year-old, not the other way round.

The most annoying thing was people asking when you were to go back. It always sounded as if they wanted to get rid of you, no matter how it was said. I was by now writing to Sylvia on a regular basis, and she had to work during the day as did all my other friends, so time at home was very precious and every second had to be made best use of. No matter how you tried though, only so much could be done, and it wasn't long before I was in contact with Bob Sumner to make arrangements for returning to camp. We finally decided to meet up on Lime Street Station, Liverpool. I arrived with Sylvia and my father. My mother would not come, as she was far too upset. Bob was there also with his girl and his family. Looking up and down the platform one could see others in the same situation. On reflection, it looked like a scene from a film later to be made, called *Yanks*. Most of the soldiers on the station would be going back to Bulford but having only just joined 25 Field we didn't know anyone yet – and I'd like to add we still wouldn't know many for quite a long while, thanks to our postings.

All over the UK many lads had to go through this ritual, each with his wife, girlfriend and family, from the beginning of the war, right through and up until the end of national service or future conflicts. Tears of departure from his hometown were shed, no one knowing what was to come. Obviously Sylvia and I kissed and cuddled, but, with tears beginning to flow, it was time to shake hands with my father and others there, kiss Sylvia for the last time in months and board the train. With Bob and me hanging out of the window we continued to wave until the train disappeared into the tunnel.

I didn't know until I returned home from Cyprus that my mother, who attended a spiritualist church, had somehow obtained an object of mine to take for what she called a reading. The idea was to get an article without anyone but the person the object belonged to touching it. I can't think for the life of me how my mother managed it, but a mother has ways and means to do things where her family is concerned. The story I was told later was that the medium said the object belonged to someone going abroad. She could see a uniform, but my mother need not worry as the person had a Union flag behind them and this was interpreted as a very good omen and no harm would befall them. They would return safe and well. I can only surmise that my mother was able to return the article because I didn't miss anything from my possessions.

Embarkation, the Dunera, Valletta, Malta and Arrival in Cyprus

With everybody back at base camp, assigned to their troop and battery, it was now a case of getting us all kitted out with what was known as jungle kit. As always we received two of everything (except for the small sea-kitbag): two hats, two sand-coloured jacket tops, two pairs of shorts, jungle green underwear, two pairs of pale blue silk-type pyjamas, and puttees (puttees fit around the boot top to keep out stones). After getting all this lot we were paraded and told to remove our division signs. We'd been told this previously so it was a case of an officer checking to see the job had been done. The officer came along the line and was happy to see us all divested of our red and white triangle div signs – that is, until he saw Sergeant Clay, who still had his American presidential citation up. Immediately the officer pounced, telling Sgt Clay to remove it. The sergeant told him it was his to keep, but the officer persisted, so Sgt Clay asked for a higher-ranking officer to verify the validity of his claim for keeping his citation, as he had been in Charlie Troop when the award was won and issued by the Americans. This meant the citation could be worn at civil ceremonies; also this privilege is bestowed on the men of the 1st Gloucester Regiment (The Glosters), who fought at the battle of the Imjin River. So it was off with the red and white diamond, and on with a black swan in a white roundel on a black squared background; eventually we'd lovingly call it the mucky duck. In years to come, I realised that I must have been the last national serviceman to be OP signaller for Charlie Troop, 170 Imjin Bty, before the troop went on to be an all-regular army unit. If any one can disprove it I would very much like to know.

The battery I was to join would be 93 Le Cateau Bty, and the troop was Fox Troop. The battery, we were told, had won its name and battle honour by repelling a German breakthrough in the First World War, at the place of Le Cateau, until the gap could be filled with reinforcements.

Having had all our big guns taken away from us, we were reissued with small arms, and for the duration of being in Cyprus we'd be subdivided from troops and put into sections. Eventually I'd end up in either F or E Section, but most of the time it would be F Section. As I've stated earlier, the lads coming in from 61 Field had had little or no training in infantry work. If we didn't learn quickly when we got overseas, we might never learn at all.

The day quickly arrived for departure, with everything packed into the big kitbag, all packs filled out and the helmet strapped to the large pack, small kitbag filled with what would be needed onboard ship. Picking up our rifles and bayonets we were mustered on the parade ground in order to be transported to the station. A battery was taken at a time; the platform on the branch line was very small with just a few outbuildings. Standing in front of one building was a weighing machine. On seeing this I wondered how much heavier I would be with all the kit I was carrying. I knew my normal weight was near 11 st 9 lb, so I delved into my pocket, found a penny, then asked Dennis to give me a helping hand with standing on the scales and being loaded up. In went the penny and the pointer went round to 16 st 7 lb giving me an extra weight of 4 st 12 lb. With curiosity satisfied, we waited for our transport. The train pulled two coaches at a time to the platform, filled six men to a compartment, then moved forward for the next two coaches to be filled, and so on until the train was full and set off for Southampton for embarkation. The date: 13 October. The voyage to Cyprus would take us eleven days.

On arrival at Southampton we got off the train to board the ship by a low-level side door and go straight to the storeroom to hand in every piece of kit except the small sea-kitbag. From here we were told where our bunks were located, so off we set to find them. We had been told plimsolls only to be worn during the voyage. The ship was called the *Dunera*, just a small vessel of about 11,000 tons. I think our regiment was the only one aboard. We were soon to find out to our regret that it was not fitted with stabilisers.

Having changed and settled in we now had time to explore the rest of the ship. On deck we could see all over the docks, and the rest of the troops coming on board as we had. To one end of the quay could be seen a regimental band; when all was ready they marched to a position and as we began to move away the band struck up and started to play appropriate tunes for leaving dock. Some lads who lived down south were lucky enough to have friends and family to wave them off, but we northern lads had no such luck.

After things had subsided we turned and headed down the Solent. In the distance coming towards us was a huge ship; the closer it came, the bigger it got, until eventually it towered above us. Its name? The SS *United States*. After passing it and other ships, before long we were in the Channel and leaving England far behind.

Darkness was beginning to fall; not only that, it was getting cold and tea time was coming up. After tea we began familiarising ourselves with the new surroundings, finding the NAAFI room where we could buy cigs, beer and the likes. That night it was strange going to bed for the first time in a bunk listening to the engines drumming away and finally sending us off to sleep.

The next morning was one of shock and horror; the ship was bobbing and rolling at all angles. (The only other time I had experienced anything as bad as this was going to the Isle of Man in July 1956 on the *Royal Daffodil* during a storm, then circling Douglas Bay nearly all night.) After breakfast we went up on deck for roll call, roll being the operative word, and some fresh air. Already quite a few blokes were ill from seasickness. We were therefore very quickly dismissed so we could fend for ourselves. As no officers ever appeared it can only be assumed that they were suffering as much as we were. Or they were being flown out later.

We were now entering the Bay of Biscay, which meant it would get worse before it got better. Being on deck sitting down with Dennis and the rest seemed to help a little, but wanting to go to the toilet I stood up and staggered over to the latrines. Just as I was about to enter Dennis shouted at me, 'Don't go in there, Al,' but it was too late, I was in. What I saw was all the slush holes blocked and everything swilling from side to side. One lad had slipped and was having difficulty trying to stand back up again. To compound all this the smell was unbearable, and it was the stench that made me begin to vomit and stagger out onto the deck, only to get an earful off Dennis for going in when told not to. For most of the next twenty-four hours we were left to our own devices. As time passed we became used to the motion of the ship and were able to settle down to an eleven-day cruise.

Nearly all the while we were able to see land on one side, either Spain or Portugal. We watched fishermen in small boats, standing on the front or rear of their vessel, bobbing up and down and swaying side to side at the same time. How on earth they could be there and not fall off I don't know – at some time or other they must have done. At night the same scene could be observed, with a type of lantern shining to attract fish. They looked like fireflies dancing on the waves.

Further south the weather became warmer and the skies were clearer of cloud, with the result that after roll call all kinds of activities were conjured up just to keep us occupied – the favourite was obviously PT; next came a refresher on small arms; but the most memorable one was first-aid training. We were detailed off into groups and given instructions on how to find pressure points, going from the ankle all the way up the body. All went well until we got to the neck. We were told to feel for the pressure point and apply slight pressure so as to be able to feel the blood pumping through the arteries – this would stop bleeding to the head! But before the medic could say any more, thump! One lad had passed out solely because he had kept his finger too long on the artery. All found it amusing except him, but at least he'd found the artery.

Another lesson concerned how to fit the putties on. They went on to the boot tops to keep out any stones, and then you tied them on so you wouldn't need to keep stopping to refasten them. The other great amusement was to have a lottery on the distance sailed each twenty-four hours. The prize was the amount that was taken in. No, the captain didn't win it every day. He and the rest of the crew were barred from entering, and the result appeared on orders each day.

Next up came Gibraltar. Although we went close, much to

our sorrow the ship didn't stop, so all we could do was take photographs at certain stages as we passed. This proved, however, that we were in the Med, and we entered more open water with no land to be seen on either side of the ship. It would be about two more days before we came to the island of Malta. In those days there were not yet travel brochures as we now know them; even so, we'd seen film of the place and wanted to get ashore.

Valletta

Entering Valletta Harbour

Seeing Valletta from on board ship was quite an experience for lads who'd probably never been further than say the Isle of Man or the Isle of Wight. Getting our shore passes, we disembarked and made our way immediately to the walled town. In a group of about four, we approached it over what looked like a causeway, with a dirt-covered football pitch on the left side. Some kids were playing a game and we noticed how good the goalkeeper was – he was diving everywhere. Did I say him? Getting close up, and much to our surprise, we saw it was a girl. She was so brilliant that we wanted to stop and watch, but couldn't.

Not wanting to lose much time we carried on through an archway into the town. Just inside the wall we came upon a large

115

courtyard with a fountain in the centre and shops and cafés all around the perimeter. After visiting most of the shops I bought a small pink handkerchief with the word 'Malta' written in one corner and embroidered in white lace round its edges – my wife still has it forty-five years later.

The Dunera *at anchor in Valletta, taking 25 Field to Cyprus –*
20 October 1958 approx

Valletta red light district

Moving on we came to the red light district – a long, narrow street. We stopped for a short while then, with photos taken of the street, we went to the walls overlooking the harbour. It was Butch Gladwin who took all the snaps of the ship at anchor, and most of the shots of our visit to the island. Time began to run short so we beat a gradual path back to ship. Back on board ship we continued our journey to Cyprus. Little did I know then, but my mate Dave from home had received his call-up and would be posted to Malta while serving in the medics, and while I was in Cyprus.

Leaving Valletta Harbour

Setting sail again meant we were on the last leg of the journey, but it was still a case of passing time away. The night before we docked at Famagusta I found myself put on guard in case someone jumped ship. I've often wondered where they could have gone to if they had done so. At dawn I had to get ready with the rest of the troop, fetch all my kit and disembark. Kitbags were thrown into designated trucks for each battery, and then we boarded trucks with just personnel and rifles. I sat at the back with Den, and who should be sitting opposite but our old friend Sgt Harris. Looking up he saw us there, then remarked, 'That training I gave you will now come in handy. It just shows how right I was not to be a bastard with you lot doesn't it?' I think he was hedging his bets a little, but he had no need to worry. We were more concerned that if we were attacked, there was only enough ammunition for half of us to have five rounds each.

The camp was on the edge of the Akrades Forest, a few miles south of a village called Yialoussa, up in what was known as the Panhandle (if you look at a map of Cyprus you will see why).

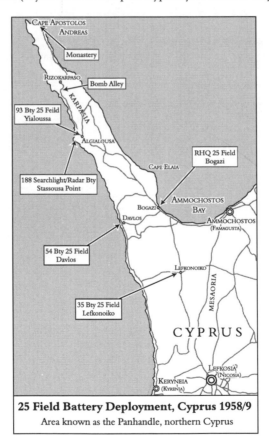

25 Field Battery Deployment, Cyprus 1958/9
Area known as the Panhandle, northern Cyprus

All got stuck in and we unloaded our kit into the tents we'd been allocated. It would be three men to a tent. Den went in first followed by Eric Lynch, who was from the Caribbean. He and Dennis took the end beds, which left me with no choice but the middle bed. The tent had a flysheet over it to give extra cover against rain or sun, but was still tall enough to stand up in, and had three wooden lockers, one for each man. The beds had boot-polish lids under the feet, which could be filled with repellent to stop anything unwanted, such as insects, crawling up the legs and on to the beds. It also had a duckboard floor. On the outside it had sandbags as high as a person when in bed asleep, obviously to stop any bullets if we were to be attacked. Also it had a little entrance way.

Uniforms should always face to the left when hung up, but I persuaded Eric and Den to put ours facing to the right. If all faced the same way it might not be noticed. The reason for facing right was that, as I was a signaller, if my trade were seen I'd end up inside Bty HQ all day, every day and hardly ever get out of camp. They could see where I was coming from so readily agreed. Den understood the argument, because he was down as a driver and the poor driver was often the first to get any flack that was going. Although we would be on active service, we knew that an inspection could come at any time.

The next thing was to familiarise ourselves with the camp ASAP. When we saw the ablutions, that was something else! The wash place had a copper pipe along a trough which acted as the basins. The pipe had a tap fitted about every three feet, to supply cold water only. When you had a shave it was necessary to fetch hot water in your mug, use it to shave, then rinse it and clean it ready for drinking out of. Hygiene? What hygiene? This wasn't the Ritz we were staying at!

EOKA's Welcome to Cyprus

I think the date was Friday, 24 October – no, I know for a fact it was 24 October. (Looking on the back of the photos I have, with the date of the 25th on them, proves it without a doubt.) For the second night in a row I was on guard duty, but this time Dennis was on guard as well. Stags had been made out so it was just a case of getting on with it.

I will call the lad I was with Z. We both went out to patrol the perimeter, the idea being to go twenty yards, stop, and wait for your mate to pass. In this way you would leapfrog round camp. With two very large coils of barbed wire stretched out encircling us, things should have been easy, yet having gone halfway round I couldn't locate Z anywhere. I moved up and down the wire a couple of times calling out his name. Having no success I made to the guard tent and informed the sergeant that I could not find Z, to which the sergeant replied, 'He came in ten minutes ago and said that you had left him.'

'You what?' I said. 'Wait till I get hold of the lying get – it was him that buggered off and left me.'

I did meet him outside, but said nothing until I got back off stag and was inside the guard tent. Then one almighty row broke out about what he'd said. As the argument went on it became obvious that, because I hadn't turned up quickly enough for him, he'd made a beeline back so as to put the blame on me for anything that may have gone wrong. The sergeant changed us round but Z still did the same to his next mate and lost him too!

Because no camp police had yet been organised, the following morning a draw was made to see who would have to stay on duty until 6 p.m. Whoever drew out the black spot had to stay on duty. I thought that I must be the unluckiest bloke in the battery when I drew out a black spot. Dennis was OK; off he went and had breakfast, while my breakfast was just a prelude to more guard duty.

Trying to look busy wasn't easy; but when news came through though that a detail was going out swimming that very morning, I really felt pig sick. I couldn't swim but at least I would have got out. It was now Saturday, 25 October. I thought it was around midday they left, but Dennis says it was more like 10 a.m. – he should know though, because he was on board the truck. Anyhow, the truck turned up at the gate all full up, with a champ in the lead and an officer named Jones on board in charge of the detail. Away they went. No more than thirty minutes later, a distant rumbling could be heard coming from the direction of Yialoussa. Being an artillery unit we knew immediately that it was an explosion. All we could do now was to wait for information.

When it did come, the news was bad, the swimming detail had been blown up outside Yialoussa police station resulting in one dead and eighteen wounded: three critically, four seriously and eleven slightly. All available personnel were pushed into service of some kind. It wasn't long before ambulances, and not just our own, came speeding past the camp gate going to the scene of carnage, then ferrying injured back to hospital as fast they could go.

Carnage of the champ and three-ton Bedford truck outside the police station

The very badly injured had to be airlifted by helicopter. It became my detail with one other to guard an area designated for helicopter landing. This turned out to be the football pitch which had been used by a battalion or company of the Welsh regiment from whom we had taken over. The bomb, we assumed, had been intended for them, but circumstances proved otherwise. Things happened so fast I can only remember helping two into the air ambulance. One, although blood-splattered, seemed to have only an internal injury, but the second man was covered in blood at his head and shoulder with a huge bandage around his neck. I don't know, but maybe it's having seen this that makes me forget anything else that day. It's even possible that two helicopters came to take all four badly injured to hospital, I just don't know.

During the late afternoon I was told that because of the situation, and confusion in camp, guard mounting at six o'clock had been cancelled and those already on duty would have to continue until the following day. That didn't mean the guard wasn't expected to be clean and tidy for the night, because the guard commander still gave us the once over. With what had happened and not knowing many of the other gunners by name or sight, it was just a matter of accepting anyone in uniform inside as friendly, and treating any one wanting to get in as enemy, no matter what they looked like. Most of the camp was in a very sombre mood, and it was very hard to find a smiling face. So this was it. Welcome to Cyprus boys; well, not any more – all had become men within one long day.

Another tale from Den is that he was one of the few left standing after the blast at the police station. He and a Sergeant Warburton chased whom they thought were the bandits who had set off the bomb. They arrived at a house but the door was closed; they knocked on the door then had to break it open and enter with caution. But they found only women and children, and the delay in getting inside was enough for the men, who had fled out the back way, to make good their escape.

Looking back on the incidents the troops on Cyprus went through, it would not be far from the truth to call them all *naked* soldiers. None that I knew ever wore a flak jacket or body protection of any kind. All that stood between skin and bombs or bullets was the thickness of our shirts, trousers and berets. The only other protection was the sandbags on the floor of the trucks we were to travel in during our tour of duty.

I was now destined to be three nights in a row on guard, checking to ascertain who was coming in or going out of camp. It was back to doing patrols round the perimeter. All went well until I came off stag at midnight. From somewhere a prisoner had been brought in and was placed at the head of a table, with four lads playing cards and the prisoner with his hands on his head. All seemed fine, but unbeknown to anyone a fifth lad was sat directly opposite the prisoner with a loaded weapon.

Someone would deliberately leave a weapon close enough for the prisoner to grab, if he wanted to do so. I think a game of cat and mouse was being played, because from time to time the prisoner would lower his arms slightly and get a response from the guys playing cards. I am more than a little convinced that the said person could speak English and knew exactly what was going on.

I was completely shattered, so after my stag ended at midnight, I found a nice little space just out of the way and got my head down. After what seemed to be only a short nap, I could feel myself being shaken awake. Sitting up and stretching I said, 'These bloody duckboards are hard for sleeping on.' A voice from somewhere then said, 'You must be joking. We were kicking you so hard trying to wake you up, that we thought at first you were dead. It was only when somebody said that it was your third night on guard in three days that we left you alone.' As it was now 6 a.m. I was allowed to go off duty.

Talking to Eric and Dennis later I found out that Eric had jumped off the truck and gone to stand in front of a white-faced wall. After the bomb had gone off he was still standing there all covered in white dust, and all the plaster that had been on the wall was now in a heap along the full length of the wall's base. Eric had gone from black to white in an instant. Trying to gather his thoughts, and looking round in a daze as the white dust began to settle, he saw a figure run across a nearby road. Lifting his rifle he was preparing to shoot at the figure when Sgt Clay pushed the weapon away saying, 'Don't shoot, it's a little old lady.' Eric lowered his rifle and let her go.

Dennis, however, was still on the truck when the bomb went off. The man to his right was the one very badly injured in the neck, and the one to his left was the one who seemed to have the internal injuries – he had damaged everything in his left arm except breaking the bone. If the bone had been broken the only option would have been to amputate his arm. The damage had been caused when he had put his arm up to try to save himself. The tragedy of this was that this lad was left-handed; and twelve months later when I was demobbed he still had his arm in plaster.

Dennis himself sustained light injuries, with just a very small scratch on his nose and badly bruised ribs from his rifle hitting him when the force of the blast shot him upward into the metal crossbars. Lieutenant Jones received minor injuries to the left shoulder and arm, leaving visible scars. If it had not been for the fact that the floor of the truck was covered with sandbags for extra protection, things would have been a great deal worse. The champs, however, had only an angle iron running up from the front so as to cut any wire that may be stretched across the road to injure the driver. The blast tossed the champ into the air about fifteen feet, turning it over in a somersault.

When reinforcements arrived a captain took charge. The first thing he did was find a local doctor to give help to the wounded. At first the doctor refused for fear of reprisals; after the second time of asking and being refused, the captain pointed his Sten gun up into the air and empted the complete magazine into the ceiling of the room where they stood. This convinced everyone that the officer was in no mood to be messed about.

It was now a case of imposing a curfew and organising patrols around the village. On inspection it was found that the bomb had been placed in a small drainage channel. The army had thought that the channel ran along the opposite side of the street, but apparently it went under the road at a crossroads just a few yards away. On going underground the culvert crossed over the road and ran the full length in front of the police station, exiting some thirty yards on at the next crossroads. It was also determined at this time that it would have been almost impossible for a fully grown man to have crawled along such a narrow opening and put the bomb in place; therefore from now on we were not even to trust places that only children could access.

Having been blown up on our very first time out, to say the lads were infuriated would be a very mild statement indeed. What followed was wrong, but none the less was fed by anger and frustration at what had happened. At each chance that offered itself the troops were as awkward as possible. One shop across from the police station had a large consignment of orange juice in crates stacked outside; as patrols passed by they'd pick up a bottle and have a drink, then put the empty back. When patrolling round houses, the troops noticed that nearly all had a well from which to get water. Although a curfew was in force people were still allowed out to get water. The patrols found that if a bucket were raised to the top and then released to plunge back down again, sediment rose up from the bottom making the water dirty and undrinkable. This seemed to them to be as good a way as any to take revenge without causing grievous bodily harm.

After two days, however, this practice was reported to our officers, who gave all and sundry a good bollocking whether they had been on patrols or not. Another accusation was that some lads had been looting when the chance came up. It was hotly denied, but all tents got searched; nothing was found at all. But Sgt Watkins was an old sweat. He got a torch, went into the latrines and looked down each one, and there at the bottom could be seen cards of spring wrist straps for watches and other small items, exactly as described by a shopkeeper. This time it was the TSM who dished out the verbal, leaving all quite certain what the consequences would be if the same thing happened again.

It was now time to unpack all the equipment that would be needed. While working, some lads removed their shirts to cool off a little, but were soon told by the TSM, Sgt Watkins, that if any of us reported to sick bay with sunburn it would be treated as self-inflicted wounds and therefore the gunner would be charged as such.

A large crate had to be opened; inside was a box, and inside this was a tubular case that held a charge temperature thermometer gauge. On our opening the case the reading showed 25°C. So in direct sun it must have been well into the nineties Fahrenheit. Even so, there was no let up until everything had been unpacked and taken to where it was wanted.

The day after it was time to empty all the water butts to get rid of any mosquito larvae, test the pumps to make sure that they were in working order, then check all fire buckets and ensure they were properly filled with sand. Another detail had the job of checking the perimeter wire for any defects or weak spots, then improving it. In passing I mention that dinner every Wednesday would be laced with salt, and I do mean laced. After the first couple of weeks lads stopped going for dinner because it was so awful to eat, but after about four weeks, things began to improve.

Some time after the bomb had gone off, we were mustered for a lecture on what was really expected of us. It being an informal occasion most of us had no shirts. Neither did the officer, 2nd Lieutenant Jones. He had all but completed his assessment of our situation, when he began to scratch his arm where his wounds were, at the same time saying that he fully intended going home with a military medal. On hearing this I turned to Dennis and said, 'Not over my dead body.'

At this Mr Jones said, 'What did you say?'

I replied, 'Not over my dead body, sir.'

'You'll do as you you're told,' was his reply.

'I never said I wouldn't, sir,' I retorted. With a few more words on the subject of soldiering dilemmas, we were duly dismissed. This encounter, though, was to be the beginning of many trivial disagreements to come.

F and E Sections, New FN Rifles and Day and Night Patrols

Not knowing exactly what was going on, all personnel except for a small detail were assembled, transported by truck to a then-unknown camp, and ushered into a very large hanger. In it were row upon row of benches on which we sat down, still not knowing what to expect. Without warning a shout of 'Attention' rang out. All stood. In came some officers and someone who turned out to be an interpreter; last but by no means least came a general. When he had sat down, the instruction for us to be seated was given. Then began a lecture on the situation we had been brought to and how we would be expected to conduct ourselves. After receiving an insight into the problem that faced us we were all issued with a little red book. It gave detailed instructions on how to apprehend a suspect and challenge them, before shooting them if needs be. It stated that the words *halt, stamata*, and, *dur* should be shouted three times before firing any shots at the suspect. *Stamata* is Greek, and *dur* is Turkish; both words in their respective languages meaning 'stop'. After we had digested most of what was being said, towards the end of the lecture, the general said they were 'bastards, bastards, bastards' and that if at any time while we were there we shot someone, to 'send for me and I'll defend you if you are put on trial.' This, believe it or not, was the exact same general who was quoted in the *Daily Mirror* as saying the exact same thing, word for word.

Within days of the bombing we were beginning to sort ourselves out, which meant it wasn't long before patrolling was being done in earnest and on a regular basis. To say 'regular' gives an impression that things were done at the same time each day, the same way each day. However, it was soon learnt and understood that to do anything this regularly was courting disaster. The only sure thing was that we would return to base at the appointed time.

As infantry now, since we no longer had big guns, the sections got made up and most occasions they would be a mixture of two with a complement of eight plus an NCO who could be of any rank. At most times a patrol would be on its own, but it might, in some cases have orders to meet another patrol somewhere else. F Section was to be my section, interchanging men from E Section. The only names I can remember now are:

Ambrose, J. Born in London of Pakistani parents, and spoke like a Londoner

Coyne, W. From Liverpool

Baker, D. From Stockton-on-Tees

Balmer, A. From St Helens, Lancs

Brindle, A. From Darwin

Beasley, M. From Birmingham

Bolton, A. L/Bd

Gladwin, B. From near London (the photographer)

Lynch, E. From Jamaica

Jones, (Taffy). From Rhyl

Talbot, A. From Jamaica (driver)

We'd be interchanged depending on camp duty rosters. At this moment I can only remember these other lads:

Worthington

Miller, F. L/Bd. From the North East

Wildman, L/Bd

Turley, Sgt

Seven out of the nine in F Section would be national service, two were regulars.

HQ was stationed at a place called Bogazi

23 Bty stationed at Lefkonico

54 Bty stationed at Davlos

93 Bty stationed at Yialoussa

After small patrols just to get us into the swing of things in Cyprus, the next major event I remember was going for supplies down in Famagusta. On this occasion the sections had been split; Dennis was with part of the other section going out on patrol. We'd driven to the depot, loaded up, and begun the journey back. At the time Taffy and I were on the last truck, which was loaded with jerrycans full of petrol, having left Bogazi and HQ behind. We sat at the back just talking and pointing out places of interest.

On the road behind us appeared a car which at first seemed to be quite happy to stay where it was, just a short distance back. However, as we began to approach the next village the car began closing right up to us. This manoeuvre made us sit up and take note of our situation. As the car drew even closer, the passenger pulled out a pistol. Immediately Taffy and I levelled our 303s at them. But as we did so I noticed a blue lanyard hanging from the pistol. Seeing this I told Taffy to hold it a second. The driver slammed on his brakes and receded.

After we had got through the village the car again came up behind us. We both realised then that they most probably were 'one of us', i.e. army people. Papping the horn and giving some verbal, they overtook us and disappeared into the distance. When we pulled into camp the same car, officer and men were there, and a complaint had been lodged against us both for raising rifles at them. They soon calmed down, however, when our BC informed them that, because of the speed in which the battery had been put together, even he didn't know all of the men under his command, and we didn't know him either. Not only that, being on this detail meant we didn't know that they were Engineers dressed in civvies going to our camp.

Now, running in conjunction with F Section was the other patrol from E Section. They were making a general nuisance of themselves. Dennis had happened to see a man acting a little suspiciously. He had informed the NCO, who had told him to go with a few others to find what was going on. Off they set, but after a short while one of them, a Scottish lad I believe, wanted to stop and do his number twos. He decided to go behind a drystone wall out of view of the main road. When he'd finished, he looked for something to cover it up with. A stone from the wall was the obvious choice. Feeling one that was loose, he pulled it out and saw a sack inside the wall. He placed the stone on the number twos, at the same time shouting to the rest of the patrol to come over to see what he had found. Pulling out the sack revealed a pipe bomb, about two feet long. With all this going on the bomber had got away.

The Scots lad slung it over his shoulder and made his way down to the road, with the rest of the section in tow. The first army vehicle that came along was a Land Rover. Slinging the bomb on board, they all climbed in and made their way back to camp. It was this find that had brought the Engineers up to camp to detonate the bomb, which we on the rations run had known nothing at all about, hence the trouble. It was taken quite a distance away and detonated; even at a safe place far from camp it still managed to break a few windows.

In some cases danger was much closer than you might think, and came even from your own people. One incident happened when I was on pump-house guard duty. A sandbagged emplacement had been built for protection and step-ups had been provided as an extra precaution. While we were sitting on a step-up with our backs to the emplacement, Dennis reading *Reveille* and myself *Tit-Bits*, the lance bombardier came up and sat close to us at about a ninety-degree angle. He had his Sten gun with him. The notoriety of this weapon I've already told of. He sat there with the weapon across his knees with a magazine attached. Placing his little finger on the bolt he drew it back, saying, 'There's a round up here.'

He continued to do this a few times more. When I suggested he went and played somewhere else – telling him he was acting stupidly and playing a very dangerous game with live ammunition – he just laughed and carried on toying with the trigger mechanism. Some five minutes went by when: Bang! Bang! Two rounds came out of the Sten gun, the first about fourteen inches away, the second much closer to us. If a third, fourth, fifth and so on had been fired, the shots would have gone right across both our stomachs.

Being very nice, I told him to go away – no there wasn't any effing and blinding, just a calm reminder of what he'd done. Away he did go, and fifteen to twenty minutes later he came back nearly in tears, saying how stupid it was of him to play around with a loaded weapon. It had taken a near fatal accident to prove this to him. Strangely enough this would not be the last time something like this would happen. My God was certainly with me again that day.

Another duty I ended up on was fire picket. With very little to do, Den and I decided to go and watch the film that was on that night. It was projected on to a white-painted outside wall at the back of the canteen somewhere. Down we sat in the back row, which was reserved for the fire picket. The film I think was *Guys and Dolls*, with Frank Sinatra and Jean Simmons. There we were, on a nice cool evening sitting outside enjoying the film, when Clang! Clang! Clang! The fire bells were ringing so off we shot as fast as possible. But it was to no avail; when we got to the actual tent nothing was left. It couldn't have taken us any more than two minutes to get there from where we were sat, but by that short time the tent had completely gone. All we could do was spot check that there was no longer a fire risk, and remove all burnt materials to a safe place.

The fire had been caused by someone hanging a towel too low over a paraffin heater, putting it there to dry after having a shower; this proved how easy it was in a tent to get into danger from fire. It spoiled our night then, but luckily enough we still saw the film later on. With nights getting cooler, though, it wasn't long before the film shows were abandoned for winter.

As time went by we had more and more patrolling to get used to. However, each patrol always had something different to contend with, so being bored was never an issue. The big problem was always tiredness. With only 175 personnel and about 200 square miles to cover, life had to be taken as it came, making the most of any rest periods. In the beginning some of the things we saw would be something of a culture shock. Passing a field, you'd see a farmer ploughing with a four-bladed plough and Massey Ferguson tractor; nothing wrong with that, you'd think, until you came to the next field and saw the farmer there, with an ox or cow pulling a one-bladed plough made from a metal spike. You could stand and watch ancient and modern technology working side by side.

Another day out on patrol we saw in the distance what looked like a walking bush. As it came nearer, it proved to be a donkey with so much brushwood on its back that the branches dragged along the ground. How on earth all the wood was loaded on to the donkey, I don't know. While on the subject of donkeys: some patrols went out at night and took the donkeys out of their stables to ride on them. It was only when the owner found his animals too tired to work during the daytime that he made his own investigations. When the reason was found, and the practice came to light, that became another job for the TSM to sort out.

We also took note of the large ants that were about; if you did not watch out for them they could soon infest your food when you stopped for a break during a patrol. The chameleons were a thing to themselves. You could find one, then let it go, and have a devil of a job to find it again, its camouflage was so good. A lot of these unusual sights fascinated only us the first time; our main priority was to stay alive, and the only way that could be done was to have eyes in our backside and trust nobody, no matter how nice they were.

One of the first contacts with a Cypriot family was when we went to a village named Ayios Theodoros. Although we were welcomed into the house it gave me a feeling of distrust, as if the owner were trying to suss us out. To be honest, though, I think he knew that the experience the battery had gone through had created an invisible barrier which would prove to be very difficult to overcome for anyone we might meet. The meeting was very much like one from any BBC Greek language programme. With plates of food on offer and drinks it was hard to believe that trouble might be around any corner. The best food was fresh oranges and *spume*, (Greek bread). In fact, ever since eating these delicious fruit, I've been rather choosy about oranges. I didn't think anything of this patrol, but it later became an advantage to know the layout near here.

Our next outing was to another village, I think it was Yialoussa but I can't be certain. On this patrol we were still checking out locations and the surrounding areas, and on entering we came across a fruit seller. I think it was Brummie Beasley who said he wanted some grapes. He went across and gave the woman two shillings (10p); what he got was enough for everyone in the patrol to have a small bunch off him. Our next port of call was a shop selling wines and spirits. Somebody else this time thought it would be a good idea to buy some brandy. Well, none of us could either read or speak Greek, so it became a lottery as to what to buy. Eventually it would be a bottle of two-star brandy, which also was two shillings. Quite pleased with our purchases, away we went until we thought we were in a safe place to relax a little and have a drink. One swig and all hell let loose. Some tried to brave it out but others of us just spat it out again. Not knowing it, we had chosen the lowest grade available, but for two bob nobody was too upset about throwing it all away. That, then, was another lesson learnt.

Barring other duties previously given, each morning brought the obligatory parade and roll and mail call. One particular morning, instead of being given individual tasks, we were all ordered to report to the armoury and line up in single file. We were then told that we were to get a brand new Belgian FN rifle each and were informed where the serial number was. Inside the armoury was a large crate full of what looked like strips of brown greaseproof paper; these were in fact rifles still factory-wrapped. Moving in line each man gave his own number, followed by the one written on the rifle. Having now got our own weapons we had to take them back to our tents and unwrap them, degrease and dismantle and thoroughly clean them, before having target practice to zero the sights in properly. Laying the rifles on the beds we began to unwrap them as if we had just got a Christmas present. It was a strange feeling to have a weapon that no one else had touched since it left the factory, and it was now your personal property; you alone were responsible for it, because your life might depend upon how well it was looked after.

Showing off with our new FN rifles and canvas tents with sandbag surrounds and small ditches. One MP in parliament said no troops in Cyprus were under canvas; with some thirty to forty thousand plus it was inevitable that some would be in tents.

*Me and my new FN, with the
waste water pipeline in the foreground.*

Dennis asked what the central bolt at the bottom of the rifle was
for, and undid it, causing the weapon to fall into pieces on the
bed. Panic, Panic! What to do next? Both Eric and I agreed that
the best thing would be to dismantle another rifle, taking note at
each step the order in which it came apart, then reassemble in
reverse order. I was the one whose rifle was to be taken to pieces.
It may have taken the three of us a little longer than the others to
clean our weapons, but in the long run we knew every working
part there was to know about an FN rifle.

The next day we were taken to a beach for instruction on the
capabilities of the FN. For this we had a bombardier who had
been in the SAS; his name was Bunny Austin. From the start it
was obvious he knew what it was all about. I think it was a
sergeant who wished to try firing it on automatic, but Bunny

advised against it, telling him that it could fire at a rate of something like 1,200 rounds per minute and would be very difficult to handle. The sergeant did try the rifle on automatic but found it very tough. Then Bunny, who was a well-built man, also tried, just to show us how hard the rifle really was to handle when on automatic. Anyhow, with only twenty rounds in a magazine, it would take only a couple of seconds to empty. He even explained various ways of carrying it, not because we were stupid but to get us up to the best standard in the shortest possible time.

The officers would probably have a pistol or a Sterling sub-machine gun, as would all the NCOs. The Sterling was very much like the Sten, with the exceptions that the Sterling had a foldaway butt and a barrel shield with holes in it. The most noticeable thing was its curved magazine, which made it distinguishable from a distance. Not long after this we would be on a range facing out to sea, firing and adjusting sights to our own liking. The weapon also had a gas port that allowed the recoil to be adjusted to the pressure of the person firing it. I set mine at number six, which to me was the right amount of kick I could handle. A half-size target was put up at 100 yards and shot at until we were satisfied with the performance and handling of the rifle.

In weeks to come we would practise being ambushed from time to time. For no reason at all (or so it seemed) a truck would come screeching to a halt and somebody would shout 'Bandits!' whereupon we'd look out of the side of the truck and start to fire at targets that had been placed in various places for us. This practice also gave an indication as to our awareness of the area we could see and where we were concentrating most of our fire power. If at any time we just had a simple target practice, a ploy would be to use some beer cans, riddle them with holes, then throw them in the streets for people to see how good we were. This was our own way of waging a psychological war on the terrorists. Carrying this rifle with a bayonet and forty rounds certainly gave us a much better feeling of security than when humping a 303 about for hours on end. The pistol grip alone gave much better handling, and the gun also had a carrying handle for marching at the trail. Even when wearing gloves or mittens the trigger guard could be tucked out of the way into the grip to give better efficiency.

Just across the road from the main gate was a small shop. Visiting it was the only time we were able to leave camp without our rifles. At the shop one day I saw a ladies' square compact and lipstick set. It was dark blue and gold, with an inscription of the island of Cyprus on the outside, inside a three-lined border. I bought it for Sylvia, hoping she would like it. She did like it, but told me that inside was a square compartment for loose powder, which was rather hard to buy I believe; the second drawback was that the spring was very strong. If care wasn't taken when opening it up, it would spring out of your grasp quite easily. This in fact is what happened in much later years, causing the mirror inside to be broken. My wife, as Sylvia now is, still has the compact, even though she doesn't use it any more.

Due to the speed in which time passed, I can't remember now whether or not the next incident happened before or after our getting the FNs. It occurred at the police station where we'd been blown up on the battery's first day out. On the first outing of day one, the section was in a ground-level room trying to get bedded down to some kind of comfort. With a dirt or stone floor, conditions were anything but good. The food was mainly from Yankee K ration boxes three feet long, full of all types of dehydrated foodstuff. How can I begin to explain what they were like! Well, here goes. Sugar, tea, in small tins the size of a small tin of beans; milk was in a container like a large tube of toothpaste. The biscuits were also dehydrated – put one in a cup of water and it would soak it all up as if by magic, swelling to three or four times its size. A small tin contained processed cheese more like a lump of rubber than anything else. The tin openers were no better quality. Bum fodder, half the time, would be a piece of newspaper.

All this in a poorly lit room didn't take long to get on the nerves of tired men. The climax came on a curfew patrol during the hours of darkness. Dennis and I with three others were up on top of the police station in the tower and gun pits. We heard the patrol go out, shutting large, high wooden gates behind them. The night was very quiet. In the stillness, the night seemed to go very slowly, but about an hour later we heard a squealing noise four- or five-hundred yards away.

No one could see anything at all in the pitch black night. Giving word to each other that something must be wrong, we got ready for some type of action. The sergeant was told immediately; as we reported back to him a much louder squeal was heard, then more squealing. Lights started coming on one by one in the distance where the noise was becoming louder still, but this time we could hear people shouting. With more and more lights coming on, the noise grew stronger as it came closer and ever closer.

Around the near corner came the patrol, running like hell, shouting, 'Open the f—ing gates! Quick, let us in, let us in!'

As the gates were opened, some of the villagers came running round the corner, also shouting, and chasing them. The rest of the guard fixed bayonets (ah yes, we had FNs), preparing to keep the villagers at bay, while at the same time letting the patrol in, then slamming the gates firmly shut behind them. The place was in uproar, orders being given right, left and centre. The Greeks were shouting like mad in their own language – we could only imagine what they were saying – while waving sticks and clubs at us. With all this commotion going on it wasn't long before the Cypriot police became involved. Eventually, as night wore on, things began to subside, but it was an uneasy calm until more troops arrived. Among them was an officer from the Catering Corps, and it was he who seemed to be doing most of the negotiations.

It came out in the enquiry that followed, that the patrol had come across what was thought to be a loose pig. Because of the food problem Joe Ambrose proposed taking the pig back to the station, to kill and eat it. At the same time he began to pull at the rope that the pig was tied up with. He had completely forgotten that because of its fat neck the animal was tied up by its trotter, and when he tugged at the rope he pulled the pig off its feet. At this the pig squealed, so Joe took out his bayonet and stabbed it – the pig then squealed even more. It was now when the villagers were beginning to wake up. Joe then tried to throw the animal into a type of trough, causing the pig to squeal even louder. By now, nearly all the village in the vicinity were out and began to chase the patrol back to the station. The following morning we were all stood to with fixed bayonets again and were on alert until after the outcome of the enquiry.

To cut a very long story short, the patrol got fined £5 for the pig, with no further charges pursued against the patrol by the owner. With army wages at an average of about £2 per week, I think the farmer got a good deal, especially as we didn't get the pig in the end. Back in camp, however, an investigation took place as to why the patrol did what it did. With accusations of poor rations having been voiced, a thorough investigation of the cookhouse stores was carried out and, among other items, a batch of thirty green, mouldy loaves was found. This one item alone gave rise to great concern and was the start of us getting a much-improved standard of food supplies – English compo ration boxes, far superior to what we'd just endured.

These were individually lettered, and you'd know what was in them without opening the box. The box with a K on it was the best, and the cooks would often open them prior to dispatch. In it would be Mars bars, steam puddings, stews, bacon rolled up in tins, scrambled egg plus tinned sausages, as well as matches, toilet paper, tin openers and self-heating soups. The sausages were packed six to a tin and covered completely in lard. They were so tasty that if these were on offer nearly everyone would go to breakfast.

Self-heating soup tins had a tube down the centre. Punching holes at the top, then removing a cap on the tube, revealed a wick. After lighting this with a cigarette end or such, within thirty seconds it was impossible to hold with bare hands. At night on stag in the cold they were a godsend.

Going back to the pig incident, all the lads later had a good laugh at the thought of nine men with rifles and Sten guns running away from villagers with only sticks and clubs, some even bearing nothing but a sense of injustice.

It was while on our first police guard that we saw a Greek Cypriot wedding celebration. I was on the roof, which gave me a good vantage point. The procession came to each crossroads, stopped, shouted out something or other, presumably about the wedding that was about to take place, then moved on to the next junction to repeat the same thing. In normal times they would also be firing shotguns in celebration, but owing to restrictions and confiscation of weapons this could not be done. The one thing that I noticed was that the groom's father was leading him by the hand with the bride more or less following on behind. It could also be seen that the bride had paper money pinned to her wedding dress. Any patrol that went out was told not to interfere in the wedding ceremony, and all went well for the wedding party walkabout.

Marching on patrol was beginning to cause havoc with our everyday footwear, and it didn't take long for us to be issued with an extra pair of second-hand boots. These had an inner sole made up of about five layers of nylon mesh, which was supposed to perform a pumping action when we walked. The boots had thick soles and were given the initials WW; we christened them cobbly wobblies. Wearing these with putties set us up nicely. Another second-hand item was a type of tracksuit with a hood attached, very, very light, and waterproof. The only problem was that not only did it keep the water out, it also kept the sweat in, and on a brisk march you would feel like a broiled chicken, so on most occasions only the jacket would be worn.

It must have been the troubles we'd had at the police station with the villagers that inspired our next piece of training. One morning after parade we were told to go and get our war bonnets on and report back immediately. Back in line, helmets on, we were introduced to a pile of thick clear plastic shields and what can be described as clubs – pick handles they were really. We were to have riot training. It looked more like shambles training. We were all dressed in boots and socks, with long, dark blue shorts and khaki shirts, and a helmet stuck on top of our heads. Looking at the state of us, anybody who saw us would be rolling about on the ground laughing, never mind rioting.

We split up into two groups, one to be the attackers and the other to be with shields. The main aim was to get the shields to move backwards and forwards on instruction without loss of shape to the ranks. Roles were reversed and the whole thing done again; then the groups were split up and reformed and the whole procedure was repeated, so as to get us used to having anyone at all next to us. I think it also sent a signal to the locals working in camp who were watching that we were beginning to mean business. Stacked in a row were fire beaters. They were like flat mops with very long handles; the ends were made from fabric. We could only be grateful that those items never had to be used by our battery.

Not long after the battery had settled in a new lieutenant arrived, and the guard decided to have bit of fun. Taking all his kit as he got off the truck they took it to a tent that was being used as a prison cell. Entering, the officer remarked on how poor the set-up was, but never pushed the subject. It was only when another officer wanted to see him that the ruse came to light. With his kit in the right place life went back to normal. This officer's name was Murray-Smith. I think he was national service, but he became a brilliant officer to the men under him.

On one occasion about this time we were all fell in, in one straight line, to ascertain our heights. The sergeant came along the line and indicated which men had to do a Governor's House guard, for which all the men needed to be close to the same height. I was left out because I was too tall. Dennis, however, wasn't, so he had to go. The lads were beginning to notice that I always seemed to end up on a cushy number out of harm's way. I had missed the big bomb, the pipe bomb find, and missed the village chasers at the police station.

Just after Dennis had left to go on the Governor's House guard, Mr Murray-Smith was asking for volunteers to go out on an evening patrol. He'd never been out on one and wanted to see what the outside was like, just to break up the monotony. No one seemed interested, so I volunteered. Within minutes more began to want to go. Having been taken aback at the renewed interest, the officer asked why. Pointing at me the TSM, Sergeant Watkins, remarked, 'Where he goes there's never any trouble.' Mr Murray-Smith remembered this remark.

Everything sorted out, off we set towards Ayios Theodoros. There we decided to go into the forest. It being dark, all that could be seen were two V-shaped gaps in the trees. Talking to himself, the officer said, 'Which one is it then?' This remark prompted a couple to give their opinion, then after a short pause I said, 'It's the deepest one on the left you want, sir. We'll go in about fifty yards then turn right along a dirt road and after say four hundred yards we should come to a crossroads, then turn left.'

He pondered for a moment or two studying his map, then off we set, going into the forest up to the junction. We turned right and had gone three hundred yards or so when we stopped. We'd come to a shallow gully that looked very much like a road. I explained to the officer what it was and that we could go that way as a short cut. (Remember, it was dark and the officer hadn't been out here before. I had, but I didn't let on. I later found out that the TSM had told the officer of this fact, seeing that most of the others hadn't been in this area.) 'No,' he said, 'we'll go to the crossroads and then turn left, I'm in charge.'

I gave my apologies for the way I had been speaking as if I were in charge, then we again set off and turned left at the crossroads. Soon it became obvious that we would end up at the pumping station. As we got closer I asked Mr Murray-Smith if I could have a word with him as to where we were headed; he agreed (now this is when a good officer shows his true credentials). I explained that the bombardier at the pump house was Bunny Austin; he'd been in the SAS and knew how to set an ambush to kill everyone. 'Sir, please, when you are challenged, don't try to be heroic, because we'll all be coming from the wrong direction and they may not know anyone is out tonight. We'll be inside the trap by the time you are asked for the password.' When we approached, the challenge came as predicted and all went well. Inside Mr Murray-Smith made it his business to check the set positions for himself, and later on thanked me for the reminder of direction we were coming in from, from the dirt track inside the forest.

The following day back in camp at around midday I noticed my blankets had been changed. Immediately I had my suspicions and went straight to the next tent and there they were. An argument broke out between me and Billy Coyne. It was he who had changed my bedding. He tried to bluff it out that the bedclothes were his, but when confronted with the fact that he had not gone on the Governor's guard because he was too small and I was too tall, and after measuring the blankets against each other, it was proved whose blankets belonged to whom, and thus ended our problem.

In the evenings with free time, cleaning kit, getting dobie ready for laundry, writing letters home, it's amazing how we found time to go down to the so-called NAAFI. This was a shop run by a group of Indians. It was the centre of our social life inside camp and almost anything we required could be got there – except razor blades after the first couple of weeks, which for some reason or other they ran out of. In the interim period we tried to sharpen old blades on bottles and newspaper, using them like a barber's strop. My advice to anyone is don't try it, it doesn't work. Other than buying everyday equipment, everybody bought themselves a sets of darts. This proved to be one the best buys we made, and we would spend many hours playing. Other squads may not have bothered to buy them, but our squad made much use of them. The next best item was a plate of egg, chips and beans. Ali the owner would always shout it out to the back as 'Egg, chips and beans, chalawhy! What 'chalawhy' really meant, or how to spell it, I don't know, but I think it meant 'right away'. It could have meant a cup of tea – where would we English be without our cuppa?

Dennis had returned from his guard duty at the Governor's House, so now our two squads were back to normal. An extra bit of info he came up with was that during his nights on duty, the Cypriots would throw stones at them. So again he'd become involved in a problem when I wasn't with him.

It was now November. Patrols still had to go out on normal duties. On one occasion though, the patrol was larger than usual: two squads with sergeants in charge. As we made our way into a village the noise of a party could be heard. Dogs began to bark, and by the time we reached the taverna, all had gone inside out of the way. After agreeing a plan of action, in went the NCOs through one door, and others in at given places. In I went but Den, the crafty bugger, stayed outside and closed the door behind me. Thinking no more of it I just kept watch on the proceedings until a young lad was asked for his identity card. He didn't have one with him, and when it was said that he would be taken into custody, he burst out crying. Others became involved in the debate, which ended in a Greek man going to the boy's house to retrieve the ID. We left and let them get on with their party. It transpired that the lad was going to England the next day and that's what the party and celebrations were all about. Dennis, however, after closing the door, was stood by a barbecue with a couple of chops on it. He swears he never touched them. The lying swine, they still disappeared, so somebody must have eaten them and he was the only one there.

If at any time a major search or roadblocks were arranged, policewomen would be available to check any females or children. When out on the road alone, however, we had no such luxury. I say this with one particular incident in mind. When I tell people this episode they don't believe me, but here goes.

As normal we'd been sent out to do a recce in a specific area and told to wander wherever we felt like. The essence of what we were doing was to be a nuisance, and let it be known that we were in the area nosing around. We'd been out quite some time and were walking along an inclined dirt track, when coming over the brow we saw a solitary figure. Nearer and nearer the person came until stopped and asked for a *passo* (ID). It was handed over and looked at, and then a discussion started. The pass said it was a woman, and her job was a navvy. Looking at this person's appearance, i.e. rough hands, sunburnt face, dirty clothing, it was very hard to make a decision regarding sex one way or the other. Ten minutes had gone by; what should we do? To break the deadlock, one lad bent down, put his hand up her clothes, and taking his hand down again said, 'It's OK, it's a woman, let her go.' I know it looks crude, but if it had been a man with a grenade or a pistol under the clothes, where would we have been? Given back her ID she simply smiled and walked away.

Patrol in the rain

I am third from left in a nine-man patrol. Other five men are out of shot

A Patrol in the Rain

Having started to run short of rations we'd gone mainly looking to see what we could scrounge. With bread, eggs, tomatoes, grapes and some tinned stuff in berets and pockets we were going along nicely when a car pulled up and out jumped a man with a camera wanting to snap our picture there and then. The sergeant was adamant that he couldn't, not with all the stuff we were carrying. A compromise was worked out: we'd backtrack a little to hide our booty round a corner, make ourselves presentable and let him take a photograph of the first four men while the other four stood guard over the proceedings. The result was a photograph in the papers soon afterwards of a four-man 'patrol' in the rain, consisting of Sergeant Turley, an unknown Scottish lad, L/bd Wildman and myself. In the picture it can be seen that we are wearing a rubber type of boot. These again were given as second-hand issue because of the heavy rain that was expected. This photograph was taken around the time of killing the pig, hence our forage for the extra grub.

It was on this outing that one night Sergeant Turley told me to stay up all night and operate the radio we had with us, but not to sign the log book as he would do that the following morning. I refused, telling him that if I stayed up all night without sleep it should be I who signed the log. He didn't know that I was a radio operator and I wasn't about to blow my cover by using correct voice procedure. I didn't want to stop in Battery HQ for the rest of my service in Cyprus.

Once we went out in a truck and parked up in the forest. In the distance towards Turkey and Russia you could see lightning flashes of far-off thunder storms. Standing on picket we began to hear what we thought was wind blowing in the trees. A few seconds later we realised nothing was moving, then without warning a very strong gust of wind got up. We interpreted this as wind pressure ahead of the rain front. I walked over to the truck that was nearby and jumped in none to soon – seconds later it began to bucket down. Some lads earlier on had bivouacked in a small gully; the rain had gushed down the slight depression and simply washed them out. News had soon got round, which meant another lesson had been learnt the hard way. Any ground on future curfews would be carefully chosen. It was soon understood that November, and then later February, were the rainy seasons in Cyprus.

We were on a police station guard and things looked quite normal, food eaten, stags changed and all seemed in control. On gate duty was the Scottish lad but a few of us were stood with him. (I'd like to point out here that after the bombing, and the pig incident, out of doors we always carried our weapons with us, even in the courtyard.)

Seeing a few kids stood round we handed them some sweets. The Scottish lad gave one little boy of about eight years of age a Mars bar. He took the Mars and backed away some twenty yards and, with the bar still in his hand, he shouted to Jock. When our lad looked up, the boy dropped the Mars bar, jumped on it a couple of times, and shouted abuse. Jock made to give chase but we stopped him doing so.

Other kids still came for sweets but we just waved them away. Some youngsters were becoming rather persistent, so we fixed bayonets and did bayonet practice on the thick wooden gateposts. This got the message across that nothing more was forthcoming in the way of sweets.

That night, Sergeant Turley made out the roster for us all, telling us which stag and whom we would be with. It was pinned on the board. It wasn't long before we were at the police station again, climbing a makeshift ladder, going through a hole that had been knocked through the ceiling, so as to get access to the roof without being made vulnerable to attack from rifle fire. We'd got on top and had settled in for what was to be an eventful night.

Forty minutes or thereabouts had gone by when we heard noises at the back of the building. Making ready, we switched on all the lights only to see one of our patrols from the station making its way along a wall. There were shouts of 'Put them f— ing lights out, you stupid buggers! Lights out right away!' and to say we were fuming was to put it mildly. If any of us had been trigger happy by now then we would have had casualties.

Finishing stag we all got on to the sergeant for not telling us that he'd sent out a patrol. He apologised, saying he'd forgotten. Much later the section returned and started to filter upstairs, asking us why the lights had been switched on, illuminating them for all to see. At the same time the sergeant was told he was wanted downstairs. He'd only just got round the corner when BANG! A bullet went into the wall through the open back of the chair where he'd been sitting. The lad's name, I think, was Worthington, but I'm not certain. I'd watched him walk into the room, go to his bed and sit down. Before I could speak or do anything, he had pulled back the bolt, taken off the magazine, eased springs, and away went the bullet into the wall. For this he was put on open arrest. (My wife and I went back to Cyprus in 1985 and visited the old police station. You can still see where the bullet is buried in the wall.)

I believe the mistakes I have just described were caused only by tiredness. I know it could have been a terrible tragedy, but I still put the blame on simple fatigue.

Mini Camp, EOKA Pamphlet, Bomb Alley and Out on Patrol

We had given our TSM the nickname of Daddio, and around this time a song called *Don't You Rock Me Daddio* was popular. Joe Ambrose thought it would be a great idea to send in a request to the local radio station. When it was played on air, with the DJ saying that it was for him, it did not please the officers one little bit. Orders were posted that in future no such a request was to be made.

One thing we liked about him was that, if we saved crusts from our bread rations when we were out on mini camp, he would sometimes make us a bread pudding. Even this was stopped though; probably the officers thought he was too soft or too familiar with us, yet that could not have been further from the truth.

As always some soldiers got unusual nicknames, Four in our eight-man section had the initial A. We were all known as Al, so when we were all together it could get complicated. Therefore, being tall I was 'Lofty', Al Bolton became 'Bomb' because he was the bombardier, Al Brindle was known as 'Rommel', mainly due to his ungainly appearance, and Al Talbot as 'Midnight'.

Al Brindle was anything but neat and tidy. In Cyprus, as long as he had a fag in his mouth he was as happy as Larry. Al Talbot, from Jamaica, really was very black, so black that on night patrols he would have to put a white powder on his face. During the daytime when out on patrol, we could ask him to go to a crowd of people and they would automatically disperse as his imposing figure got near them. Eventually he was given the job as driver.

The two lieutenants were very different. Mr Jones was plain Mr Jones, while Mr Murray-Smith we nicknamed Murray Mint. When we were out with Mr Jones he'd leave us by the side of the road, telling us to wait there. Then he would take the NCO into an orange grove, get himself some oranges, come out again then carry on without so much as a kiss-my-arse. Mr Murray-Smith was a different officer altogether; he'd stop us by the roadside, shouting at us all to face the orange grove. Then he would order us to walk in some twenty yards, keeping an eye open for anything that might be suspicious; then on his command we would turn round and come out again. After he had checked we were all present, away we'd go, orange problem solved.

A mini camp would help to cut down a lot of legwork. F and E Sections took beds and tents along as well as a water trailer, and would set up a camp with wire all round. This meant we would be there for quite a few days. A section went out, and the other section did guard as well as digging a pit for you-know-what.

Using spades and a pick to get through the rock, it took a good four hours to dig it deep enough for our requirements. Close by we placed the water trailer with the Bren gun on top, and we'd sit on it looking through binoculars surveying the area.

The start of the cess pit, Taffy on sentry

Cess pit finished and showing camp layout

'Gunner Z' was with us at one camp and, on the third day, Taffy and I said we'd stay on stag from midday till midnight so that the others could get a decent rest. We'd started to get ready for bed when the wind began to get up, which indicated a squall was coming. I shouted as loud as I possibly could, 'Batten down the hatches,' waking everyone up. The storm lasted for only a few minutes, and everyone grabbed hold of the tents and saved them from being blown away. Much to my surprise I received a compliment from Mr Jones for my quick thinking in rousing the camp as I did.

With no armoury, the only course of action was to sleep with your rifle and ammunition in bed with you, or in very close proximity. I wrote home telling Sylvia about having to sleep with my girlfriend at night. She at first didn't understand, then began to realise that it was the rifle I was writing about.

Troops don't always write home and tell of their true situation; instead they will say things are OK, and tell loved ones not to worry. However, on one patrol a batch of EOKA pamphlets were found in what was known as a letterbox, i.e. a hole in the ground with a tin box in it with papers inside. Dennis has kept his and it appears on the following pages (I've lost mine). It is a single sheet printed on both sides (one side in Greek, the other English) and gives casualties of British troops for October 1958. In later years some members of parliament would say Cyprus was not a war zone; why then issue death blankets, dog tags and a medal? Now, read the transcripts of the pamphlet for October 1958 and digest the contents.

Back in bed, within minutes we were all well away, but surprise, surprise, it was Gunner Z who could be heard saying, 'Sir, I can hear some digging down the road.'

'Whereabouts?' he was asked.

'Two hundred yards away.'

At this I piped up, 'But it's solid bloody rock down that road. They'd need a jackhammer to dig a hole there. Anyway,' I continued, 'how are they going to cover up the change in the road colouring?' Nevertheless, an alarm had been given, so all had to get dressed and off we set. From 1.30 a.m. until 5.30 a.m. we trudged up and down that road, even extending the search area, but nothing was found. I think the officer took it on board when I remarked, 'Some use us doing a twelve-hour stag to give the lads a rest, then being up all night looking for phantom bloody diggers.' After three hours' searching that night we were all back to square one, knackered.

E.O.K.A

<u>SIDE ONE</u>
THE BLACK OCTOBER OF THE BRITISH
BRITISH CASUALTIES 21-31 October 1958

		DEAD	WOUNDED
21/10	- At Varossia. Bombs against a military vehicle.	2	1
	- At Larnaca. " " " " "	?	?
	- Near Agios Nikolaos Lefkonikou. Ambush against a military vehicle, which fell down a 50 meters precipice.	1	3
	- At Geroskipou. Bomb against a military vehicle.	?	?
	X Near Akordalies Paphos. Bomb against a military vehicle.		2
22/10	- At Karavas. Bridge exploded whilst a military vehicle was crossing.	?	?
	- Near Kiperounda. Ambush.	3	?
	- On Kokopetrias Street-Kiperounda. Ambush against two military vehicles.		3
	- At Assian. Mine against a military vehicle. Its rear part destroyed completely	?	3
	- At Dali. Ambush.	1	
	X At Rizokarpasso, Mine against four military vehicles, one of which was thrown off the road.	?	?
23/10	X At Agios Vassilios Skilouras. Ambush.	?	?
	- At Trahoni Limassol. Ambush.	?	?
	X At Polemi Paphos. Mine against a vehicle.	?	?
	X At Akaki. Bridge exploded whilst a military vehicle was crossing.	?	?
	X At Palaiohori. Ambush. A vehicle was damaged and some soldiers were wounded, it was unknown how many.	?	?
	X At Kolokossis camp. Bomb. Fire in military tents.	?	?
24/10	- At Nicosia by pistol	1	
	- At Nicosia. Bomb against a military vehicle.	?	?
	- At Kaimakli. Mine. A vehicle was overturned.	?	?
	- At Limassol. Bomb at the hotel "Metropol"		5
	- At Agios Andronikos-Famagusta. Mine against a military vehicle.		1
	X On Ardanon Street-Agios Elias. Ambush against two military vehicles. one of which was blown 5 meters high and committed to flames due to the ignition of the tank and after fell into a ravine 50 meters deep. Inside the vehicle were 10 soldiers who should be badly burnt. A helicopter took off to get them.	8	
25/10	- AT YIALOUSSA........Police? station. Mine. Two vehicles destroyed. Casualties: 1 dead, 18 wounded. 3 of them were critically, 4 seriously and 11 slightly wounded.	1	18
	X At Nicosia near Metohi Kykkou?. Mine against a vehicle which overturned with 7 soldiers on board.	?	?
	- At Larnaca a police vehicle was set on fire.	?	?
	X At Tavros. A NAAFI vehicle was set on fire		
26/10	X In area Mirtou-Kormakiti. Ambush against a military vehicle.	?	?
	X Near Giolou-Paphos. Mine against a military vehicle which fell into a ditch.		2
27/10	- Near Natan-Paphos. Mine against a vehicle.	?	?
	- Near Chrisohou Gate. Mine against a vehicle.	?	?
	- Near Libia. Mine against a vehicle.	?	?
	Total:	17	38

The first side of an EOKA pamphlet found in what was known as a letterbox, i.e. a hole in the ground with a tin box in it with papers inside. It lists casualties of British troops for October 1958

			DEAD	WOUNDED
	SIDE TWO	Brought forward	17	38
28/10	- At Marathovounon. Ambush against three military vehicles. An armoured vehicle was blown up.			2
	- At Arediou. Mine against a military vehicle which exploded and later on was moved away by a crane. <u>There are casualties</u>		?	?
29/10	- At RAF Airport in Nicosia. From an explosion of a time bomb.		?	10
	X At Lakatamian. Ambush		?	?
	X Near Frenaros. Mine against a military vehicle.		?	?
30/10	- Near Akrotiri Elaias Karpasias. Mine against a military vehicle. Two dead one of whom was a major.		2	
	X Near Lissin. Mine against a military vehicle.		?	?
	- At Kepir village. Mine against a military vehicle.		?	?
	X At Flamoudi-Karpasias. Mine against a vehicle.		?	?
31/10	- At Varossia by revolver.		1	
	- At Varossia. A patrol steam boat destroyed.		?	?
	- At Varossia. Two NAAFI cars were set on fire.		?	?
	- At Prastion Mesaorias. Mine against a military vehicle.		?	?
		Total:	20	50

Total casualties 21-31 October 1958:

-20 Dead

-50 Wounded

British casualties from 1-20 October (as it was published in our publication)

-45 Dead

-91 Wounded

Some more casualties <u>were ascertained</u> between 1-20 October:

11/10	At Risokarpason		2
13/10	At Giola Kyrinias 3 wounded instead of 2		1
14/10	At Limassol	1	
16/10	At Aheritou	3	

That is, total of casualties between 1-20 October:

-49 Dead

- 94 Wounded

Total of British casualties during the <u>BLACK OCTOBER 1958:</u>

-69 DEAD

-144 WOUNDED

EOKA

The 1958 EOKA pamphlet continued… Despite assertions by MPs in later years that Cyprus was not a war zone, there were a significant number of British deaths.

With Bren gun as main armament, the bayonet is for the Belgium FN Fal

Me eating a Mars bar, with Dennis sat on the Land Rover

Nearly every day a patrol of some type would go out, and inevitably little incidents would happen. Once we went into the forest and found a tree with pomegranates on it; somebody said it could be booby trapped, but as kids might well eat them we didn't think so. Still, not taking chances, a search was made round the tree to make absolutely certain it was safe. The pomegranates were nice and made a change from oranges. The next incident occurred on a dobie run, i.e. laundry run. After unloading, instead of standing around, four of us began playing football with a stone. As if by magic, two MPs turned up and started to get on to us for not taking more care. We pointed out to them where our two pickets were and that they had come past them to get to us. They then remarked on our scruffy appearance and asked which unit we belonged to. Given the answer, they just nodded and left.

Another incident occurred on a night curfew. We'd been given a length of track to patrol – maybe two- to three-hundred yards long. It would go dark rather early so information from the first ones out was often most helpful. The incoming stag was given warning of a small bush to be careful of. On the right side going down was a building with washing on a line; beyond that after some short distance was a large olive tree. That was the end of our patrol. The night being pitch black, we stumbled over the small bush a few times, but with thunder and lightning going on there were some occasions when the sky lit up and it could be seen easily. After the flash though you couldn't see a thing for a second or two.

Well, things were quiet and everyone was settled until Gunner Z went on stag. For most of his stag all went well. Then, as he passed the house with the washing on the line, the lightning struck. Seeing the clothes on the line he shouted his challenge to halt. Of course, nothing happened, so he opened fire, shooting the clothes to pieces. He was given an MID (Mentioned in Despatches) for this, but others began to ask how he had reacted so quickly. The answer was very simple: he always had a round up the spout with the safety catch on. Even as he left through the camp gates you could hear him activate the bolt and put a round up the spout. It wasn't very long after this that he was given other duties.

Finding a chameleon when on patrol in the area patrolled at Bomb Alley;
88 set under left arm with headset

On many outings we took (I think) an 88 set for radio communi-
cations with base. In the beginning the lads had problems with
technicalities such as voice procedure. It was only when Dennis
said that my trade was as a signaller that I began to be asked how
to reply to certain messages. I categorically stated that I would
only give the answers if they never divulged who the real flaggy
was in the section. They all agreed to keep shtum as this was one
way they could all have a go at operating.

On one occasion we were searching 'Bomb Alley'. This was a
road that went into a valley and had a high cliff on one side,
which made it quite easy for an attacker to throw a grenade of
some type over the edge and not be seen from the bottom.
Walking round we found a donkey in a terrible condition – so bad
in fact that we thought it was dying. After we reported back to
base, an officer turned up, looked at it, then sent for the owner.
The farmer couldn't have cared less and just wanted to leave it
there to die.

Bomb Alley

This very much seemed to be the way of life that went out there; if it could no longer work, the animal was of no further use.

Another outing turned out to be very funny – well it was to us. Because of the prohibition of firearms the fowl population had increased somewhat. This day, as we sat having packed lunches, ducks and other feathered friends came to visit. At some point it was suggested we try to catch one or two. Setting up the usual bowl and stick with a string-pull attached, we waited patiently, but with no success. One bright spark then came up with the idea of shooting one. Good idea – but if we used our rifles, the ammunition could all go, leaving us vulnerable. Ah, brainwave, use the Bren gun. It was very accurate so just one shot should be enough for what was needed.

Everything was meticulously set; bread was left in a certain place, and, hidden out of view, a lad named Smith who was a marksman waited with the Bren. Closer and closer came the ducks. Then instead of a single shot a burst of fire came out Brrrrrrrrrrrr! Somebody had put the Bren on automatic. What a sight! All that could be seen were feathers. The poor ducks didn't stand an earthly chance. That put an end to that little game. Just think though – who'd be daft enough to go duck shooting with a Bren gun? Well, obviously F Section would.

Not long after the bombing, the Yialoussa police station, along with its station guard, was relocated in the outskirts of the village, nearer to our base camp. The house belonged to a sea captain and was rather new. Except for one side it had a clear, open view of the surroundings. It wasn't long before the frontage got a facelift in the usual army manner of a white-painted oval shape of stone with the Artillery badge and 93 Bty written inside. This building would serve as the station until our return to Blighty.

Culvert clearing had to be done every morning, and our section of road to check was towards Bogazi. F Section decided to change tactics when it became our turn to do the job. We were up and out on the road by 5.30 a.m. At thirty yards from every gully we would dismount and spread out into the fields on each side checking for wires. Going on another thirty yards we would return to the road, mounting up and checking every culvert we came to in the same way until our boundary had been reached. Then we turned to come back. However, instead of returning as normal we thought we would repeat the procedure all over again back to camp. Everything went without a hitch, but getting to camp we knew we were about five minutes late (if that) for breakfast.

When we got to the canteen the Scottish corporal told us we were too late and would not get fed. 'If you don't come early enough, you don't get breakfast,' he said. Seeing one of the Greek workers sitting down eating his breakfast really infuriated us. Pointing our weapons at the cook, we said, 'If you can feed the f—ing Greeks in this camp you can f—ing feed us as well, otherwise you're f—ing dead, you bastard.' The speed at which word got round was amazing. Within what seemed seconds, sure enough it was the one and only Sgt Watkins who came up and began to defuse the situation. The cooks were arguing that we'd turned up late so therefore it was our fault. The sarge could see the Greeks eating just the same as we could. Looking round to let the cooks see that he had taken stock of the situation, he ordered the cooks to get our breakfasts sorted out and do it with out any animosity. The cooks also had instructions to give breakfast to any culvert clearing team, no matter what time they returned to camp.

Back to the lighter side; writing was our only major contact with home, and a habit of only one of us bringing the mail to the lines became standard practice. Sylvia wrote and asked what I thought of the top twenty on Radio Luxembourg if I ever listened to it. As I've said a few times now, tiredness was a big problem. Not thinking straight I picked up pen and paper and wrote a letter back immediately, saying that if she thought I would stay up until two o'clock in the morning just to hear someone like Johnny Mathis she must be bonkers. I posted the letter late that night and went to bed. The following morning, however, I went to breakfast thinking, what the hell have I done? It's not her fault that Cyprus is two hours ahead of UK time. At the first possible moment, I wrote another letter apologising for what I'd written and the tone in which it was written. I never knew until I came home that she received the apology before she got that letter – lucky me! After this mistake I decided to number my mail; this continued until demob.

Another thing that started at this time was to put acronyms on the back of the envelope, like 'Swalk', or 'Burma' (Be Undressed Ready My Angel); another was 'Capstan': Can A P— Stand Twice A Night? The reply might be 'Natspac': Now And Then Some P— Are Capable. Many others were sent, but it would be too long an exercise to write them all down here.

On the coast of the Panhandle on the Turkish side of Cyprus is a tiny outcrop about two miles to the north of Yialoussa. At this point was stationed a detachment from 188 Searchlight/Radar Battery. I believe the place was called Stassousa Point. One night in complete darkness we approached the gate. After replying to a few words of challenge to clarify who we were, we got in quite easily. The section went into the NAAFI they had there, and the sergeant into the NCOs' place.

How long we'd been there waiting I can't really say, but it was quite some time before the sergeant reappeared and came back to us. He seemed a little worse for wear with drink but still capable of command. Off again into the darkness we went with the sergeant ahead. Twenty minutes or so had gone by when the lance bombardier asked where the sergeant was. Looking round, nothing could be seen of him anywhere. Then from behind a low sand dune he appeared, staggering slightly, saying, 'Bang, bang, bang, I bloody got you all then, didn't I?' The lance bombardier, looking slightly uncertain of himself in the situation, remarked that the sergeant must be drunk; what should we do now? Should we just take his magazine off him until we got back to camp so he could not do any harm to anyone? That seemed to be the only solution. This the lance bombardier did. Then off we set for camp. We arrived and entered OK, but not before giving the sergeant his magazine back. The small arms were returned. Everyone went off to bed happily, sleeping until the next morning.

The following morning after parade, Sgt Watkins shouted that he wanted to see me.

'What do you want me for, sarge?' I asked.

'It's about last night and the sergeant coming in off patrol drunk.'

'What do you mean, drunk? He wasn't drunk when he came in with us,' I said.

'He was drunk when he came in, he just virtually fell into bed!' was the reply.

'Well, he must have got drunk in the sergeants' mess after he came in then,' I said.

'Who put his Sten away then?' the sarge wanted to know.

'I suppose he did, I don't know.'

'You are one lying bastard,' the sergeant said, with a broad grin.

I still said, 'Well I didn't see anything last night, it was dark.'

'You're still a lying get. Go on, off you go,' and so I did, no proof, no action, and no pack drill.

As far as I could ascertain, 188 Bty was split into smaller units, then dotted around the island at strategic points. The British navy, who had the job of patrolling the coastline, would often call upon the camp we'd visited the previous night. When the navy arrived, they would exchange some of their rations for the army rations, plus probably anything else they might need. It has never been broadly put about that the navy as well as the air force had a vital part alongside the army in the policing of Cyprus during the troubles there. In fact for one particular meeting to be held in Athens, President Makarios would not leave the island unless the British escorted him. This must have been done by either the navy or the air force. Makarios thus made certain that he would give the British the responsibility for his safety and that he would be guaranteed a safe passage.

Setting up an ambush was another detail we needed to learn. It is bad enough knowing you might be walking into one, but to actually lie in wait is another thing altogether. As you lie for hours nerves can start to go a bit. Any noise is magnified and then imagination creeps in; you are seeing things that are not there and hoping no one gets trigger-happy.

The location of our chosen position was at an offset cross-roads. To make matters more difficult it was to be set at night, and this was very soon after the bombing. All was still and quiet, with just the sergeant coming round checking; in fact it was really becoming boring, just lying there in wait. Looking at the skyline I noticed two figures coming over the hill in front of me, something like two hundred yards away. In a low voice I called and informed the sergeant of what I'd seen. The sarge then started scurrying round telling all to get ready.

Den and I were together and I was hoping the rest of the lads weren't getting stirred up by the sarge. We waited until the two figures were dead centre of the ambush before giving out the challenge. Happy to say, all went well. Later the TSM remarked that he had been dubious and a little bit nervous at coming to the set-up, until he found out it was F Section out there. A bit of an unruly mob we may have been, but we had learnt quite early on the importance of having a great deal of confidence in the man next to you in the field.

We had no such luxuries as mobile phones, so written letters were the main link with home. If a lad had problems at home of any kind his mates would try to help him out. With this help in mind, Joe Ambrose began to get at me to write a letter for him to a girl he was in touch with. After weeks of pestering I agreed to write a letter informing the young lady that Joe had a broken arm and was finding it difficult to answer any letters. Joe read its contents, then happily sealed it and posted it off. Thinking back on this, I often wonder why or how on earth I let him talk me into doing it. Maybe it was because Den and I would help Eric to write his letters home and word them so as not to worry anyone about our situation. Den should take most of the credit though.

However, a couple of weeks later, I received a letter from this girl telling me in no uncertain terms what she thought of the attempt to con her. I didn't like what I'd done but thought it wiser not to get into any correspondence with her. Many weeks later Dennis told me that if I had started writing to her, he would have written and told Sylvia what was going on. So I was being chaperoned by Dennis, wanted or not.

From time to time in with the mail my father would send me the local newspaper, the *St Helens Reporter*. In it was very often an article written in local dialect. Den would ask me to read it to him in my Lancashire accent. In the beginning it was another language altogether for him to get to understand, but as weeks passed by he started to pick it up and found it easier to follow the dialect if I happened to drop back into it. I think it was probably because I used dialect when I spoke, then spoke in a completely different way on the radios, that I threw some of the lads who came from not too far away from where I was born. I also confused the Signals bombardier, because when on radio operating my twang wasn't as pronounced.

Keeping up with local news was great, especially the time I opened one paper delivery. The headlines read St Helens 46, Australia 4, (or something like that); the Saints had beaten the Aussies' touring team by a huge score. I read the report a few times just to let it sink in. The problem though is that every time an Aussie touring team comes to Knowsley Road rugby ground, it wants to wipe that score clean away with a bigger one against the Saints.

Having patrolled Bomb Alley a few times it was now time to take a convoy through. On the outskirts of Yialoussa, as we were all ready to proceed, an NCO told me to go and get by the side of a particular truck he pointed at. I went towards it then turned and came away from it. As I did so, the NCO told me to get back again. 'No way,' I said, 'it's a petrol truck. I want to be able to have a chance of seeing anything that may be thrown over from the top, and I can only do that if I'm a short distance away. I've been sat on a petrol truck once before, so I don't intend to push my luck too far again.' The NCO nodded in agreement when he learnt what was on the truck. I then repositioned myself and walked some twenty yards behind all the way through.

Near to here, at what I suppose could be called the head of Bomb Alley on the Rizokarpaso side, a mini camp was set up with an officer in charge. From this location it would be less tiring searching the local countryside and checking traffic coming through. One check we did was on an orange wagon, fully loaded, going to the Keo factory to have them pulped and made into orangeade. The driver got out of his cabin and watched us do a thorough search of his truck. When we'd finished he was signalled to go, but all he did was to stand and stare at us, looking first at one, then the other. Then without a word he jumped up on to his truck and began to throw oranges to us. It was normal practice to stop one of these wagons and take any oranges that were needed, but, because we hadn't taken anything off his lorry this time, he may have thought that we were setting him up for something. So he made sure we got some fruit by throwing it down to us himself. Even as he drove away we could see him continually looking into his driving mirror expecting something to happen.

Back at the mini camp they were having trouble getting a signal through to Battery HQ owing to the terrain being so undulating. It had not gone unnoticed that a peculiar looking set of wires was with the radio set. No one knew what they were for, until I told them that it was a ground aerial. Most lads thought I was joking when I told them that it should be spread out on the ground like a spider's web, then the radio signals would bounce off the ionosphere in a V formation. If the battery station was in between the bounce you'd get no reception at all, but if it was on the rebound a good signal could be had. Spreading out the aerial and plugging into the radio we obtained a very good reception. So it proved we were in an excellent position to receive. We later had a visit from the Artillery Signals NCO, who asked a lot of questions as to how we'd set up the aerial. After receiving a load of waffle about us putting the aerial on a pole, then on a tent, then finding out when someone threw it on the ground we got a reception, he went away satisfied.

Later that night I wanted to go to the toilet. It was the custom when out like this that somebody had to accompany you, so I went with torch in hand and Dennis as my minder. As we walked along I heard an aircraft overhead coming rather low. Silly me. I decided to shine the torch at it, just to see if anything would happen. The plane circled and within some fifteen to twenty minutes a radio message was received of the sighting of moving lights at our position. This was proof if needed that the RAF was on full alert the same as everyone else. So not only was the navy keeping a watchful eye around the island on water, the RAF was doing its bit also in supporting the army in the air.

It was while at this camp we woke up one morning to be told that a curfew had to be set up during the very early hours of the morning by the rest of the battery. At first light a radio message was received. The lance bombardier was operating; thinking it was a hoax, he gave some unsavoury replies. Little did he know that he was in conversation with the BC (Battery Captain). His remarks cost him his stripe.

Anyway, my place was at an open piece of ground covering a back road. On my own, I settled down, with some others a few hundred yards away. This would be for the full day or there abouts. Late in the morning, what should I see but an old Greek man sitting on an ox cart coming slowly towards me. He was dressed in the traditional small black waistcoat with white shirt and wide black pantaloon trousers and boots; he also had the usual handlebar moustache. I signalled the old man to stop. He got off the cart, while I was saying, 'Curfew'. The old man nodded that he understood what I'd said, unhitched the animal, then went and sat down on a rock at the roadside. As an hour or so went by we just looked at each other. He shrugged. I nodded, and taking pity on him I offered him a cigarette. He took it, lit it and sat there contented. A little while later, I gave him another.

All at once two lads came galloping towards me, both on the one horse. The horse was lathered in sweat – all down its neck was a type of white foam. They must have been riding it really hard. I told them to dismount, but they hesitated. After I waved the rifle, and following a few words from the old man, they did as bidden.

We'd all been there for maybe forty minutes when I gave the old man another cigarette. Within minutes one of the lads stood and began to walk to the horse. He must have thought I was a soft touch, but immediately I shouted at him to sit down. He thought he would ignore me. It was then that I loaded my rifle and raised it. At this, the old man began a full tirade at the young lad, whilst at the same time I gestured the boy to go back to where he'd been sitting. When he got back to his place and sat down, from a distance I shouted for his attention. When he looked, I took off the magazine, drew back the bolt and a round fell out to the ground. Once again the old man went berserk, no doubt telling him how lucky he was that I hadn't shot him.

I have often been asked when telling this story, if I would really have shot and killed him. Well, without being boastful about the matter, I later put four rounds in the head and six in the body of a half-size target at 100 yards. I knew full well that if he jumped on the horse and made a getaway without me stopping him, I would be liable to get five years' jail for dereliction of duty. I wasn't too worried though, because I also knew if I didn't get the lad I'd get the horse. After this things soon got back to normal.

Searching in a village for weapons

Ambulance Duty

I can't fully remember the start of the next episode, but I know we were getting ready to go on parade before going out on an assignment. All of us had our rifles and were standing about waiting, when the TSM shouted at four of us to get into the ambulance – an accident had happened near Rizokarpaso. A vehicle with six people in it had rolled off the road. All the occupants were injured and some were children. Diving into our vehicle, away we went at breakneck speed.

Reaching the scene we split up and took charge of one person each. I got a young boy and each time I tried to go near him he would start to cry or whimper. Not knowing exactly what to do I asked if anyone could speak English and translate for me. I got someone to tell the boy that I was not trying to hurt him but to help him. I also found out that he had broken his left arm, which before, without knowing it, was the arm I had been touching. No wonder he cried when I went near him.

One of the other injured was a woman who had a very bad wound in the groin area. To get to the wound her clothes needed to be at waist height in order for the medics to be able to apply the pressure bandages. (I have always felt proud of the way she was well treated by the medics in attendance and respected by the rest, even though she was in such an unladylike state.)

After we had made everyone as comfortable as possible, off the driver took us as fast as possible, round bends in villages with lights blazing and flying past houses at the roadside. Passing one of these houses we heard a thump. He'd hit and killed two chickens. We soon got to the hospital in Famagusta, where the emergency unit were waiting to take charge. The young boy I was with walked out of the ambulance, so I made it my duty to inform one of the staff of his broken arm. They looked at me rather quizzically, maybe wondering how I knew.

With everything sorted out we began our return in the same

manner (like a bat out of hell). Because it was starting to get dark, we raced to get back to camp as soon as possible. It wasn't long though before another loud bang was heard; this time, though, the driver had hit a pig. The brakes were slammed on and out jumped two lads who slung the dead pig in the ambulance. Away we went again to camp, with us thinking, what a bloody driver, he's killed more than he's saved. The ambulance had a plaque inside telling of a baby that had been born in it; such is life.

Not all ambulance duties were as hectic as this; most times it would simply be a case of being on stand-by. Luckily we didn't need the vehicle a great deal. Oh yes, the dead pig went to be butchered and served up in the officers' mess. The lads who killed it didn't even get a smell of it, which was only par for the course I suppose.

Pastimes

Darts remained the main pastime at night – well, any time really, especially if you were on guard and had spare time to yourself. We played three main darts games, rugby, cricket, and killer. The rules to rugby were that you had to get the inner or bull to gain possession of the ball, and then go for a treble or double. But if you got a treble, i.e. scored a try, your next throw had be for a double to convert the try. If that dart missed you carried on as usual – but you must have the ball to score. In the meantime your opponent would attempt to get the inner or bull to get the ball so that he could go for points.

For cricket, it would first be decided whether it should be a five-wicket or an eleven-wicket game; then we would decide who would be batting by throwing for closest to the bull. When the match began, a bullseye was two wickets, and an inner one wicket. The game had to start by the bowler going for the bullseye. The batsman could only score runs if he scored over forty points, meaning a score of say sixty-nine would mean only twenty-nine runs recorded. As with a normal game of cricket, when all the wickets had gone the roles would be reversed.

The third game, killer, was often the most popular, owing to the short length of time it took to complete. Each player would have to throw one dart with his weakest hand to obtain his number, and no two players could have the same number. The idea would be for the lowest number to throw first and go for the double of the person he wanted to knock out. If or when three darts had gone into your number you were out. With just a couple playing, this game wasn't too bad, but if it got to maybe six or seven players you might throw only the one dart, for your number, with the poorest hand. This game proved to be the most popular because if any player was called upon for a duty, it didn't interrupt the game. With these three games being played on a regular basis the lads really became expert at darts, and nearly always had darts on their person somewhere.

The battery had a driver who was a New Zealander. One day four of us were playing darts waiting for afternoon parade when Al Talbot (the black lad) started messing about. Without thinking I said, jokingly, 'I'll black your bloody eye for you if you don't give over.' Smartish he replied, 'You can whiten it boy, but you'll never blacken it.'

'Sod off,' was my reply, and away he went laughing.

As we began our next game, a shout of 'On parade, Fox Troop' went out. At this the Kiwi told us to get off the board. We told him to get stuffed. With only five wickets to go down we would finish the game and then get on parade. With only six darts each the game had both innings played and all wickets down in a matter of minutes. I know this sounds far-fetched, but that was how good we were becoming.

Muster Parades

I soon learnt that when I was early for parade I often ended up on a special detail, so I began to make a habit of being last, or there abouts. One morning I got in line with four others. TSM Watkins came along the line and gave these four cookhouse duty. At this they all complained that I hadn't been given a detail as well. To this the sergeant answered, 'If he's late and you come on parade after him, you must be late, so just shut up.' I didn't get more privileges than anyone else, because I never pushed my luck too far – it was just an easy way for the sarge to get us together as a unit.

On another morning I'd been out on culvert clearing, had had my breakfast and was standing near the POL point (petrol and oil). Who should come walking past but TSM Watkins. 'Good morning, sarge.'

'Good morning, Balmer.' He carried on a few yards, stopped, turned and looked me, then said, 'What are you doing there?'

'I'm waiting for parade, sarge.'

'You are what?' he said. 'Oh no you're not. If you're here the rest of the troop's late. Now bugger off back to your tent until parade is called.' So back to the tent I went after being bollocked for being early for parade, with rifle and tail between my legs. Let me put all this in the right context. When I say that I was nearly always the last man to fall in for parade, it is not that I was minutes late, just seconds. I might even be just in the last bunch to fall in.

The next tale isn't very nice to tell, but it shows how some people can't give orders without trying hide behind their stripes. One NCO in particular couldn't address anyone without using abusive and derogatory language. It was f—ing bastard this, f—ing bastard that, with other uncalled for remarks put in as well. I decided to try to put a stop to it. I had been told to send home for my birth certificate. I don't know why, but the battery office was uncertain of my age, perhaps because I was enlisted at the age of twenty and not the usual eighteen or twenty-one. After two weeks it arrived so, putting it in my map pocket (the leg pocket), I went on parade. The NCO in question was taking parade. He came along the line as usual with his foul gutter language and stood in front of me, but before he could utter a word, I said to him, 'I've got my birth certificate in my pocket and if you call me a bastard I'll f—ing well flatten you.' Obviously taken aback he looked at and said, 'Fall in two men – he's on a charge for threatening an NCO.'

'What's up with you, you soft get?' I replied, 'I've said nothing yet, and I've got two witnesses, one at each side of me, to prove I've said nothing.'

This really infuriated him. Without thinking he went to make out a charge or a complaint, little realising that he was thereby telling other NCOs he was greatly disliked. Within days he was moved to another troop or section – problem again solved.

I'd like to stress it wasn't what was said, but the manner in which it was said and done, that was causing all the trouble. Also, when men have rifles and ammunition you can't take a chance that someone won't lose his patience one day.

The Curfew, Christmas in Cyprus and More Patrolling

Most of the time trouble in the ranks came only when silly orders were given to very tired troops. One such occasion was on another mini camp we were at, near the top end of Bomb Alley, covering all the area surrounding it.

Road going into Bomb Alley from Rizokarpaso end

The officer in charge was Mr Jones. I have a photograph of me on the side of the road. I was sitting with the rifle across my knees when up came Butch Gladwin with his camera. 'Stay there,' he said. It's a cracking photo that he snapped and I think it is one of the best he ever took of me.

Photograph of me on sentry curfew, at Bomb Alley, showing dog tags and rubber boots

About 100 yards from where I was sat we'd set up camp, from where we could go out into the countryside quite easily. It was after one of these outings that trouble arose. We came into camp just before dark. As we got in grub was up, so off I went with my eating irons, got the food and went back to the tent. As I went in Mr Jones shouted, 'Lights out!' The light was left on so I could finish my supper. The tent flap flew open and the lance bombardier again ordered lights out.

'OK, as soon as I've eaten up and got changed,' I retorted.

'Well, if you're not going to turn it out then I will,' said the lance bombardier coming closer to the light.

'You touch that and I'll put your f—ing light out! I'm not eating this grub in the dark for any f—r. Piss off!'

Flustered at this reply, he went out of the tent saying, 'Mr Jones sir, Mr Jones sir, Mr Jones sir. They won't put the light out until they've eaten their supper.'

'Well make sure the light goes out when they've finished eating.'

Within minutes we were changed and in bed. We didn't need rocking to get to sleep, either.

It may sound as though every patrol was one long argument, but it wasn't. Most outings were quite mundane, going along dusty roads, tramping for miles, monotony to be broken up only by moving over open country. But going over the countryside had its pitfalls. Our coming over a hill would most times cause a shepherd to start whistling a very high-pitched note, no doubt to warn everybody in the area that we were about. What made it more infuriating was that on many occasions you could see the sheep but you had to scour the terrain to find where the shepherd was.

The main areas we searched would be around the villages of Ayios Nikholaos, Ayios Georgios, Ayios Andronikos, Ayios Theodoros, Leonarisso, Vasili, Vothylakas, Neta, Ayios Symeon, Koroveia, Galinoporni, Melanarga, Lythragkomi, Koilanemos, Yialoussa, and of course, Rizokarpaso.

The word *ayios* in Greek means 'saint', so a village is so named in much the same way as St Helens. The battery had a complement of about 175 men with 200 square miles to patrol and search, and many times we tramped for miles without an incident at all.

Well after Christmas we were on a quiet patrol going along at a steady plod, with me tail-end Charlie as usual, when somebody mentioned that we should be getting a medal issued to us for policing the island. Minutes went by discussing the pros and cons before Brummie Beasley, in a Black Country accent, shouted out, 'I reckon we should get a medal as big as a f—ing dustbin lid for all this walking we're doing.' For most of the day after this, it was one long moan as to why we should be better treated. With things being as they were we didn't get our ribbons up or medals issued until back in Blighty.

On another patrol, again with me as tail-end Charlie, all was going well until we entered one of the villages. In most places there was no such thing as a pavement. The roads could be narrow and bendy, as in this village. With Joe Ambrose ahead of me we went round two short, quick bends. Unconcerned I carried on, while the villagers began to close the doors and shutters on their windows as I passed. I thought to myself, surely I'm not that ugly? I soon began to realise, however, that the reason was that I was on my own; I'd lost the rest of the section. All that I could do was try to keep a steady nerve and continue in the general direction the others were going, hoping that I might meet them along the road, or get out unharmed without being attacked. More alert now than ever – talk about having eyes in your backside – I was beginning to get a little worried to say the least. I carried on, until I did eventually come out of the village.

Anxiously looking about I saw that I had emerged some two- to three-hundred yards away from the patrol, and hundreds of feet higher up. Putting fingers to my mouth, I gave a shrill whistle to attract their attention. Seeing me all on my own they looked at each other as if wondering where the hell I had been. When I rejoined the section, a discussion began as to who was responsible for my being left behind, and what needed to be done to make sure this didn't happen again. That day my God was with me all the way. If the villagers had been hostile and challenged my presence, it would have been proved that I was virtually lost in the village and on my own. Was I glad to see my own patrol!

One escort duty was to HQ. At this place Dennis and I met up with an old pal, Pete Barlow, another lad who'd been in training with us. We stood round talking and coming up to date as best we could, as well as trying to find out what the others in our intake were getting up to in whichever batteries they were in. The RSM, who'd been watching us, came close to start eavesdropping on our conversation. He must have been happy with us because, unusually for an RSM, he walked away leaving us to natter on. Another 'cabbie' (ride) was to 54 Bty, but this really was a flying visit. Butch Gladwin or someone just about had time to snap a half track that had been blown up. (A half track was a vehicle with wheels at the front and tank tracks at the back, heavily armoured.) The cab had been rearranged with the force of the blast and was at an angle of thirty degrees or so. When snaps had been taken we were off again.

Taken at Davlos Camp 54 Bty, 4 November 1958
Champ believed to be from the explosion of 30 October 1958

It was now nearing Christmas and mail arrived with regularity. Weeks previously Billy Coyne had written home asking his mother to post him some money so that he could send her some oranges for Christmas. Word had got round that for 10/- (50p) it was possible to send a crate of oranges back to England. So when

Billy got the money – along with an inference from home that they thought he was on a fiddle – he made certain that he filled in all the necessary paperwork to have four crates of oranges sent home in time for the holiday period. After Christmas he received a letter from his mother telling him that she'd got so many oranges that she had given all the kids in the street some.

At Christmas our section was in camp, so it came as no surprise that the padre came to give a service of communion and the likes. First a trellis table was put up with a white cloth over it, then the candles. When everything had been set up, the various denominations were called out. Your turn came, if you wished, to make your peace with God. Strange as it may seem, it was only at this moment I found out that Dennis was a Catholic. I was then a Congregationalist, and years later became a Methodist, when I got married to Sylvia. Religion never became an issue between us; in fact, I think that if I counted all my friends up, a great many would be Catholics.

A week before Christmas all our beer rations were saved up. We also bought bottles of wine, plus two bottles of brandy. I think it was on Christmas Eve that the camp party had been arranged. All the cast taking part were obviously soldiers. Best remembered, other than the singing, was a joke by Joe Ambrose, telling us that he'd often heard of an intelligence officer, but he'd never heard of an intelligent officer. The biggest cheer of the night went up for this one. The other big hit was an act or trick done by a sergeant. He pretended to be hypnotised, then was told to stand rigid. He was then picked up and suspended between two chairs, supported only by his head and feet. Being close I could still not see any way that this was a trick – it was brilliant, just brilliant. The usual party for the local kids was held the following day I think, but by then our section had gone or was going on police station guard.

Going back to Christmas Eve: we got a large pot from the kitchen and poured in Watney's Pale Ale, Newcastle Brown Ale, two bottles of brandy and the rest of the red and white wine. It all got stirred up and taken in the next tent. With mugs at the ready we all set to the task of having a good time. The following morning the NCO tried to wake us all up, but got the normal polite army response. At nine o'clock we were all still in bed with hangovers. The outcome was that we were told to be on parade at twelve o'clock ready to relieve the police station guard, so that they could get back to camp and have their Christmas dinner as well. All the hampers that had been received had almost certainly been eaten. It would be commonplace to share a parcel with others; because of quick movement plus poor storage, the food never stayed very fresh for long.

With kit on a wagon, away we went to the newly located police station. After we had settled in and sorted out our stags we got down to the serious business of playing darts. The most noticeable part of this guard duty? You had to be blind not to see the snow that had fallen, Yes, I said snow. There we were in Cyprus, on Boxing Day, on guard in the snow. I did have a photograph of me standing at the back of the police station in the fields, wearing my greatcoat and carrying a rifle, but it seems to have vanished into thin air.

Within a week the temperature went back up so quickly that on New Year's Day we were out again up the coast a few miles past Rizzo skinny dipping. One lad got his mate to take a full-length photo of him and he sent it to his wife with a note saying look what you're missing! The only other photograph I still have of the day out is one can taken from a distance.

Another example of light relief is a story of how a Scottish lad had gone three months without having his hair cut. After he had taken two weeks getting to Cyprus without seeing a barber his hair was rather long to start with. He hadn't had his hair cut simply because each time the barber came to camp he was out somewhere doing a job. With two-and-a-half months' hair growth, his mane was hanging over the scarf he wore. It only came to light how bad it was after he'd been to hospital, near Nicosia. Caught walking along the main road that goes across the plains, he was picked up and reported for his unusual hair style. Back in camp it was made certain that his hair got cut, with the result that his beret was now too big and he had to get a new one. Converse to this story, a full bombardier named Bunny Austin, along with another soldier, decided to have a Mohican haircut. A third one had his head shaved bald. In camp they looked unusual, but outside when they had headgear on you couldn't tell the difference.

In the NAAFI other things besides food were available. One item I bought was a small tablecloth to fit a coffee table. It was in sombre gold and red colours with Arab motifs of horsemen woven into it, and three-inch tassels all round its edge. (It's now forty-seven years old and my wife still has it.) Also Ali, the man in charge, was bringing in settee cushions, but only in pairs of the same design. I kept pestering him for four of the same pattern. It took weeks upon weeks, but I did eventually get them. The NAAFI workers had their own tent hidden away from the rest of us behind the back of the building. We could watch them having their food from a large round platter, always using one hand only. The reason for this, we found out, was because the redundant hand was used for doing their ablutions. That though didn't bother them one jot when serving us our food.

One devious trick was tried when on a patrol in a village. Which village I can't remember, but the section doing its job normally came upon a taverna in the village with quite a few people inside. The usual practice was to use a different taverna at different times of the day, and this is why one taverna would be full to overflowing and others empty. Most of these customs we picked up as we went along. Anyhow, the place having been surrounded, I was to be the one to go in. (Remember, I was the lucky one.) Inside the atmosphere changed immediately, from one of rowdy talk to one of near silence. Looking about, seeing an empty chair I took my time, and walked towards it. I noted its position, then sat down. The man at the table began to speak and a conversation started going on. Five minutes had elapsed when the young lads in there began to get a bit cocky. The man spoke to them in Greek, then turned to me, saying, 'Sorry about that, but I'm telling them you're not on your own.'

'I am, there's only me in here.'

'Yes, I know that, but your pals are outside waiting for something to start,' was his reply. 'You've only come in here to set a trap and cause trouble.'

Again I denied his accusation. All the while during the conversation he kept turning to the young lads and saying something in Greek. In the end he said, 'Please shout for your friends. I was in the British army in the last war, in the Engineers, and know how you people operate. Please shout for them.'

Knowing the game was up, I shouted, 'Den, Brum, Eric, Rommel!' at the top of my voice and faces appeared at the doors and windows. The man then began to speak to the lads, who in turn looked at every door and window; it was plain to see by the expression on their faces that they had grossly underestimated the situation. Waving to my comrades and saying that all was OK, I shook hands with the man and departed.

Each troop's section seemed to change and cross personnel with another on a daily basis, but even to this day I don't know exactly how many sections there really were in the battery. The only time I know of that both troops met (other than at the meeting with the general) was at the battery football game. I think it can be safely said that most of those who played that day were off duty. My job, with a dozen or more, would be to guard the perimeter while the match was in progress.

As I waited for the game to start, a Cypriot came along the touchline to me and started talking of certain things. He knew that we'd taken over from the Welsh Regiment and began to talk of unusual happenings. He didn't make it quite clear exactly who was to blame but he was saying he'd been shot for no reason at all. Lifting his trouser leg then pulling down his sock, he revealed a scar at the ankle joint where the bullet had gone in and out.

By this time I'd been joined by one or two others from the perimeter guard and they were listening into what he had to say. He said he was praising the troops and began to give the V sign as Churchill did in the war, showing us how he had done it, and then had been shot in the foot for his troubles. We started laughing and he wanted to know why we thought it was funny. Obviously it took a minute or two to explain the difference of having the back of the hand on view, as opposed to the palm of the hand. It would be quite confusing for anyone seeing Churchill giving this sign during the war years, as even he often gave the V sign the wrong way round to the crowds following him around. Having had the problem explained, the man went away satisfied. Or at least I think he was.

The two teams came out and kicked off. The match was just like any other. As the game went on, though, the TSM of Echo Troop kept shouting for the ball to be given to him. As the game wore on the more he shouted, because no one was giving him the ball. Eventually he was bellowing at the top of his voice. 'The next so-and-so that doesn't give me the ball is on a f—ing charge.' Well it had to come, didn't it? He shouted, someone passed the ball to him, whereupon every player on the pitch gathered round to get it off him. When everybody had dispersed you could hear him shouting, 'Even my own bloody team was tackling me to get the ball off me! You're all on f—ing guard tonight, the lot of you!' And that I believe was the closest I ever got to Echo Troop.

I do know that Echo Troop had its moments the same as we did. The occasion I remember was when a section from E Troop had been sent out to bring in another section from the troop that had stopped at a taverna and got drunk. The locals were afraid to ask them to go in case things got nasty. The solution was to send out another section to bring the first one back in – so you see how the stress got to us all, one way or another, in the end.

A section, or maybe two, from Echo Troop went out taking the second-hand sleeping bags with them. The area they would be searching had chicken compounds in the smallholdings. Some clever bloke thought it would be a great idea to bed down inside one of these shacks for the night. They must have been city dwellers, because as any country lad, or those who had dealt with chickens before, would know, that chickens are notorious for fleas. These chickens were no exception. What made matters worse was that the lads involved kept quiet about the problem after they came back to camp, then without saying a word handed their sleeping bags back in to the QM stores. Any kit that came into contact with the sleeping bags also became infested with fleas. This episode happened midway during the campaign, so it didn't take too long for us to be known not as Le Cateau Bty, but Flea Cateau Bty. As can be imagined, with the changeover of kit from the QM stores it didn't take long for many more of us to become infected with fleas. Time proved how hard it was to get rid of them too.

One of the Cypriot camp workers had been boasting that his wife was due to have a baby, and he pointed her out as one of the women in the fields working. It soon came to light that she didn't have very long to go before the child was born. He would sit in camp, doing as little as possible, telling everyone how well she was, until one day it was noticed that she was missing. The Cypriot man came into camp, as proud as anything telling all how happy he was. He kept on and on as to how well mother and baby were. We all put up with his happiness until the following day, when a patrol came in and said that they'd seen his wife in the fields working. Without batting an eye he said, 'Yes, she is all right, the baby is all right, she can go back to work now.' With an attitude like that, I've often said that no way did Mary ride on the donkey to Jerusalem. If anybody rode the donkey, it would have been Joseph.

Another day we noticed four women in the field at the back of camp, with not one man in sight. They cleared an area, then began digging. Some days later an investigation was initiated to see what they were up to. It turned out that they were digging a well. It was just after Christmas that they'd selected the site for the well. Each day that followed they could still be seen digging away, and they were still digging at it in March when we returned to England. We often stood and watched those four women labouring away, but very rarely did we ever see any men digging at all.

Back in camp, bringing a mug of tea back for anyone who didn't want go for breakfast, was a practised habit for one reason or another. One morning Eric and I were up and ready, but Dennis said he was tired, so he asked if we would bring him back a mug of tea. Thinking no more of it, we went to breakfast, ate up, and with a mug of tea in hand returned to the tent – only to find Dennis asleep again. He'd lit a cigarette then fallen back to sleep, letting the cigarette fall on to the bed sheets which had caught fire, resulting in a hole in the top sheet about a foot across, smouldering round the edges and growing bigger by the minute. Thank God it hadn't burst into flames. Eric and I then set about waking Dennis up, while at the same time stamping out the smouldering sheet, then lifting up the tent flaps to remove the smell of smoke. The next step was to strip the bed, fold up the sheet and put it into the blanket square we made each morning, then get it replaced as soon as possible. This was a further warning of how easy it is to set fire to a tent by smoking in bed then falling asleep again, especially if you are on your own. I was rather stunned that Den hadn't already learnt this lesson. But again, fatigue was a major player in this little incident.

Christmas had been and gone, so it was back to the grindstone. One morning Dennis went for the mail and on entering our tent handed me my letter, saying, 'Here, you've got a Dear John.' The reason for his remarks was that the letter was written in red ink. I said, 'Well if it is, there's nothing I can do about it out here.' With Christmas just gone, it was almost certain that she would have met someone else I thought, but upon opening the letter I discovered my fears unfounded.

There was no hint of any kind as to her wanting to finish with me, or even finding another lad. It was instead a letter about going to my mother's, and having Christmas at home and at her granny's. Her granny was absolutely great; she found by way of Sylvia that I simply adored the scones she made. Each time I was at home on leave she would be sure to cook scones for me to take back to camp. Little did she know, I liked them so much they never got anywhere near camp; they were nearly always eaten though before I left home.

Satisfied, I replaced the letter in the envelope and put it away, only to have Dennis, then Eric as well as others, asking if it was bad news I'd received. I kept telling them all one by one it was OK, but after a while the only option I had was to let Dennis see it and let him tell the others. One lad had already received a Dear John and put it on the noticeboard for all to see. It does seem a little drastic to do this, but when you are given a rifle and ammunition every day, it's always advisable to keep a close watch on anyone who may have a problem of some kind.

Another incident was very unusual indeed. As was normal procedure, a patrol had gone out, but this one included people other than personnel attached to our unit. They'd taken with them a dog handler and a medic; both carried pistols, not rifles like the rest of us. Now, what I'm about to write can perhaps be discredited, because I was in camp when the incident occurred, and I am giving this account second-hand, or maybe third-hand, from information gathered after the event. The story goes that the two men were playing about pretending to be gunslingers of the old Wild West. No one seems to know the exact details, but the medic accidentally shot the dog handler, whereupon the dog immediately became uncontrollable and began to run amok. After the wounded man was attended to, sections had to be sent out to tell the locals that the dog could be dangerous. If they saw it they should inform the soldiers right away or the local police. It is reported that the animal was eventually found and had to be shot because it had gone wild. I cannot stress enough that anyone who was involved could undoubtedly improve its accuracy.

Myself, Eric Lynch, Billy Coyne and Alan Brindle

With two to three months now gone by, most of us knew what was expected when doing patrols, but then we learnt we would be doing house-to-house searching. It was only to be expected that the villagers would do their utmost to disrupt our efforts. We would search a house and when we'd finished put an X on the door frame or wall, then continue to the next and so on. The villagers, however, rubbed off the marks every time we left, which obviously meant that it would be searched again, and again. They thought this would confuse us, but we soon cottoned on to it and began to play them at their own game. It got to such a state that an officer asked what the hell was going on when he saw four lads come out of a house, put an X on the door, and as they walked away four more went up to the same house, rubbed off the mark, then walked straight back in again. It wasn't long before the villagers realised that it was now becoming a case of them having to watch us and not the other way round.

In one house I went into, after going into a small room I shouted, 'Hey Den, come and have a look at this!' I pointed to a single bed covered with Jaffa oranges. When I shouted the woman of the house came in quickly, as she also wanted to see what the fuss was about. The oranges were piled up the full length of the bed in pyramid fashion, all as green as grass and as big as a size-one rugby ball; these were to be exported somewhere.

From another part of the village quite a stir went up and our section was called to the scene. It turned out that the local prostitute had made accusations that the section in front of us had stolen her money. The men denied it, of course, so a driver was sent to camp to bring an extra officer back, to conduct a body search of the men she pointed out as the ones involved. With the extra officer taking command, all the lads had weapons taken off them. Then they were lined up and one by one brought forward and in full view of the woman thoroughly checked. Even after all this charade she wasn't happy and still complained bitterly about being robbed. Without further evidence there was very little that could be done. I think she then lodged an objection through normal channels, but having no evidence she had no chance. The matter was closed and never heard of again.

We carried on until around tea when we were ordered back to camp. That evening, after cleaning the kit, we went down the NAAFI for our usual game of darts. As we went in things seemed a bit boisterous. Getting settled in as normal we were asked if we'd like a drink. Why, had somebody got some cash from home for a party? No, they said, it's the money that was stolen from the pro. Don't worry, she'll soon get some more.

Now, what had happened was that, when the officer had sent the driver to camp to bring back another officer to conduct the body search, the lads had handed the cash to the driver. While he was in camp he put it away in his own locker, so that if he was checked they wouldn't find any money on him either. It was only a slim chance that he might have been searched because he never went into the house in question. And a good night was had by all.

Beyond Rizokarpaso and Practice on the Ranges

Our adventures now took us up to and beyond Rizokarpaso. (After the partition of 1974 the Turkish people renamed it Dipkarpaz.) On a corner of the main road stood a coffee house which I believe is still there. The road turns a sharp right down a hill then up along the coast. Instead of turning right we went straight ahead, then to the left. A few miles further on we were told to dismount from the vehicles and were each given a long metal rod. Then we had a lecture on how to prod for mines. Verbal instruction over, each in turn received a hands-on lesson as to what was expected; then it was put to the test, with us all abreast across the dirt track advancing slowly. The sergeant was watching and giving tips as to where we might be going wrong, thinking it a huge joke. Our interest soon waned.

Carrying on to the end of the road we came upon an expanse of ground right by the sea. Here we'd have our packed lunch. As always, it wasn't long before a recce of the vicinity was done. The road came to a halt near the sea, and to the left was a house with kids playing; directly ahead was a dip to the right going to the water's edge, but the piece that stayed level had large shelf jutting out over the sea. Looking down through a large hole one could see beautiful clear sea water. We were maybe thirty feet above sea level, but it was so clear you could see the fish swimming about below, darting in and out of the rocks and weed.

Dotted about were pools of water as if a storm had blown the sea water into the holes in the rocks. When one of us prodded about in one of them something moved. Shouting to the others to get some more probes, we began to fetch the creature to the surface. When a tentacle came up we knew we were playing with an octopus – it was only small but it was frightening the living daylights out of us lot. The commotion brought a little boy to see what we were doing. After watching our feeble attempts to get the octopus out, the lad pushed his way past us, grabbed it, upon which it wrapped itself around his hand. All the boy did then was to wipe away its tentacles, leaving suction marks on his arm. He then turned it inside out, bit a blob that stuck up, then threw it back into the pool. The water went jet black as the creature squirmed and wriggled for a few minutes, then died. Picking it up with one finger stuck in what we thought was its mouth, he offered it back to us, but as it was of no use to us we beckoned him to keep it; he ran to the house shouting. His mother then came out of the house and offered us bread (*psomi*), olives and grapes, but as we had just eaten we declined.

On the very edge where the water lapped the rocks could be seen salt sparkling in the sunlight. Even tiny puddles had crystals forming as the water evaporated leaving just the salt behind. Tasting it proved without a doubt it was salt. Having done what we came for, and enjoyed an afternoon out, we now had to gather up our weapons, jump on the trucks, head back to camp and see what our next outing would be.

It was our turn to do cookhouse or camp duties. What free time you had depended on the chore you got, and the camp duty not only involved checking the perimeter wire, but seeing to the animals that had been acquired. We had almost every type of beast that was on the island; the argument was that they were lost and we had saved them from starving. Knowing most of the senior officers and NCOs were out of camp, by doing the job quickly we could get into the NAAFI for a quick game of darts. I was still pestering Ali for the two extra cushions, but the saga of the cushions would go on for some time yet.

The following days involved one ambush practice and a target practice. For the target practice Dennis and I knelt down with ten rounds to fire at a half target 100 yards away. We had a discussion and decided to put four shots into the head and six into the body. A voice from behind told us to stop messing about and get firing. When the shooting stopped, and inspection proved that we had both indeed done what we had said we'd do. Mr Murray-Smith then remarked it was 'bloody good shooting'; and that, may I add, was some of the strongest language our officers would use. Is it any wonder an NCO was threatened for abusive bad language?

My turn to fire, TSM Watkins and L/Bd Fred Miller looking on

It was from an ambush practice that I got the side blast from an FN rifle. As always on these tests, we were going along at a steady pace when out of the blue we screeched to a halt as someone shouted 'Ambush'. We turned outwards to look for targets, identifying them and then opening fire. When the lad next to me opened fire he was uncomfortable in his position, so he took a step backwards to get a better view. At the same time without realising it, he put the muzzle of the rifle level to my left ear and started to shoot off his rounds. I got the full blast in the left ear and for days afterwards I was as deaf as a door post. As always happens, later in life I began to experience problems, but because I hadn't tried to claim compensation within three years I had nothing to get.

It was on one of these ad lib types of patrol that we went to the armoury to get our weapons. Giving my number I received the rifle with ammunition and stood there waiting. The armourer wanted to know what I was still waiting for. I told him I still had not been given my bayonet.

'You're not getting one,' came back the reply.

'Well, I want one,' I said.

Again I was told I wasn't getting one. At this I told him I was putting my neck on the line out there, not him, so I wanted a bayonet to go with the rest of my stuff. The other lads were in agreement with me, but still no go. So handing back my rifle and ammunition I asked the armourer to keep them until I could get a full issue.

It was now taking so long for us all to get on parade that the TSM came through the door asking what was the problem. The armourer had his say, stating that it was not necessary for us to take bayonets with us so he wasn't going to dish them out.

Turning to me, the TSM said, 'I suppose you are to blame for this? Why won't you go out without your bayonets?'

'Yes I am, sarge,' I replied, 'because it's as you have pointed out – you can't shoot a hole in the ground if in trouble, and you can't open a tin with a bullet either, but you can dig a hole with a bayonet, and you can open a tin, and if we run out of ammo and need to put the bayonets on, and get somebody stuck on the end, they must be bloody close.'

This confrontation had to have a backlash of some kind, and we found out the next time we went on the ranges. Setting up targets as usual we began to fire, and lo and behold we couldn't have hit a barn door if we'd been sat on the latch. Getting back to camp the armourer was told of the problem, but with a sarcastic grin on his face he said, 'I've zeroed them all.' His face soon changed though when he was told that he could be going out with us on our next excursion, having to rely on us to protect him if attacked.

On one roadblock, I'd been left with the responsibility of what might be called a holding area. That's to say that if anyone was stopped from entering the forbidden area they would be brought to where I was, and it would then be my job to take care of them. At first it seemed a cushy number, but as things went on I was getting more and more people to look after, so I had to think of something quick. I solved the problem, but not long afterwards an officer came and began to remonstrate with me about not being careful enough.

He then saw a pile of shoes and asked why I put them all in one heap, to which I replied, 'Have you ever tried to run over stones and corn stubble with a bullet chasing you, sir?' His response was to look at the shoes again, then at the people and say, 'Carry on.' He then walked away.

On other days I might be on an escort of some kind, or standing by ready to go at a minute's notice. Oh, yeah, and the women were still digging the well.

Injured Civilian

As I've said before, I'd got the reputation in the section that no matter where I went, trouble went the other way. On one trip Mr Murray-Smith was in charge, which meant that Two Section were going out. Where to was really of no consequence, knowing we were going out was simply just enough. Dennis and I took our usual 'rations' of a pair of socks, extra cigs, foot powder and a bottle of water. Trudging all over the countryside we eventually came to a T-junction, Mr Murray-Smith pointed to his left saying, 'F Section that way,' then pointing right said, 'E Section right.' He took a couple of steps then stopped dead in his tracks. Turning and looking at me, he said, 'I'll get you yet! It's E Section to the left and F Section to the right.' Still looking at him I said, 'You're wasting your time, sir, it won't work.' So off we set in our designated directions.

We'd been going half an hour or so, when it came over the radio that E Section were being attacked by some villagers, and that the policeman who was with them had had his head split open with a brick or stone, and required urgent assistance. On hearing this message, the officer replied, 'I give up. Come on let's go on the double.' As we were on foot, reinforcements from camp had got there well before us and had the situation under control.

The man who hit the policeman with the brick had been captured and was now in the one-ton truck or Land Rover waiting to be transported to HQ or somewhere. The vehicle departed with a sergeant and six gunners. At intervals one gunner would shout a warning, to make the sergeant look away; as soon as he did a gun butt would come back and hit the prisoner. When the prisoner got to his destination he was bundled out of the vehicle, falling and breaking a leg. An enquiry took place, but what the outcome was I don't altogether know. No one in our battery, as far as I know, received a reprimand of any kind.

Before any do-gooders think this was wrong, I should like to remind them of what had happened to our unit without us even mounting a concerted patrol of any kind.

When a high-ranking officer pays a visit, most of the unit get sent off somewhere out of the way so the camp can look nice and tidy. Even though we were on active service it didn't stop us getting a visit. A day came when an OC (Officer Commanding) visit was due. About forty or fifty of us were told we would all be going out together on an exercise. As always we gathered our bits and bobs to see us through the day. In our sections, everyone got into the trucks and off we set.

Most of the time we never bothered where we were going and this outing was much the same. Having been deployed, each section set out on its designated assignment. After trudging along for a few hours we heard on our radio that we would have packed lunches sent out to us, instead of us returning to camp for lunch. With new co-ordinates, off we went to our rendezvous where sure enough a truck with an escort turned up and unloaded the lunch packs. Away it went leaving us all to get on with eating. Our section found an open piece of ground which contained a rather large boulder. Sitting down in a circle with our backs to the rock we began lunch. About three quarters through lunch, I heard TSM Watkins asking, 'Where's Baker? Have you got the water?' Jokingly, in a Geordie accent, Dennis said, 'Who, sarge? Me, sarge?'

'Don't "who-sarge-me-sarge" me,' said the TSM. 'Just give me the f—ing water here.'

Still laughing, Dennis replied, 'I've not got it, honest, sarge, I've not got it.'

'Well if you haven't got it the other awkward get must have it. Where is he then?' the sarge wanted to know.

'Round the back somewhere I think,' Dennis replied. I'd been listening to the conversation from my position behind a large rock out of view from the sergeant, so I knew exactly what to expect when the sergeant major came round the boulder. 'Right, Balmer, where's the water then?' I just sat there, turned to look at him and said, 'You know, sarge, I'm just thinking of all them cookhouse duties I have to do tomorrow.'

'Give me the water here,' he said, 'or you'll get double f—ing cookhouse duties tomorrow you blackmailing—' Taking the water, he turned and offered it to Captain Friend, who had come with him and heard all that had gone on. The TSM said, 'I told you, didn't I, that one of these two would have some water, sir. They are the best two soldiers I've got for looking after each other. If one doesn't have it the other one does.'

I hope readers don't think that I didn't do duties like the other lads – I did. They weren't cushy duties either. Sergeant Watkins was always fair when giving out details. He also looked after us when need be. I have mentioned that early on we found out he could cook a brilliant bread pudding, so if he was with us on a mini camp we'd ask if he had the time and if so we'd save all the crusts and some Carnation milk. When he gave orders he didn't bawl and shout very often – just an ordinary instruction sufficed. I have photographs of him standing by our sides giving instruction and encouragement on the ranges firing out to sea. TSM Watkins and Sergeant Clay were in my view two of the best senior NCOs I ever served under in combat. This does not mean that the other NCOs in Echo Troop were not good. Because I did not serve in Echo Troop regularly, I did not get to know them equally well.

On My Own

To show what I meant about Sergeant Watkins: a scheme was set up to try to disrupt EOKA activities and tempt members out and about at night into taking risks when moving from place to place. On this night we had to go out to a location and pretend we were doing our work properly, but when smoking cigarettes let them shine slightly through the fingers, and, when speaking, talk just a little too loudly or possibly cause a noise if moving about. The detail I was given, however, was one of guarding a bridge over a small culvert. The general idea was for a section to go out and cross this area. When going over the bridge one man, i.e. me, was to detach from the group then hide until relieved. With this manoeuvre completed I settled down for a very long wait. In no time at all I could hear small creatures scurrying through the undergrowth. Every noise seemed to be amplified: the rustle of the trees, farm animals roaming round and the occasional sound from the direction of the wagons. It didn't help wanting to smoke, knowing full well I daren't.

I can only hazard a guess as to how long I was out there; I would think that it was for three hours or more. In the end I heard footsteps coming from the direction of the wagons. The figure came and stood some feet away. A voice whispered, 'Balmer, Balmer, where are you?' It was Sergeant Watkins. I just stayed where I was, yet never replied to him. He then began to walk slowly around and at odd times call my name. He eventually came upon my position – treading on my foot, he stumbled and came out with a few choice words. After he'd carried on a little bit further, he said, 'When you're ready, come in.'

Again, I let some time go by before deciding to return to the unit. As I approached I could hear the officer asking why had I still not come in, but the sarge reassured him things were still OK. At that moment I made my return known. I was asked by the officer why I had not answered when called by the sergeant. I pointed out that if the sergeant couldn't see me, yet he knew I was there, anybody else would have one hell of a job to see me. I told the sergeant that it was my foot he'd fallen over, and repeated word for word what he'd said.

The officer then enquired why I didn't make myself known and return with the sergeant. Again I explained that if anyone had tried to get Sergeant Watkins, I'd have got them, and the only way to make sure was to let a short space of time elapse before returning myself.

One of the biggest let-downs of being out there on stag was missing the self-heated soups (not only would a light shine but you could smell them miles away), but as I've pointed out the TSM always made sure that all his lads got their equal share. Because went dark early I don't think it was past ten o'clock. Although time was not really important – if you had to go out, you did, and that was that – the only thing we wanted to know when the exercise was over was: Is the NAAFI still open?

Operation Mudlark

One operation got into all the local newspapers because of the terrible conditions and the fact that a large contingent of other regiments would take part. It was somewhere near a place called Gypsos, a village further down the island in the Bogazi area, but a few miles inland. The weather started out OK, but coming into February it could bucket down at any time, and this is what happened to us. The area we were in was rather flat and on the outskirts of the village. Our job was to cover the area by day, then as night descended to advance slowly towards the village.

Everything went well; we'd got into position and donned our ponchos and bush hats, knowing full well that it was going to rain. Rain it did, and then the thunder and lightning started. With the rifle covered up under the poncho we slowly moved forward on unsteady legs into newly ploughed fields. The mud began to stick to the rubber boots, making progress even more difficult. The lightning would strike giving a full view of the landscape ahead, but in an instant it was pitch black again making it impossible to see after such a blinding light. With this would come an almost instantaneous clap of thunder so loud as to make you shudder. The rain, pelting down as hard as it could, didn't do any thing for morale or the nerves either; standing in the middle of a field during such a storm, with the nearest pal about thirty feet away, is an experience I wouldn't recommend to anyone.

All wet through and up to the ankles in mud we returned to our area for supper. When we arrived, with mess tins and eating irons ready, hot food was a welcome sight. It was still raining hard and, being the last in, as we then thought, we didn't have any cover – unless we went inside that is and mudded up our room. Our only option, with rifle upside down on the shoulder, hands poking through the cape to get our food, was to stand in the rain trying to cover the mess tin with the brim of the bush hat, and to keep the water from coming off the hat into the grub.

Standing there gnawing away, I heard a voice from behind shouting, 'Hey, you!' I ignored it. Then for a second time, 'Hey, you!' I still ignored it, but Dennis at the same time said, 'He's talking to you, Al.' In a low whisper I said, 'Balls to him.' Then a third time, 'Hey, you!' I still ignored him, then on the fourth time he said, 'Gunner!' At this I immediately turned round. 'I'm talking to you,' he bellowed out. 'Why didn't you answer when I shouted?'

'Because I'm a gunner, sir, and not hey you.'

His response was to tell me to wash his mess tins. I did, but not before finishing my own food. When I handed his mess tins back to him he looked at them, then gave them back to me saying, 'They are not clean enough, clean them again.' I picked them up and went over again to the wash area, swilling them round once more, then returned and handed them back to him. 'They're still not clean enough,' was his answer.

'They're as clean as mine, sir,' I replied.

'Clean them again,' he said.

'Begging your pardon, sir, I am not your batman. I was given £52 worth of kit at Oswestry, and told to look after it and I think you must have been told the same at Sandhurst.' With a conversation like this going on for so long, it was a racing certainty that word would get round, and it was at this very second the TSM came into view. Bawling me out to keep my mouth shut, he then asked the officer if he could speak to him in private for a moment inside. As yet I have not mentioned that this officer was Mr Jones, the one I always seemed to get into trouble with. Also, while this conversation about cleaning mess tins was taking place between the officer and myself, I was still in the pouring rain, while he was stood under the cover of a veranda, in silk pyjamas, wearing a silk dressing gown, with silk slippers on his feet. A rough synopsis of the TSM's intervention was that we had enough to do cleaning our own kit, and that Mr Jones should not have been standing on the veranda at that time dressed as he was.

I was to have one more argument with Mr Jones before my demob. But that would be way in the future.

About fifteen to thirty minutes had passed when Mr Murray-Smith came into camp. Like us he'd been out in the mud and rain. He started to take his poncho off and other wet things. I asked him if he'd had his grub; finding out he hadn't, I asked him to give me some of his kit so I could clean it for him while he was eating. Taking this as a cue the other lads offered also to do some of his kit. Who should then walk in but the TSM. Looking at me and pointing he said, 'Pack it in you! Finish what you're doing, get your head down and stop stirring the shit.' Mr Murray-Smith looked a little bemused and the TSM said, 'It's OK, sir, I'll explain later what's wrong.' The remainder of the scheme passed without any further trouble, and the weather later began to improve.

Grub up, on Operation Mudlark. Notice the mud on boots

199

A usual, Dennis late for Grub up. Again

I'm not too sure of the location of the next incident, but I think it was past Rizokarpaso further up the panhandle; the time and dates are also a little obscure. The scene was a fork off the main highway. Where the road divided was a house where a family of four children lived. An army wagon would use this by-road to go for water. This again is a second-hand tale, so details may be inaccurate.

It was said that an RAF lad had been on the island for some two weeks and had never left his camp. He asked if he could swap with the guard and go on the detail in his place. When the truck was unable to get round the fork in one go it had to reverse round the bend, and on this manoeuvre the truck was blown up killing the RAF lad (what happened to the driver I don't know, but I believe he was killed also). When the army got to the scene, all that was left that was recognisable was part of the cab.

Soldiers went to the house trying to get more information on the event. The woman of the house was found to have been badly beaten and was in a distressed state. Only two of her children could be found; the other two, along with her husband, had been abducted. She had been told they would be killed if she didn't sit outside the house so as to make it look as if nothing was wrong. Her dilemma, she thought, was that if she didn't tell the army they might beat her up and put her in prison along with her children, and if she did tell the army, EOKA would kill her husband and children. Worst of all, she would have to sit and watch the carnage happen and say nothing to anyone. As always, a search of the area was made, but to no avail. I think sometimes a visit to the scene was ordered so as to keep us on our toes and aware what could happen if we let our guard down. This also could have been the reason that we began to go further up the Panhandle on our patrols.

Another short stint was done at the new police station, and the only incident while we were here was that one of the lads got an abscess on his bottom. This was one of the only times we saw a decent female who was the doctor's nurse. It was thought though that she was an EOKA sympathiser, so if she was about you needed to be careful of what you said or did. In fact, I didn't trust the police either – the surgery was only a very short distance.

The best of this short duty was we were able to keep up our dart practice. I was still chasing Ali for the extra two cushions; thank goodness he got them for me, because it turned out in the long run I'd done the right thing.

Up the Panhandle

Pushing up past Rizzo further than we'd ever gone before, we set up a camp. This time we had Mr Murray-Smith in charge, and this was one camp where TSM Watkins cooked us a bread pudding for dinner. Billy Coyne had volunteered to be cook for a short while.

It was on this stay that our officer began to understand the lads he had under him. One morning I went for my ration of cigs and beer and to pick Dennis's up at the same time. Mr Murray-Smith told me I couldn't have Dennis's rations, he would have to get his own. At this the TSM remarked that he would get some earache now from Baker. No more was said until I reached the tent and gave Dennis the news. Straight away Dennis got up and went to the Q tent saying, 'This isn't on, not letting Balmer get my rations, sarge, what's wrong?' It was only then that Dennis realised it was the officer who'd refused to give them to me, not the sarge. Smiling, the sergeant turned to the officer saying, 'I told you something would be said.' Typical Geordie banter – Dennis got out off the situation, but still mumbling at me because I hadn't told him it was Mr Murray-Smith who had refused the ration, not the sergeant.

Anyhow, sections went and came back as usual and all went to bed. The following morning with everyone having had their obligatory wash and shave, breakfast was served. All had been served, or so we thought, when Dennis came out of the tent and asked Billy for his breakfast. Billy told him that it had all been dished out. Upon hearing this, Mr Murray-Smith told Dennis to take *his*. Dennis said, 'No, it's all right, it's my fault for being late sir.' The order was repeated again, with the same answer coming from Dennis; this time, however, Mr Murray-Smith said, 'I've told you, get my breakfast eaten. If you don't eat it and do as you're told, you're on a charge. You forget, I can go back to the mess and get a breakfast. You can't, you have to walk all over these mountains all day, when I can sit and watch.'

From that moment on, Mr Murray-Smith's standing with all the lads went sky high. If an action can prove a point this one certainly did. The lads already thought a great deal of him, but this pushed it up a notch further.

It was Billy's turn later on to drop a clanger. While we were all milling around doing various jobs Billy came up, saluted, and in the quick Scouse twang said, 'Mr Murray Mint sir, err, err, sorry sir, Mr Murray-Smith sir...' then delivered the message. Mr Murray-Smith, then said to Billy, 'Don't say that again, otherwise you'll be on a charge for certain.'

Later at this camp we searched up into high hills and mountains and at one point stopped beneath a rather high vantage point. With what seemed to be an afterthought, just to give us something to do, Mr Murray-Smith gathered us together. Then he began telling us which area we would search up this particular mountain, while he would cover us with his Sterling (Sten gun). I noticed that he didn't have a magazine on, and remarked to Dennis how it would be a bloody good trick to cover us lot with no magazine on.

Off we set, enjoying ourselves looking behind all rocks and stones. At the top we were having a rest when Mr Murray-Smith shouted, 'Hold it, I've lost my magazine. All spread out and search the area thoroughly.'

'You've not lost it, sir,' I said.

'I know I have,' came the reply.

'You've not, sir,' I repeated.

'How do you know I haven't?' he wanted to know.

I then told him what I'd said to Dennis at the bottom concerning the magazine; he took a very long look at me, then said, 'If the magazine is not down there when we go down and count up, you are on a charge without a doubt.' At the bottom a feverish check was made on the ammunition. When we were satisfied all was correct, a sigh of relief went around camp, and life got back to as normal as could be.

At a very quiet time Mr Murray-Smith came to me and asked why I hadn't said anything about him not having a magazine on his Sterling. 'Because you're the officer, sir, not me.' Pushing me, and knowing the run-ins I'd had with Mr Jones, he again asked why. 'Well,' I said, 'with the length of time we'd been at the bottom of that hill, if EOKA were going to have a go at us they'd have done it before we went up there. Not only that, you may have had the magazine in one of your side pockets, and I thought it would be very unlikely that an ambush would be set up for us on top of a mountain, because we've never been up there before today that I know of.' I think from that moment on he realised how his sections trusted him and his judgement of any given situation and also knew he led from the front.

The view when searching up the Panhandle Mountains

While in the area a patrol of F Section was sent out further up the coast road, to the very end of the island which is called Cape Apostolos Andreas. Dennis was lucky enough to go to the very small island on the end of the peninsular, by way of a dinghy with some other lads, while the rest of the group searched the nearby hillsides until they returned from the island. The weather was improving almost every day now, so we started to wear lighter clothing. I know it may seem strange that in later years people would book holidays in Cyprus and lie on the beach to get a nice tan, yet here we were, all dressed up in heavy clothing to keep warm, and only now coming to the end of February did we start to think of lighter clothing. Going back to the job in hand, the lance bombardier on this trip would be Freddie Miller. He'd signed on as a regular. He was a tall lad, taller than me in fact, whose home town was somewhere in the North East.

Part of a patrol at rest, from top centre: Fred Miller, Eric Lynch, myself, Alan Brindle. The last one not known

The landscape as usual was a little sparse. After marching along for a distance in a direction we thought would bring us to a large beach we'd seen when up the mountains, the section swung right towards the sea between sand dunes. Getting through them brought us on to a magnificent beach front with gentle lapping waves. It was hard to believe that a conflict was raging on an island like this. That though was the problem: how not to get sucked into a state of false security. This was the same beach that was used for the dip just a few days after Christmas.

Moving towards two large rocks, Fred Miller said he was intrigued to find out how far a bullet could go into the rock. He had got himself a spare round when on the ranges so as to be able to test his curiosity. With everyone standing behind him to avoid any ricochet he stood about ten feet away and fired; all he got was a hole just the same as had happened in the police station when a round was accidentally discharged. With that curiosity satisfied we took a meander through the dunes before being picked up by a truck, which took us to the monastery at the very end of the peninsular. We did a search of a kind but weren't there for any length of time before returning to the mini camp. It wasn't long after that before we made a full return to the base camp.

On parade the following morning both E and F Sections were detailed for police station guard, so gathering our kit and rifles both sections fell in to be transported up to the station. Arriving, we encountered the normal problem of finding an empty bed space to doss down in. The building had not long been built and was rather modern for its time. The radio room was on the top floor as was nearly always the case. NCOs were on the ground floor taking the next best areas available, with us lot, the scruffs, sleeping in the basement.

The very first thing was to organise stags or patrols into the village of Yialoussa. Life became one long drag, with most of the time being spent just playing games of darts. It didn't take a great deal of persuading to get a patrol together to go out no matter what time of either night or day; the only other thing you could do was hang around outside talking to the police. Seeing as we didn't trust them either, the only thing left was to bull the kit, and keep clean and tidy. Anything was better than sitting just doing nothing at all but look at the same four walls every day.

The Inquisitive Policeman

One policeman in particular singled me out, and at every occasion possible would ask me to let him handle my rifle when I was either on guard or cleaning it. Two or three days went by and he was still at me to let him handle the weapon. I was really getting fed up with his constant pestering. When I was once again sat cleaning the rifle he asked again. I asked him, 'Do you really want a good look at my rifle?'

'Yes,' he said.

Standing up I asked Dennis to give me orders for bayonet drill. Dennis looked a bit puzzled but agreed. I placed myself in front of the policeman, then Dennis gave the order to fix bayonets. Click, click, on it went. 'On guard.' Up came the rifle with the bayonet pointing at the policeman. Next order: 'Advance.' I slowly went towards him and he began to back up. Back, and back he went until he could go no further. He was in a corner, arms spread out, on tip toes with my bayonet only four inches away from his throat.

Dennis then intervened, saying, 'Don't, Al, he'll shit himself or have a heart attack. Give over.' I then asked the policeman whether he'd seen enough of my rifle. In a stuttering voice he said, 'Yes, Johnny, yes.' At this reply I lowered my guard and backed away. The others who had watched what had happened also came to me, saying that they too thought I was serious and was going to stab him or do something silly. I told them I had to make it look real, otherwise he would keep pestering me. 'I don't think he'll ask any more,' I said, and he didn't.

Even playing darts can get boring, so if a jeep or truck stopped over we'd try to get what news we could – and of course the mail was often in a delivery. Being very close to a house on one side gave us an insight into the lifestyle of the Cypriot family. One day the old lady wanted a chicken for the table. She slowly trailed the bird she wanted, but somehow it seemed to know that she was after it. None of the other chickens bothered as she got near to them but the one she wanted just kept moving away. Eventually she caught it and brought it to the front of the house, placed it between her legs to trap it, then simply began to twist its neck off, to kill it. I've often heard of wringing someone's neck, but to see it done to a chicken in this fashion was awful. A bombardier who was standing watching went over to her, took the bird away from her and broke its neck the way we would kill a chicken, then threw it on the ground until it stopped twitching. She then sat outside as nonchalant as anything, plucking and cleaning it ready for cooking.

A day later I was on the gate again. The policeman I'd had problems with was also there. Within the length of time the army had been at the house a dog had been brought in. Being an Alsatian it was not a small animal at all. When it was my turn for stag, the policeman came to my side, telling me that it was his dog and it would do anything he told it to do. He showed me how he could get it to do tricks and fetch objects. Having got this far he then told me he could make it go for me. He stupidly began to point at me and tell the dog to fetch. The dog looked at me and made a slight move as if not knowing exactly what to do. It did this a couple of times, then I got fed up with him telling it to go for me, so I told the dog to go for him. It did, and all my mates shouted at me to stop the dog as it would damage his uniform. Everybody said I was a swine setting the dog on him, until I told them he'd been trying to do the same to me for the previous ten minutes. My reply was, 'F— him, he didn't care about me.' I don't think that the copper understood that it nearly always stood on the front gate with us. We fed it, and we all had the same uniform on – say no more!

The Radio Relay Set-Up

We had been at the station for all of three weeks without a break. I was downstairs on the bed reading a *Tit-Bits* or the likes when Dennis came in and said, 'Hey, Al, there's been an accident on the other side of Rizzo. They can't get through on the radio – any chance of you having a go to see what you can do?' Getting off the bed I made my way to the radio room and began listening to what was going on. I also noticed that it was a 72 set we had (or it could have been a 62 set – on research I couldn't find a 72 set listed anywhere), the type often used by air OPs. The problem with these sets was that they had two tuning dials. If you hadn't used one before, it could sometimes prove difficult to tune them in.

It was obvious the lad operating our set in the police station was inexperienced on a 62/72 set, so he couldn't really help. Asking him to move over so that I could get to the set, I sat down and started to tune in to Control. When I'd completed the task, I listened to the other vehicle try to get through, still with little success. I then decided to set up a relay station. Breaking in I asked Control how they were receiving my signal; loud and clear was their reply. Getting this answer, I told them, 'Wait out to you.'

I then asked the other station (which I'll call D, because it was the Dingo driver who was in trouble) to tune in on my signal. After he had done so I again asked for the signal strength. Getting back a loud and clear reply, I then signalled D and told him he had two aerials erected – remove one. In the same transmission I said, 'I say again you have two aerials up – remove one.' A few seconds went by, then I asked for his signal strength. Having two aerials up he had been giving off a slight distortion, causing unnecessary problems in the reception of a signal. Deeming both stations loud and clear I began to relay messages about the accident situation and its location.

I was rather perplexed as to why the station had not been

made into a relay radio before, because, once patrols started to stretch out up the Panhandle, reception nearly always started to become weaker and weaker. This only went to prove that the distances we had to cover on our patrols were greater than some of our radios could cope with.

We were told later by one of the control room ops that immediately they heard a relay being set up the Signals sergeant became very interested, and started asking which section was at the police station – did they know who it was? Who was a flaggy? No one knew, so it proved my section had not spilled the beans on me. He had his suspicions confirmed when the instruction to take down the second aerial was given to D. The Dingo driver thought that by having two aerials up, the signal would be better. Not true; what it did do though, was to put out 'shadowing', a vibrating effect on the transmission which made it more difficult to hear when the transmission signal was weak.

I'd been operating for some thirty minutes, when the top lookout guard shouted down that the sergeant was coming up the road in the jeep like a bat out of hell. Somebody took over from me and I went down to the basement by way of the back steps out of sight of the oncoming sergeant. All of a flutter, in the sergeant came, demanding to know who had been on the radio when it had been set up for relaying. The lad who had taken over from me said he had been on the radio all the while. At this statement the sarge said, 'Don't try to bullshit me. As soon as the champ came over the hill, within seconds the voice changed; I'm not that bloody stupid.' He'd obviously been listening in on the radio he had in the jeep when travelling to the police guard.

I was stretched out on the bed with my beret over my eyes. I could hear him coming down the stairs, getting closer and closer, still ranting and raving, still threatening to charge every one of us if nobody owned up. When he came to me I took the beret off my face and said in Lancashire dialect, 'Aw reet, sarge, it wer me tha wer o' set aw' time.'

'You?' he said looking at me. 'You can't operate a f—ing tin opener, never mind a radio. I'll get the bastard when you all get back to camp.' Then off he stormed, and thanks to the lads he still didn't know who the flaggy was.

Even to this day I can't understand why he didn't ask any of the NCOs who were with us on walkabout. Maybe he did, and even they wouldn't tell him.

It came as no surprise when we were told to pack up as we were heading back to camp. Having got back there and dumped all our kit it was time for tea. I don't know how exactly the next little half hour went, but it was a bit like this. I think it was because either Dennis or I had to drop off the rifle or something. Anyhow, we'd got separated and Dennis was in the canteen. I was walking along following him, when TSM Watkins shouted me over and told me that I had to pack up all my kit, as I was going home at six o'clock. It was now about 4.40 p.m. so I didn't have much time. 'You've no chance,' I told him, 'I'm not going home without Baker.'

'You'll pack your stuff up and be on that truck at six o'clock.'

Turning away I was still mumbling. I went into the canteen, got my grub, saw where Dennis was sitting, and went and sat beside him. As I settled down, Dennis started telling me that Daddio had told him to pack all his gear as he was going home tonight, and he'd told the sarge that he wasn't going home without me. At this precise moment a hand came down on each of our shoulders. It was the sergeant saying, 'Now, are you two buggers happy that you're going home together?' He was laughing his head off that he'd set us both up.

Then he told us that he'd chosen the advance party before we returned to camp, then at the very last minute had been told he had to get two more. Knowing Den and I were as thick as thieves, and that one wouldn't go without the other without giving an argument, he knew we two were the prime candidates for the job. As we would be on our way home in just over an hour, it was swallow down the grub, and with the help of Eric and others all the stops were pulled out, and we were ready by about 5.50 p.m. Jumping on the trucks, with accompanying shouts of 'You lucky buggers', off we set for Limassol Harbour.

Homeward Bound and a Pass to Gibraltar

The treaty had been agreed upon (if not completely), therefore hostilities would cease. With two other units across the island 25 Field had to go back to England as soon as possible. Back in the tent, I grabbed pen and paper to tell Sylvia that she might not get another letter for a while as I was going on a scheme. I also asked her to let my mother know. When I was to get home though, she would tell me that she already had a very good idea why there'd be a lapse in mail. It had been in all the daily papers that troops would soon be coming home.

Having written a letter, I began putting every piece of kit that would be needed on board ship into the sea-kitbag. Everything else, including the cushions and tablecloth I'd bought, was put into the large kit bag for storage. It's amazing how fast you can pack when you know you are on your way home. All packed up, we were at the parade point and ready to go well before 6 p.m. It felt strange getting into the truck without a rifle at my side; even so, we still had an armed escort.

We were going to Limassol to catch a troop ship the following day, the HMTS *Empire Fowey*. It was coming from the Far East through the Suez Canal, then had been diverted to Cyprus to pick us up the next day. That night we ended up in the customs sheds, finding a space to put down the kit. Here we'd stay on a hard, bare floor until being taken aboard.

Taffy Jones was in the party, and Mr Jones his namesake was in charge of the group. During the last hours before going to sleep Taffy began coming out with sayings like, 'Who said Jones was a —?' or 'Who called Jones a —?' And 'Who said Jones is f—ing rubbish?' With Taffy having the same surname as the officer, it would be hard for Mr Jones to prove that the jibes were meant for him. It got to the stage, though, that Taffy was told by one and all to pack it in; it looked as if trouble was looming if he didn't stop. Thankfully he did.

We were catered for by the NAAFI people, the finest people ever. Serving tea and food, working at all hours, they would still ask if everything was OK. Washing and shaving were our biggest obstacles – there were so many men but so few facilities. Breakfast over we all got on the trucks and were taken down to the quayside to get on board ship. A bit of a swell was running, which didn't make it easy getting into the tender to take us to a pontoon that was alongside the ship. At the pontoon the tender rose and fell about four feet; it would also move away a few feet at the same time.

To help us get on board, two MPs were watching the proceedings. First we would sling up the two kitbags on to the platform where the MPs stood. It would then be a matter of waiting for the right moment to step on to the pontoon. All went well until one lad slipped and fell. The MPs grabbed his shoulder straps, and as he started to dangle over open water, they pulled him to safety. From then on it was up a stairway at the side of the ship and down to the storage to get rid of all the excess kit.

Having been given our bunks, we now faced the reverse process of five or six months earlier, again getting to learn the layout of the ship and the gangways to and from our bunks. The major difference was that we had no officers in charge of us as such – every morning we had roll call done by an NCO, and that would more or less be it for the rest of the day.

One morning we woke up with rather a heavy swell developing. This was obvious because the crew were coming round, checking on all or any equipment that might need seeing to, then tightening all the hatches. Going up and down on the swell was fairly easy to get used to. Six times was OK, but on the seventh swell, the ship would almost certainly hit the wave head on and shudder as it went through, emerging with the sound of propellers whirling aft as the stern came out of the water.

On roll call no one was seasick, so away we went to do whatever. Down among the bunks, the deck we were on was all awash. As we tried looking around to find out why, the ship again hit the seventh wave, plunging deep into it at the bow. The creaking of the ship could be heard, and as if by magic a huge torrent of water came pouring in through a porthole. That was because some idiot had left a porthole wide open to let in some fresh air, but had forgotten to close it again. In quick time it was shut and clamped down before more water could come in.

It was on this trip home that I first met Jimmy Smith, obviously better known as 'Smudge', or 'Smudger'. I got to know him very well, so well in fact that he told me of his past experiences as a younger man and how he had had to make sure he survived whatever came his way. I reassured him that I was only interested in now, not the past. He was a really good guy to know. Of an evening sometimes we'd play a daft game of trying to catch each other's thumbs; we'd sit opposite each other with fists touching but with thumbs stuck up; the idea was to try to get your opponent's thumb at the slightest hint of movement from him. Daft I know, but at least it passed the time.

Other than this it would be cards. The tables were bolted to the deck so that wasn't a problem. On top they had a ridge around to stop things sliding off and in each corner a pull-out where you could put a pint if it was rough. The weather I mean, not the pint. Dennis was on board but he too had made new friends, so it became easier to mingle with the advance party.

It was after a game of cards that Jimmy said he could tell a fortune by reading the cards. This was taken lightly, but he insisted that he should try. He told me to box the cards, then deal them out in a square of sixteen, four across and four down, with the face side up. After I had done as he said, he then came to my side of the table, looked at what I'd dealt out, and came out with a few choice words. In all the sixteen cards only two were black, a deuce and a queen; all the other fourteen cards were hearts and diamonds. He said he'd never seen anything like this before. Pointing at the two black cards he said all he could deduce from the position of the cards was that I would need to look out in the future for two women who might possibly cause problems. Other than that my life would be one of not wanting for love or money. I have never paid great attention to what he predicted, but I must say with hindsight that I have never really been found wanting for love or money too much.

In the galley the food was very good. As usual, plimsolls had to be worn. The floors were of lino so if anything got spilled on it, it was like a skating rink. Every mealtime a check had to be made to ensure no one had wet the floor. The galley was to the right, hidden behind the kitchen, and the first person I saw get caught went sliding down with someone shouting, 'And another one,' into the bulkhead spilling all that was on the tray. A huge cheer went up as everyone enjoyed the floorshow (no pun intended).

The weather was nice and warm, which meant going on deck was enjoyable. One thing I liked very much was we could go right to the front of the ship and look over into the breaking bow wave and watch dolphins playing in and out of the waves. On one occasion all I could see was a single fin sticking up out of the water. It was about thirty feet behind the bow and twenty feet out. I was mesmerised how it stayed in the precise position at all times, poised on the crest of the wave made by the bow. I then began to suspect it was a shark, because there was not a dolphin in sight anywhere. I had always thought that there weren't any sharks in the Mediterranean, but it really was a shark. They say seeing is believing; well, I'd seen, so from then on, I believed.

The next tale to tell is one of an RAF corporal. I don't know why, but for some reason I think he thought I was homosexual, which I am definitely not. He continued to pester me day after day with all kinds of remarks. One day I was on the stairway with Dennis when he tried to pull rank and get me to go below and agree to his demands. This only made me see the deepest of red. Turning on him, I told him in no uncertain terms what I thought of him. Dennis tried to intervene, telling me he was a corporal. I couldn't give a monkey's what he is, I told Dennis, he's not getting up my backside, and if he comes anywhere near me again, he'll be bloody swimming it home to Blighty, not sailing. He'd been so clandestine in his approaches that Dennis hadn't noticed, or Jimmy for that matter, what had been going on. He must have mistaken a very good friendship between Dennis and me for something else. From then on he kept away from me and I never heard anything more from him.

The next place for us to see was Gibraltar. It's strange how thing worked out. When I was going to Cyprus my mate Dave from back home was still in training and it was then we stopped at Malta, as part of the outward journey. Now I am coming home, I thought, he's stationed in Malta, but we're going to stop at Gibraltar. It would have been great to get a photo of us both in uniform. Sadly it wasn't to be.

Smudger in his vest, Dennis behind him, me in full uniform and Al Bolton with his head in his hand.
Unfortunately I don't remember the names of the other lads

I have not mentioned that one of the other lads on board was none other than Bob Sumner. This was another strange occurrence. I had travelled home by train on embarkation leave with him, and sailed out abroad with him, but because he was in a different battery to me I never saw him at all while out in Cyprus. Yet there he was on the same ship as me on the advance party coming home.

At Gibraltar a four-hour pass was given so we could get ashore for a short spell. Off we set, all four of us, Dennis, Bob, myself, and I think Jimmy Smith. The obvious place to go would be the tourist shops to see what we could get. One shop had musical ballerina jewellery boxes. Bob looked at one in particular and thought it would be just the ticket for his girlfriend, Marie. When he dipped his hand in his pocket and pulled it out again the rest of us saw a look of complete disappointment on his face. We knew straight away he didn't have enough. The price was an astronomical £1, yes, £1, and four of us had to club together to get it for him. (The financial problem was caused by the way we were sent home so quickly. We'd left camp on the Wednesday, pay day was Thursday, so we hadn't been paid properly, for nearly two weeks.)

Behind us were two RAF sergeants and their wives. We'd knocked the shopkeeper down in price, which gave them the opportunity get what they wanted. Moving off again they tagged on behind and at each shop would let us do the business of haggling.

In one shop, the proprietor was very reluctant to have so many inside. He said he'd been robbed when a gang of soldiers had come in before and he couldn't keep an eye on them all. When most of the lads had left, we went back in and began to look around. What caught my eye was a piece of black Spanish lace. It was absolutely gorgeous, the type of lace that Ava Gardner wore in the film, *The Barefoot Contessa*. It must have been six to seven feet long and maybe three feet wide. What a present! We haggled and haggled and got the shopkeeper down to ten shillings (50p), then found out that we didn't have ten bob between us. Yes, you've guessed it – a ten-bob note was pushed into the hand of one of us, who then bought it, and handed it to the sergeants outside the shop afterwards. We then started to make our way back to the ship, still doing a bit of haggling here and there, just to see how much we could have knocked off any item if it could have been bought, and then reminiscing on what we could have had if we'd had the money.

Although only ambling we soon reached the quayside where we needed to pick up the tender to get back on board. Standing there in our way was a little old man dressed in a long black overcoat. His features showed he was very old, and he had sagging lower eyelids with tears running from them. He stopped Dennis and asked if he would like to buy a watch, at the same time showing him the one he had in his hand. Looking at it Dennis told him the dial was cracked. The old man put his hand inside his overcoat, then brought out an identical watch. We made excuses about not wanting the article, then everyone got on board the shuttle for the ship.

The rest of the voyage passed with little incident. When we had a shower on board there was plenty of hot water, but it was salt water. Trying to get a lather was nigh on impossible. The only way was to have a special type of soap. As we had none it was just a case of putting up with it.

The day before docking, Mike Bury – whom we knew from training days and who was also with us – was getting a bit concerned about customs, and what we were allowed to take into the country. He asked me if I wore a watch. I didn't, so he handed me one to take through customs for him. His main problem was that he smoked a pipe, and he was trying every way he could think of to increase his allowance, including putting pipe tobacco in cigarette cartons. How successful he was I can only guess, because after going through customs and handing him the watch back I didn't see him again. He must have been in a different area in camp from me. But I do know his apprehension about customs services would prove only too correct when we disembarked.

The ship was making steady progress up the Solent, so from now on it became a case of retrieving all our kit in readiness for disembarkation. In all the excitement, it is very hard to remember all of what went on, but obviously all was sorted out.

Southampton Customs Check and Going Home

Coming into dock to tie up at the quayside is a memory I will never lose. As we slowly approached the quay a band played all the pertinent tunes that go with welcoming home a troop ship. With flags flying, and crowds of people waving and shouting, this was a scene that would next be seen again for troops returning from the Falklands War.

I suspect (and I don't mean to take anything away from the other troops, returning from the Far East) that the celebration I witnessed was mainly to welcome the troops from the troubles of Cyprus.

I looked over the side but couldn't get a good view, so I moved forward to a less crowded part of the ship. Looking down I could see the beautiful sight of a young girl. We began waving to each other. The other lads came along, wanting to know who she was; I told them that I hadn't got a clue and couldn't care less. I just looked upon her as my own girlfriend Sylvia, and kept waving like a person who hadn't seen a decent female in months: I hadn't! The impression that someone was waving to you and to you alone, whether she was or not, felt fantastic.

With all the excitement dying down it was time for the friends and relatives to make way for our disembarkation. Having been mustered into our respective troops, we picked up our kitbags. In a slow procession we gathered all our kit from the hold, then made our way down the gangplank and into the customs hall. There stood a long line of tables with customs men at each, seemingly ready and eager to pounce and disembowel our kitbags.

After we had each been directed to our particular table, we were asked what we had to declare. As if not believing a word we'd said the officials began to go through our belongings in the sea-kitbags. I was asked how many cigarettes I had; I told the man two hundred, not counting the fifty packet I was already smoking. Asked what other things I might have, I told him all I had was a

219

tablecloth and a set of cushions. When asked again if I had any more, I replied, 'No, we were pulled out that quick we couldn't get anything else.' His next question was, 'Why? Where are you from?' 'Cyprus,' I said. At this answer he looked at the div sign on my shoulder, leant back and shouted along the line, 'The *Black Swan*!'[6] Later I found out that they thought we were the only ones returning from Cyprus, when in fact there were two more detachments coming home. Putting a cross of white chalk on each of my kitbags, and then pointing to a low barrier with a wicket gate in it, he told me I could go that way out.

Still standing just inside the area, I could see Dennis being checked to the extreme. His officer had cut open the washing he had, dirty laundry from when we'd been on guard at the police station some two or three weeks before. He was diligently and very slowly picking up each item between finger and thumb. Coming to the underpants he used the pencil he had in his hand. I was so engrossed watching the procedure, I didn't take much notice of the customs man who came up to me, then asked if I'd been checked through yet. When I answered yes, and showed him the chalk marks on my kit, he suggested I go out through the wicket gate, otherwise, I'd be dragged through all over again. Taking his advice, outside I went to wait for the others; I now realise that on doing so I must have been the first soldier to return to British soil, by ship, after the conflict had officially ended in Cyprus.

Inevitably, some smart arse MP had been watching and waiting for me to come out of customs so he could show his authority. In the distance I saw, nick, nick, nick, a redcap coming in like an air-to-ground missile. Standing in front of me he began to ask me questions in the normal bombastic manner. The dialogue went something like this:

'Where are you going to?' he asked.

'I don't know,' I said.

'Are you getting on the train?'

'I don't know.'

'Are you getting in the trucks?'

---

[6] Divisional sign on our uniform shoulder, consisting of a black square with a white roundel that had a black swan insignia inside.

'I don't know.'

'Who is the officer in charge?'

For the fourth time I said, 'I don't know.'

With all these negative answers he was beginning to get nasty. He then tried to get at me by saying, 'You're a right funny f— aren't you?' My reply to this was, 'No funnier than you.' As this conversation was going on, an MP officer in the background could see his man getting very frustrated, getting nowhere fast and being unable to get me to move. He approached and wanted to know what the hold-up was. The corporal then said, 'I've asked him where he is going – is he getting on the train or the trucks, or who is the officer in charge? – all I get out of him is, "I don't know." ' Turning to confront me, the officer asked, 'What is your regiment?'

'Twenty-five Field, sir,' was my answer. At this the officer turned to the corporal, then wanted to know if he, the corporal, had read Part One Orders, because if he had he should know that there would be two more detachments besides 25 Field coming in from Cyprus on this ship this day. Of these, nothing was known, only that we had to be met by an officer, who would have the necessary information to take us to our destination. Only this officer would know which transport we would be taking to get us to our new barracks.

I was told to stand near a support pillar and gather the rest of the unit to the area, until contact was made by our officer. Being the first out meant I had one heck of a wait, but if I hadn't been waiting outside I'd only be doing the same inside. It must have been a good half hour if not more before our officer arrived. It was none other than Captain Friend. He always seemed to have a nonchalant attitude, and even in this hustle and bustle he was still the same.

I can't really remember much of what happened next, but it must have been by truck to a camp about twenty-five miles north of Southampton, where on arrival we got all our kit into the billets we'd been assigned to. Dennis was put into a different billet than me and so began our separation from each other, being in different billets for the rest of our service until demob.

Over the past few months we'd all got used to setting up new locations, so it was no hard task to get stuck in and sort ourselves out all over again. The biggest shock we got was from the cold weather. As night fell so did the temperature. Our only source of heating was from a huge pot-bellied stove in the centre of the billet. (Quite a change from the central heating of Jalalabad Barracks, wouldn't you say?) The beds were made up, and out came the death blankets (the one you'd have been wrapped up in if killed). The old greatcoat came out and went on the bed as well, as we knew from being at home that the nights were still very cold in England.

That night in camp we got to know that the evening paper in Southampton had given the customs men a right-going over for the way they'd treated the troops coming home from Cyprus. They'd gone through everybody's kit as if all of us had something to hide. No one was to go through unscathed – that is until they found out that the Black Swan shoulder insignia was from Cyprus. In defence of the customs officers though, I must say that it was rumoured all over the ship that drugs were on board coming in from Hong Kong. That though didn't excuse them from not finding out that three regimental advance parties were coming home and not just the one.

Next morning on parade we were given details of our duties until dinner and what would be expected on our return from leave. After securing our kit in lockers and dinner over, we were then given our passes for disembarkation leave for our individual destinations.

A lot of what happened travelling home is just a blur now. My next clear memory is of knocking on the front door at around 10 p.m., my father opening it to let me in, after which he shouted upstairs to my mother, 'Lizzie, there's somebody here to see you.' My mother wasn't in very good health, mainly I think because of my being abroad. Each day bad news on the radio, or the scenes of devastation on the television, had only made her condition much worse through her worrying over me, as I'm sure other mothers did. Shortly after entering the house I heard footsteps coming downstairs. There she was, standing there, sighing with emotion and relief. I put my arms around her and she hugged me saying, 'Oh son, I'm glad you're home.' Each time I see the homecoming scene in the film *Sergeant York* it reminds me of this moment. It being so late at night I had little else to do but unwind with small talk, and gather information about all that had gone on while I was away.

Next morning, having got used to an early routine, by eight o'clock I'd had breakfast and was just wasting time really until I could see Sylvia. Getting on buses, I was often given a long inquisitive look from people not understanding why I was so brown, even though I was in uniform and had a medal ribbon on. The hardest stare I got was from a black man with tribal markings on his face. At the same time as the Cyprus engagement the army was, or had recently been, involved in an insurgency in Africa, against the Mau Mau. That didn't bother me though, I was home and glad to be there.

Sylvia was due out of work at five thirty. So as to make certain I didn't miss her, I got to the Co-op at four thirty. It soon got round that I was outside waiting; the manager found out and sent her home early. Everyone came to the front to see our reunion. I later found out that if I'd gone for her even earlier he'd still have let out early without pay being stopped. From then on all had a good time. As always when you are relishing the situation, time just flies, and so did this – so much time to make up, and so little time to do it in. To put it politely, my mother said if I wasn't careful I'd be going up with the blinds, so if nothing else she knew what was going on.

One thing happened then that I thought was funny. While I was home on leave an election was held, whether for council or parliament I don't rightly know now. Off I went with my parents to the polling station, and as I got to the door I realised I didn't know which candidate was for which party. I asked which was which, and my mother blurted out, 'Vote Labour.' The policeman on the door said, 'You can't tell anyone what to vote, Madam.' To which my mother replied, 'Well if he doesn't, he'll not get bloody fed.' At this I had to explain to the constable that I'd only returned from abroad two days before, so didn't know much about the candidates and which party they stood for. Thankfully, seeing my dark tan and uniform, I think he grasped the situation, and I fully understood that he had to make his remarks heard for everyone else to hear. It was now becoming obvious that, after only a few days of my being at home, Mother was feeling much better and coming back to her normal self.

Barton Stacey C Camp

After leave we headed back to our new camp. It was found to be of all-wooden structured huts of Second World War design. The location was Barton Stacey, and immediately opposite the main gate was a REME (Royal Electrical and Mechanical Engineers) regiment.

The days were warm enough and work was very easy to do. Knowing the ETA of the regiment gave us the chance to work out roughly how many lockers and beds needed to be installed into each billet on a daily basis, leaving time to clean up any eyesores around camp. In this camp we again encountered civilian workers doing some of the jobs for us. They'd be refitting windows and checking they would open, also doing doors and refurbishing the offices. They may have been drafted in because the regiment was returning so soon before completing a full tour of duty. One Friday morning not long after breakfast, when Captain Friend came to see how we'd been getting on, we gave him the information that another four billets had to be fitted with beds and lockers. 'Ho, it's a shame,' he said, 'if the job had been finished by four o'clock you could all have had a twenty-four-hour pass.'

'Get the passes ready, sir, we'll work through our NAAFI break!' This was a unanimous answer.

'I thought you might do,' he replied, smiling. Off he went knowing full well the job would be completed in no time at all.

Now coaches started to come to the camp every Friday evening to take lads home on 'forty-eights'. The weekend pass happened to be one week before Easter, which signified that it would be the holiday weekend in camp for the advance party. We'd had our embarkation leave, so it was now the turn of the full regiment to be off on leave, with just the advance party left in camp as a skeleton guard. Being on guard again didn't pose any problems from the personnel point of view. With everyone being on leave, most doors were locked up until the regiment came back off leave. The only places to keep a sharp eye on were the quarters of the few on camp plus cookhouse, boiler house and gun park.

It felt rather strange walking round in a greatcoat to keep warm with nothing but a pick handle for protection, and then walking along all on your own doing the rounds listening to the crunch of gravel under the hobnailed boots. After always having had a buddy with you, as well as a rifle bayonet and ammunition, and trying to keep as quiet as possible each time you made a move in the dark, this was definitely something very different. This was the other side of soldiering, which we had to get used to once more.

It was during the Easter weekend that I began to write a letter to Sylvia, stopping and starting it whenever I felt like it. Over the weekend I wrote as many as twenty-three pages – not bad really for a bloke who could manage less than twenty-three lines at the start of my service.

On one of these weekend passes home I saw something I didn't think was possible in England at this time. I know it must be one of the early trips home from this camp, because it was one of the only times when, because of lack of people, the coach went through Birmingham instead of the usual route up the A49. Going along a major road not far from Edgbaston the bus slowed down because of heavy traffic. On the left-hand side of the bus, a dance hall came into view. Outside was a placard on which was written the words: Blacks Only Tonight. I couldn't believe my eyes. Not long having returned from a conflict where black and white lads had to depend upon each other if trouble started, I found it very hard to believe it; yet here in England, just a short while later, segregation was alive and well.

I tried as I might to convince my old mate Tony that this sort of thing was still going on, but he wouldn't have any of it. I can also understand people saying, well there must have been a Whites Only Night as well. That I know, but it was still hard for me to understand. Just think, I'd been sleeping in the next bed to Eric Lynch for nigh on five-and-a-half months, depending on him for protection if anything went wrong on patrol, sharing thoughts as well as cigs or a drink. Yet here was a sign that would stop us going in the dance hall together. I thought these were very sad placards to read.

With very little to do the days dragged terribly. The place often looked like a spaghetti western ghost town, with just the one or two blokes knocking about. Being so bored I embarked on writing a letter to Sylvia. If you remember the very first letter was one of five or ten lines; this one ended up with thirty-two pages. Not only did the letter contain endearments to Sylvia, but it was also a running commentary on life in camp over the Easter period. At night it was either the NAAFI or a pub called the Bullington Cross, located on the crossroads of the A34 and the A303. Until demob this would be our local hang-out. Having time to sit down and think about the situations we'd all been through, I came to the stark realisation that all the lads I had been with from training days had virtually served in three regiments. The first regiment was 61 Field. First, doing basic training after which we joined as fully-fledged gunners to be trained up as a service regiment ready to be called on at any time for action as field artillery.

The second was 25 Field, losing all our big guns and being sent out as infantry to do a job in Cyprus, for which we had *not* been fully trained, learning tactics and methods as we went along, walking almost everywhere we went. It was quite a change from riding in trucks or champs when going out with the guns on to the ranges for practice.

Then back again to artillery, still with 25 Field, after having been stripped of our small arms and getting the twenty-five pounders back. We had to begin retraining as an artillery unit, then rejoin the division as a proper fighting force, and serve in England until needed again or disbanded. To be in just two artillery regiments is bad enough, with their varying ideas and standards, but this seemed to go beyond the pale.

Back to Basics, Rumbled as a Signaller and Retraining with Guns

When the regiment returned it was back to basics. The first concern was to get rid of the habit of swinging only one arm (owing to always carrying a rifle). Marching in squads started again, the way it used to be in training. Being shouted at to swing our arms, and pick up our feet, and knowing what to expect, we soon got back into shape.

One memorable day it was decided to take the entire troop on a route march. The officers stood in front of the column as if to say, we'll show them how to do this. Away the column went at the normal artillery pace. The distance would be around six miles. After plodding along for some time we came upon a pub. Having halted us and given the order to fall out, the officers went inside for a drink and left us lot outside to fend for ourselves. Close by were some nice farm fences to get our feet up on to, to get the blood back down the legs. Rest period over, out came the officers fully refreshed and started us off again. We couldn't have gone a mile, when a champ turned up; the driver said the officers were wanted in camp right away. They hadn't fooled anybody – they'd rung the camp for a vehicle to come and pick them up, no doubt because they were knackered. What they had failed to realise was that a six-mile route march was only half of the daily distance we did in Cyprus, over stony ground too, and we had gained knowledge of how to recuperate.

When we were satisfied that the marching was OK, we were given lessons on gun drill or assigned jobs. Dennis wanted to be a driver, as I did. Dennis was already a qualified driver, but it was still necessary to go into the Signals class before going on to be a driver. The first day in the classroom was for me complete and utter boredom. The second day, sitting at one of the tables at the back of the room, I began to play a game of matchbox rugby. This was played by flicking a matchbox on to pre-set lines: if the box landed on the line it was a try. Then you'd try to flick the matchbox over your opponent's thumbs on his up-turned hands, which symbolised the goal posts. Even while playing the game I could still follow the lecture easily. This though was to be my downfall, because out of the blue the sergeant shouted at me, 'What am I talking about here?' With brain in neutral, I replied, 'You're talking a load of rubbish. You've got two OPs sending orders to two different sets of guns, and never once have you given a call sign. You'd have everybody shooting all over everywhere.'

He turned to look at the board, stopped halfway, turned back and threw the chalk at me saying, 'You are the b— I was looking for in Cyprus!' Grinning and trying to get out of the hole I'd just put myself in, I said, 'Me? What have I done wrong?' 'Don't try and bluff your way out of this one, you're the only one out of twenty-two blokes who knows that I'm talking crap, and has proved it.' The next remark was one I didn't want to hear: 'Go on, out you go.'

Everybody was now looking round at each other wondering what was happening and why. 'I'm not having you in here any more,' continued the sergeant. My spirits sank like a lead balloon. I'd had my heart set on getting a driving licence, but I now knew I'd well and truly blown it. I went out, but had nowhere to go. All I could do was hide more or less until 4.30 p.m. which was the end of the day.

The following morning I again went into the Signals lesson, only to be told that a champ would be coming out shortly and I would be assigned to it as the regular signaller. I didn't have long to wait, because as I went out the predicted vehicle turned up, with none other than Captain Friend in charge. From now on I was to be his new OP signaller. All I had to do now was to more or less waste time until the classes had finished their courses. When all the instruction courses were complete, the troop began its training programme again in earnest.

Early on, existing equipment around the camp area needed to be checked, including the fire truck with all the gear on it. This was done on a Saturday afternoon when the parade ground would be empty. The fire team had done all its checks and was rolling up the last length of hose, when across the main road in the REME camp the fire bell sounded. In the distance over the road a plume of smoke could be seen swirling up into the air.

All the crew jumped into the Land Rover and drove through our main gate across the road into the other camp and proceeded to put out the fire. The fire consisted of old crates and oily rags which, unknown to the 25 Field crew, had been deliberately set on fire by the officer on duty at the REME camp, to see how fast his team would be at getting to a fire. You can imagine the scene when he saw our team first in action to put it out. It was impossible to convince the officer that the only reason the Artillery was so quick was because they already had all their equipment out and were just putting it away again when the bells sounded. Those poor lads were at it for hours after, for no fault of their own, trying to beat the time it took our truck to get there and put out the fire.

It would be around this time that I met another old pal. Bob Ashcroft was his name, and I'd known him from when we were in primary school together. Then at secondary school we had been in the same school house, and played rugby, cricket and football, and even been in the athletics team together. His trade was as a mechanic, and this is how he came to be in the REME. Who could have known we'd meet up again like this? On one occasion he gave me a lift in his car back to camp. I think this was the time I had a problem getting my pass from the TSM. I didn't see him much after this, and don't have any recollections as to what happened to him afterwards. He may have been posted somewhere else.

I was in the NAAFI one night having a cup of tea and what I can only describe as a savoury pie, which was absolutely delicious. I started to feel something biting just inside my shirt. Putting my hand inside I gently felt around and got a little pinhead object in between my finger and thumb. Extracting my hand from the shirt I kept rolling it round to stop it moving. Opening my fingers slightly I could see it was a flea. Getting a cigarette lighter, I lit it, then dropped the flea into an ashtray over a flame. As it burned you could hear it go crack. It was one of the fleas from Cyprus.

With a saddle on its back it could have won the Grand National that year. That flea must have been in my kit for about twelve weeks; if not, it must have come from the kit of one of the other lads when he returned off leave.

In the billet would be about sixteen men, because all signallers were together and Dennis had got his driving job. Dennis and I were now in separate billets. The only original ones left from F Section were Al Brindle and Butch Gladwin. Butch asked one day which town I came from. When I told him St Helens, he asked if I could get him some stonies (marbles) the next time I went on a weekend pass. (As the story goes over a few weeks I'll finish it in one go.) I came back with a very small case; inside must have been a hundred marbles or there abouts. He was more than thankful and put them in his locker, hoping a locker inspection wouldn't take place before he could take them home. In St Helens was the main glass factory at the time, making television screens, where would be found railway wagons full of marbles as cullet with which to make the screens. Obviously the wagons were a magnet for all the kids wanting marbles, but if anyone worked there it was easy to get them. Butch took them home for his nephew and came back telling us of the good time he had. This was borne out when a few nights later we could hear him talking in his sleep, dreaming like mad about the games he was playing with his nephew and the marbles.

Most schemes were the same as before with just a few varia-tions, except that the quad and limber had been done away with and in their place would be the three-ton Bedford to take both ammunition and gunners all in the same vehicle. One scheme, however, was notably different. Today I think you have to pay to go anywhere near the Stonehenge monoliths; well this day found us in the OP champ just fifty feet from it, if that. As this was a night camp, Salisbury Plain being MoD property, and us being army, getting to Stonehenge was quite easy. However, the main order of the day was to make absolutely sure that the site was left perfectly clean and tidy.

It should go without saying that we did have a good look around, first touching the monument, then wondering how on earth the people put the stones up on top like a lintel. Jimmy

Smith was driving this day. When the order came to move out, having already packed up, into the champ we all got. Jimmy started up and drove off at breakneck speed, on to the road turning left. Captain Friend asked 'Where are you going?'

Smudger replied, 'We are on the move, sir.'

'Where to?' he was asked.

'I don't know, sir, but we're on the move.'

'Well turn round and let's go thirty miles an hour the right way, instead of sixty miles an hour the wrong way.'

I think this small mistake cost Jimmy his job as the OP driver, because after this episode he was put on the J truck, which was the TSM's one tonner.

After carrying on for a few more miles, Jimmy was ordered to turn into a field. 'But it's a cabbage field, sir,' Jimmy said. 'It's MoD land. Drive in, the farmer is using land he shouldn't be using,' came back the answer. In Jimmy went and an OP was set up, and that is the only thing that happened on that shoot of any interest.

I was told that on one particular scheme the safety officer seemed to be prancing round looking for faults. When entering one gun area he began to kick at the cartridges that were lying around on the ground. He kicked at one cartridge, but before he could touch another he was half hit and pushed away from the position. He had completely forgotten that the transition from quad limber and gun had taken place, or he had mistaken which cartridges were primed and which had been fired and empty, because now the gun position was one of a three-ton truck and gun with loose ammunition laid out on the ground around it. This lapse in memory nearly caused a catastrophic accident.

It was during another one of these schemes on stand-down that our officer again started up a conversation as to what I though of all the foreign nationals coming into the country. Without giving my reply much thought I said that they should all be sent back out of the way. To which Captain Friend answered, 'What me as well? I'm from South Africa.' Once again, foot in mouth disease.

On another time out the conversation concerned our possibly having to go against the miners if they went out on strike. I stated that I was a collier's son who also had two uncles working down the mines. That being the case, I thought I would have to refuse the order to go against my own family if I was sent to the area where I lived, to try to force them back to work. We then debated the fact that an army was supposed to defend its people, not attack them on the whim of a government. This job should be left to the police, not the army. We had many more discussions on other topics. If nothing else it gave me a better understanding as to what others may think and believe.

Because the regiment had come home with a medal, it became our regimental responsibility to supply a detachment for a Queen's Birthday parade. We'd only been home some two months, and I was one of the troops chosen for this task, so for at least the next two weekends I would be unable to get home. But during the middle of the weeks normal training for gun deployment still went on. On Saturday mornings with 303 rifles in hand we'd parade with other regiments, including the QARANCs or the WAFs. The worst problem was the change in the marching tempo of the music as each regiment passed the stationary band. As a detachment passed by, the speed of step would change, but only at a certain distance, meaning that only the front lines of each group marched at the new tempo. At the first few attempts it looked like a load of trainees on parade, but with perseverance the problem was overcome.

The other thing we had to get used to was putting the rifle, which weighed in the region of nine-and-a-half pounds, on to the shoulder in readiness to fire the salute. On the day of the parade it would be loaded with three blank rounds, in readiness for the salute which was called a *feu de joie*. Putting our rifles into a vertical position our shoulders, pointing skywards and easing springs would give a rippling sound effect, first going along the front rank of the first three columns, then continuing back along the middle ranks, and then the other way again along the rear ranks. The parade commander then gave the order to come down to the port arms position; then when reloaded we would repeat the manoeuvre until it had been done three times in all.

One very naughty action took place during the weekend practices, and this concerned the female ranks. For the first few commands they took the brunt of some very crass humour. Each time they were given the order to attention or stand at easy, most of the lads would make a squelching sound. At first it went unnoticed, but as soon as the RSM heard it, all hell broke loose, resulting in the normal threats of what would happen to all, not just one, if he heard it again.

The big day in June came, and off to Winchester we went. It didn't rain that day, so luckily everything went according to plan. The ripple of fire made quite a brilliant show. The crowd watching clapped and cheered, so at least they enjoyed it all; the kids must have had a field day picking up any empty cartridges that had been missed after the clean-up.

One weekend during our settling-in period, we had a football match between ourselves on the sports ground. The next obvious thing was to go and have a shower. With the showering finished, making our way back to the billet with only boots on and nothing else, jabbering away and swinging towels, we began to approach the gym. As we passed it a voice bellowed out, 'You men get dressed properly! There's women in here.' It was Mr Jones. Thinking the camp would be empty he'd invited others to join him for a game of badminton in the gym. His demand only met with innuendos like, 'Send them out here, we'll show them a shuttlecock or two. They could have choice of any fifteen to play with.' Seeing he was getting nowhere fast, he tried to bluff his way out by the usual threat of charges; but it was pointed out to him that women were not allowed on camp – and not only that, he was not in uniform either. Still jeering and cheering we carried on, cock-a-hoop you might say. Nothing was ever done about it and no women ever came on camp again as far as I know, but it was a talking point for a few days.

On one scheme as OP with Captain Friend in command, I found we were in what could only be called open country. Off the Land Rover and starting to walk along, I hadn't gone more than a few yards when I tripped over something and went sprawling headlong. Getting up I went back to see what it was – a strip of black wire. One end seemed loose, so I started to tug at the other end and discovered that it disappeared into the valley and across. I thought, Right, get out the empty cable drum and take it all in. I'd been winding in for some fifteen minutes when the cable went very slack. Unperturbed I carried on until I had it all on the drum. As I was doing this, all three of us at the OP saw a parachute coming down; yet looking into the sky we could see nothing, nothing but a clear blue sky, so where had it come from? Who was it?

Putting the drum in the champ I went off with the captain to where the figure had landed. We found it to be a dummy dressed in what looked like air force clobber. All around and up into the sky not even a vapour trail could be seen or a sound heard, so it was decided to leave it where it was and carry on as normal.

Later on in the day I was asked to get a 'meteorological report'. I was told that it was unavailable because someone had removed the landline to the met station. I wonder who?

On some of these outing, an officer might make it his business to call up a colleague. I don't know if it was this scheme in particular, but Captain Friend took us to a certain location, very near to an RAF place. Getting there I was told to go with him wherever he wanted to go. Searching for a way to get in through a barbed wire perimeter fence, we met an RAF corporal on patrol with an Alsatian dog. He challenged our right to be there and asked what we wanted. Captain Friend told him he wanted to enter to see a colleague; his entry was denied. Still pushing the issue, my officer said he was a captain and would come in anyhow, to which the RAF bod said, 'Maybe, but the dog doesn't know what rank you are.' All I could do was stand and listen. Eventually, with great calm, Captain Friend returned to the vehicle and we went back to the scheme. I have often wondered if this was part of an exercise, because the question is, why didn't he use the main gate?

On one occasion a sports day was organised, just for fun I suppose. I had a go. In the 100 yards I didn't do too badly, yet in the 220 I did something like twenty-four seconds, which, considering all I'd been doing for the past six months was walking up hill and down dale was pretty good going. In the long jump I did nineteen feet six inches but I must admit that the sand was well below ground level. The difference between 25 Field and 61 Field was now becoming obvious, because the following weekend

I was asked if I would like a game of football against the pay corps. I declined with some excuse. On the afternoon after the game, the lads were coming in all tired and full of mud when one lad shouted, 'Did you know what that team was like?' 'No, why, what happened?' I asked. 'They slaughtered us sixteen nil,' was the reply. I didn't know if this was a case in point, but it was often the army habit to put all the good players from the First Division clubs in a regiment where they could easily be sent for if needed to play for their club at the weekend. I was told that the other team kicked off, passed the ball to three players, and it was one nil to them; nobody on our side had even touched the ball. Games like this were regularly arranged.

Mr Murray-Smith was an officer I went on a scheme with once. I can't think of anything that happened on the outing – it was afterwards that the incident occurred. It was normal practice to have passes given out on a Friday after the return from a scheme, but only when all the equipment was cleaned and put away. Being an old hand at it, I was soon well and truly finished and down at the battery office asking for the pass. At that same time Mr Murray-Smith arrived. He heard me ask and then get refused by the new TSM. Mr Murray-Smith butted in and told the TSM that I could have my pass, as all my equipment had been put away and I'd been dismissed. The sergeant refused, saying he was in charge of the passes, so I would have to wait until everyone else got their equipment stored away. At this Mr Murray-Smith hit the roof, reminding the sergeant that he was the officer, and he said I'd finished and could have my pass.

I got the pass, but with it the evil-eyed look from the TSM, so I knew that somewhere along the line I would have to pay for what had just gone on, although it had virtually nothing to do with me. So it proved. I asked the same TSM for my pass two weeks later, but he made an excuse that he had to do something else first, I waited and waited until he'd given everyone else their passes, then he asked me which coach was I going to catch. 'The big green one,' I said. 'Just a minute,' he said, and, as the coach started towards the gates, 'Here,' he said, 'see if you can catch it now.' I had known it would come some day. I just thought I was lucky that it was only something like this that I could get out of easily. All I did now was one of the very few hitchhikes home from here. The plus side was that I still had some cash in my pocket when I got home. This is the one weekend I think that Bob Ashcroft gave me a lift back to camp in his car.

On some schemes the full regiment would go out, but before doing so it had to line up on the regimental square for the CO's inspection. Everyone was lined up, or so we thought, when who should come on to the parade ground but Smudger in his little one-tonner. It was the J truck that was assigned to the TSM. Round he came and parked up by the side of us (the OP), but no sooner had he jumped out of his vehicle, than he was told to go somewhere else. Off he went, only to be told a second, third and fourth time to move on, each time driving past the CO, who looked up to see what was going on. As a last resort Jimmy drove up near to where the colonel was inspecting. He jumped out of his truck, went up to the colonel, saluted him and asked him to sign his POL papers because he was running out of petrol. He was then ordered to a position and told to stay there until the regiment moved out. There's more than one way to skin a cat.

On the ranges I sensed that I was getting more and more time off than I would normally get. Basically it was because a new lad had joined us; he was Scottish and came from one of the islands. He had a very strong accent but, as always with the Scots, when on a radio his diction was perfect. Being spare, I asked if I could go down to the wagon lines. Given approval, off I set to see if I could see Dennis and have a scrounge round. I know what happened next but I just can't think how it came about. When I arrived at the lines, the cooks had all the grub laid out. I was asked if I wanted some – of course I did. 'I'll go and get my mess tins,' I said. 'You'll be too late if you do, we're throwing it away now,' one of the cooks answered. A mate gave me only one of his tins, so I went down the line, spuds in, veg in, gravy in, sweet in, custard in, then all topped up with tea. I can't fully remember what I used to eat with but I ate as much as I could.

Having finished, washed up, and seen my mates it was scrounging time. I didn't do too badly either. At the OP I could see another officer there as well as Captain Friend. As I stepped inside the area the officer told me to put my beret on, but Captain

Friend intervened and told me to put the stuff away, then put my beret on. Our visitor was surprised to see half a loaf, and a packet of butter, along with a tin of sausages, appear out of the beret I didn't have on, plus four eggs. It was Mr Jones I think, and he still hadn't got the gist of what was going on.

Our local pub, the Bullington Cross, was situated about a mile and a half from camp. I went up there one evening with Dennis and I think Mo Beasley, plus another lad whose name I think was either Worsley or Worthington. It was decided we'd have a game of darts, a pint and a hot pie out of the heater that was on the bar. We'd been playing for some time when in came a man and woman. They watched us playing for a while then asked if we'd let them join us. It wasn't long before they asked if we wanted to put any bets on. We declined, laughing that we didn't want to take their money off them. The landlord had already warned us that they were both the pub champions and what to expect.

Playing just for enjoyment was all we wanted to do; we four played a round robin of two different players each game. As the night wore on, others coming in began to watch with growing interest. No matter which pairing they played, the local couple never won a match. At the end of the night the publican remarked that it was the first time he'd ever seen this happen to this pair. When we told him where we'd come from, and that when off duty all we had to do in camp was play darts, he understood. Not only did we play well, but we also knew which numbers were the favourites of the partner we were playing with. I think this experience was one the pub champions wouldn't forget in a hurry.

Returning to camp in the evening meant a nice leisurely stroll along grass-covered verges. From time to time we'd come across little fluorescent lights of glow-worms. They look like caterpillars with a green light coming from their rear. Us lads from up north didn't see this type of insect back home, owing to the very cold weather in winter. This being the case, on our first sighting we stopped for a few minutes to have a good look at them. It soon became common for us to see them when returning to camp and knew straight away what the little lights were.

It was now in midsummer, and quite a relief for me because

my second blouse was wearing through on one of the pleats at the front. This meant I was using my best tunic more often, so it too was getting rather tatty. Making matters even worse, my pullover had now got a hole in the left elbow. On nearly every morning parade I was told the same thing: go and get it changed. I tried to explain that, each time I went, the QM told me that I only had a few months left before demob, so I couldn't have another new pullover.

One morning Mr Murray-Smith took the roll call, giving me the same instruction as the others had done. I explained the situation to him and he ordered me to go with him to the Q stores. Inside the Q repeated what he'd said on the other occasions, trying to get out of the problem by saying all he had was officers' pullovers. However Mr Murray-Smith made it quite plain that I had to have a new one even if I only had a week to do; he would not have one of his men walking round with holes in his clothes. The sergeant was right though – I did bring the pullover home when I was demobbed.

Going back to retraining: it was more than a change to have an extra pair of hands to help out; it was absolute heaven. After having been on my own (apart from a driver) most of the time, if not all of the time when I was in Charlie Troop with Captain Pettifer, I now found tasks quite easy. On one scheme the exercise would be how to deploy and set up a picket gun. The idea came I believe from the Germans. It was simple really: out of a line of four guns, one would be detached from the rest of the troop, along with a makeshift command post, and sent to a position either in front of or behind the existing position, depending on how the action was being fought. When in place the OP sent new co-ordinates to the lone detachment by using a different call sign. Most times it would range on to more than just one target, but always stay short of it, so as not to let it be known that the target could now be bombarded if need be. The remaining three guns carried on firing as if they were four guns when given the order 'troop fire'; if the word 'gunfire' was used, each gun just fired its allotted rounds. They would carry on firing until the time came for them to redeploy at their new location. Getting there and setting up meant they could take on the new co-ordinates from the picket gun for all targets recorded. This enabled them to start firing immediately on any target that required it, thus saving what could be valuable minutes, which could prove crucial in battle.

Later in the scheme Captain Friend went off to play in an RA golf tournament, leaving us with Mr Jones, who took charge the evening of the last day and once again was determined to show how good he was. All was well until the following morning. I went out to bring in the outlying equipment. When I came back I enquired about breakfast. 'Mr Jones has eaten it all,' was the answer.

'Have you eaten all the breakfast, sir?' I asked.

'Yes,' he said.

'But you've eaten food for four men,' I replied.

'I was hungry this morning.'

'Don't you think I am now, sir?' I asked.

'Well, if you can't get back in time it's your own fault.'

I simply replied that this was supposed to be a team, not a one-man band, and that I'd been out recovering the remote equipment. His retort was the obvious one: 'You're on a charge when you get back to camp.' I said it wasn't me who could go any lower in rank. Told to shut my mouth, that was exactly what I did.

The morning shoots went on, and at dinner time Mr Jones told the driver to get dinner ready. 'We've got no food left, sir, the last went this morning,' was the answer. With this the driver was ordered to take him to the wagon lines, where he got something to eat. Whether the driver did or not I don't know, but I do know we two didn't, the two remaining at our position. All we could do was make a brew and wait for their return.

After a few more shoots in the afternoon, and getting on for 3.30 p.m. orders were finally given to return to camp. Going into camp the driver was told to drive to the cookhouse, whereupon Mr Jones took us inside. As tea had finished, he gave instructions to the duty cook to knock up some grub for the three of us, telling him we'd had nothing all day. That was wrong though – actually, we'd had nothing to eat since tea time the day before. Dished up were five sausages each, with beans and bacon, the usual bread and jam, and a nice amount of tea to drink and satisfy our hunger.

The next parade was on Monday, which saw me being singled out by Captain Friend. I was informed that he'd heard all about the argument over the food and told to forget it; but when I mentioned the fact that I was to be put on a charge, he emphatically made it clear that I should forget it. I did as I was told.

I put in for leave and got it without any problem. I caught the evening train from Andover to Waterloo, then on to Euston, and then the Red Rose Express to Wigan where I boarded the Liverpool train to St Helens. I'd been home a few days when I received a telegram to return to camp immediately. I shot off to town to tell Sylvia of the situation, and our plans for the night had to go on hold until I came back. I travelled back the way I came overnight, getting to camp as soon as I could. On arrival I was told to report to the battery office where I was then told that I would be representing the regiment in a sports meeting that afternoon.

I had lunch, then got my plimsolls and shorts and off we went to the meeting. Some of the contestants had proper spiked shoes and tracksuits to keep themselves warm between races. The race I was down for was the 220 yards. I came last (I'm not surprised really because with all that travelling I was well and truly knackered).

I got back in camp in time for tea and again was told to report to the office. In I went, only to be handed an extended pass for the inconvenience I'd been through. Very nice I thought. Doing a quick change, then getting something to eat, away I went again on a journey back home again in reverse to the one I'd done the previous night. The rest of the leave went well, and at the time on the pass I returned to barracks.

As I stood on parade, as normal all jobs were dished out – but I was left standing there like a lemon. TSM Watkins looked at me and asked why I was back in camp. I told him my leave was up, and was told that according to his information sheet I was still on leave. Going through his paperwork again, he glanced up and said, 'All you can do is get lost until tomorrow morning.'

On a Charge, Final Exercises and Theft of Cap Badge

I'd been on leave and returned as normal. I went into the ablutions to have a wash and shave, when in walked Lance Bombardier Freddie Miller. He asked me what was I doing in this washroom. He asked me my name and I told him he should already know it, because we'd been in the same section together in Cyprus. I thought he was just pulling my leg or something. Saying nothing else away he went but, that evening, in came one of the lads saying I was on regimental orders, on a charge. Not understanding why, I went and had a look for myself, and sure enough my name was there, for using the wrong washrooms. The following morning, all dressed and ready with five others, I stood outside the battery office waiting to go in.

I must try to explain the configuration of the offices. As you went in the main door down the corridor, it turned in an L shape to the right. At the right angle were three doors, all together, separated only by the door frames. Two doors were on the left and the third was directly ahead. Now that the scene is set, I hope you can follow the proceedings. Given the order to only 'off caps', we knew right away that at the most this would be an arse-kicking contest.

The next order was in rapid-fire language: 'Defaulters attention, right turn, quick march, right wheel, left right, left right, left turn, mark time, halt.' Now tittering started. The officer we had to see was in the second room but owing to the speed with which we'd been marched in, the first two defaulters were in the room directly down the corridor, facing a wall only two to four inches away from their faces; the second two were in the room they should be in, but one behind the other, with a dividing wall to their left; the third pair were in the first room on the left, also one behind the other, but with the same dividing wall to their right.

The officers and clerks in the rooms we should not have been in were wondering what the hell was going on. We took the usual blame from the TSM for being stupid, then had to get into the charge room as best we could.

When we were all in the correct room we were still tittering; until, that is, the officer made it more than plain that the next one to laugh or giggle, would definitely be on a charge. With everything now quietened down, it was explained to us that an order had been issued while we six were on leave, saying that if you did not belong to Echo Troop you could not use the ablutions that we had used. Because we'd been on leave and it was impossible for us to have read the orders, the charges were dropped. With hindsight I think I can boast of being one of the few men to be placed on a charge for having a wash and shave.

Before all this Freddie had bought an old Riley motorcar and had on some occasions given lads a lift into town of an evening. At one time he told us of a slight accident he had had with his car. Going round a sharp bend in the town, he said, he came up against a cement wagon and gave it a glancing blow. Much to his amazement when he got out to look at the damage, his car had a slight dent in the wing but he had knocked the hub cap clean off the wagon. When we enjoyed this kind of rapport in conversation I really was quite stunned at his complete change of character in reporting me. Especially after we had served in the same section while in Cyprus.

I still can't see what had got into Freddie, because it wasn't long afterwards that I was detailed to the sergeants' mess. I'd not been there long, when I realised I'd forgotten my cigarettes. It was no sweat getting permission from the sarge to go back and get them and on the way back I decided to go to the toilet – the correct washroom this time. As I washed my hands, in again came Freddie. 'What are you doing?' he wanted to know. I started to tell him, but before I could get two words out, he ordered me to clean all the ablutions. So following the last order, as a good soldier should, I did just that, but at my pace, hours went by. Dinner came and went and I was still cleaning up. With other lads coming to use the toilet, it was no wonder that at one stage the sergeant from the mess found out where I was. He came down to tell me to get back up to the mess. Off I went, and all I can say is that I didn't have any more trouble with Lance Bombardier Fred after this.

As I've said, I was often now becoming surplus to requirements. On these occasions I'd team up, if I could, with the J truck. This being the BSM's truck it had a radio in it, which meant I could still keep in touch with what was going on. I'd sit in the passenger seat talking to Jimmy most of the time.

On one scheme we were night driving in convoy. All vehicles had their lights out, except for a very small red light at the rear. If, when in convoy, this light was missed for any reason, every truck that was behind yours would end up in the wrong place. No, we didn't lose ourselves at any time, but going over rough country made it very hard for the driver to hang on to the steering wheel, as he didn't know where any undulations were. I helped Jimmy by holding on to the wheel from the side. I don't know if it did help but Jimmy said so. I think he'd say anything though, just to get a rest for a minute.

The new lad at OP with me was now also in the next bed to me in the billet. He was the one who came from one of the islands off the Scottish coast, whose brogue was so strong in conversation, yet on a radio he could be understood quite easily. One day we visited Imber village. This was an old, derelict place, where the Infantry would do its house-to-house warfare practices and so on. The day was warm, and I was in shirt-sleeve order eating my lunch, when over the radio came a message that something called a tiddler was to be sent to us. Jock Russell had obviously never had one of these messages before, so I told him not to panic, but just put down all that was sent. Then at the end of the message, I would explain what the signal was he'd received.

All having been gathered in, I asked for his pad and began to go through it slowly, so as to make certain he understood everything. As I finished the explanation, Captain Friend came round to the back of the champ, looked at me and said, 'You do know your job, don't you.' Now it wasn't what he said that had me puzzled, but the way in which he had said it. I thought on this for quite a while, and when I couldn't fathom out his statement, I took the bull by the horns and asked him what he meant by the remark. I was stunned by his answer. He told me that when I'd become his signaller earlier on without going through the training room, he'd written to my old captain, Captain Pettifer, more or less asking for a reference. The reply, he said, was that I knew all there was to know about OP work; and that was one of the reasons, I gather, why Captain Friend appeared to be so relaxed when giving me orders. It was now obvious that he was using me to help teach Jock, the man who would take over after my job after demob. This was why he let me roam about like I did.

In the billet one day Jimmy Smith came dashing in, wanting to know if he could borrow a writing pad. He had to write a letter to 'our Shee' (his wife's name was Sheila). Having got the pad he went to the next lad and asked if he could borrow a pen, then to the next for an envelope, finally asking if anyone could let him have a stamp. All equipped, off he went, sat down in the middle of the room and wrote his letter to Shee with everything borrowed. It looks as if Jimmy was skinny with his money – far from it. Pay day was on a Thursday and, one Wednesday evening, Jimmy walked in the room smoking away saying, 'Look what I've got,' at the same time waving a five packet of Woodbines. He opened it up and lit a cigarette to a chorus of 'Twos up on your dog end, Jim!' or, 'Give us a drag, Jim!' In the end he got the remaining four and said, 'Here, take the f—ing lot then!' He simply gave all his remaining cigs away. Who couldn't help liking a bloke like that.

My time in the army wasn't far off coming to an end, but that didn't put a stop to training, oh, no, far from it. On this outing very little happened of any consequence, until that is on a stand-down, because Echo Troop OP had the full battery to itself for the afternoon. Captain Friend told me to follow him and off he set in the direction of the shell bursts. After some time the sound of shell after shell could be heard going overhead. We still went forward and it wasn't long before we were only a matter of some six hundred yards from where shells were landing, and I began to drop behind. Turning round he asked me if I was frightened; the answer was a definite *yes*. 'I don't want to get killed by a bad ram,' I said (that is shell that has not been rammed home into the breech properly). He smiled and said, 'OK then, let's go back,' then added, 'You'll do – you know when to get frightened.'

One day a new bombardier arrived, a right cocky get he was too. No one knew for certain, but the way he strutted around with shoulders back and an attitude of 'look at me, I'm in charge', it seemed certain that he'd come from a training regiment. Nobody bothered with him much because he was a miserable sod as well. It must have only been a week at the most after he arrived that I was going home on a weekend pass, while Jimmy was going home for a week. Jimmy had put his bedding away before finding out the times of his trains. Realising that he'd missed his connection, he decided to get his bedding out again and stop overnight. Nothing wrong with that you'd think, except the next morning at reveille Jim, being on leave, was still in bed. Who should come along but mister dirtbox. Seeing Jimmy, he tipped him out of bed.

The story now goes that up Jim got, and laid into the bombardier with all the experience he had gained as a younger man, and how he had to make sure he survived whatever came his way. I reassured him that I was only interested in now and not the past. Jimmy didn't have a mark on himself, but the bombardier had one hell of a face, with all his left side black and blue. The lads that witnessed it said Jimmy was like some kind of madman. He later spoke to me about it, I think mostly in the hope that I wouldn't be afraid of what he might do, but after the antics we got up to on board ship I had no such worries. No charge was ever brought against Jimmy because the bombardier knew what the outcome would be for tipping someone out of bed.

During this period in 1959 injections for polio had become available. Believing the government would not put its army at risk I decided to have the first of three injections, the following two to be given at intervals. However, on reflection I realised that the last one would be after my demobilisation from the forces. I would be sent notification of when, with details of which type of vaccine I'd had in order to take the last one.

One of the last exercises, indeed I think it was my last, involved doing experiments with certain types of shell. The troop had all its guns deployed in a normal spread and each gun had to fire rounds of airburst. Apparently these were of a quite different make-up to the normal issue. The nose cone of the shell was transparent and a lot of workings inside could be seen. A gunner would put a setting on the nose cone, and the shell would then be loaded into the breach. Every cartridge used had the super charge and charge three removed, leaving just the two remaining bags of cordite. At any moment an aeroplane would fly low in front of the guns; then the order to fire was given, as if to try and shoot the plane out of the sky. This was repeated many times after further adjustments to the shells.

One thing that may be hard to believe for anyone who hasn't actually seen it, is that if one stood directly behind the gun when it fired, the projectile (shell) could be seen going away into the distance. It was strange watching the plane come into sight, then watch the shell travelling towards it. The main idea was for the aircraft to try to explode the shell while travelling to its target.

As the shoot went on more and more cordite accumulated, until a small pile some two feet high had developed. When everything had finished the cordite had to be disposed of. Quite a few volunteers came forward for the job of igniting it, but TSM Watkins made it known to everyone that he and he alone would do it. He explained how volatile cordite was, which meant great care had to be taken when disposing of any excess. To this end he laid a trail of cordite some eight feet long leading away from the main pile, then, giving warning, lit it. The flame shot to the pile as if drawn by magnets. The flames went into the air twisting and dancing in various coloured lights. It was all over in a couple of minutes. After seeing how quickly it burnt we understood the sergeant's concern.

Later in the day as evening approached, it was found that we at the OP were running short of bread. Captain Friend said someone would have to go and get a loaf and some milk from the nearest pub, which turned out to be one called the Bustard. The others volunteered, but I was told to go. I set out in dimming light in the direction of the pub. It wasn't long before I got there. Going inside I asked if it was possible to obtain bread and milk. I explained that we were the ones doing the firing just down the road – not that that would make any difference, it was just a case of trying to reassure him that I wasn't AWOL. I got the stuff and returned in pitch darkness. I was greeted by Captain Friend asking me if I'd enjoyed the pint. I told him I would have had one, but I was skint. At this he said that if I'd asked, he would have given me the money until pay day. Now he tells me! The grub got us through the following day until we returned to camp after a few more shoots.

With the end in sight, I was asked if I would like to have a game of rugby. I'd never played since leaving school at the age of fifteen, so I thought I'd give it a try. The position I was given was scrum half; seeing as it was rugby union, a tall half back wasn't out of the ordinary. On the opposite side, playing in the same position, was a bombardier, whose first name was Andy, who had played a few games for Castleford rugby league club I believe. I was enjoying the game when I saw Mr Jones hurtling towards me. I thought, please get me out of here, I want to be a gunner, not a goner. However, about four paces from me, he seemed to stoop down as if intending to knock me out of the way, but this only slowed his momentum. Going underneath his arms I was able to bring him to a halt. I was almost certain, that because of all the problems we'd had with each other he would have trampled all over me just to get his own back, but he didn't thank goodness.

The only other incident was when I came round the scrum and, instead of diving and throwing the ball out, I stayed on my feet and did a grubber kick into the corner. This seemed to catch most of the players on my side by surprise. I chased the kick and got to it before my own wing man. Because of this I gave him a rocket for not being more alert. (There's no rank on a football field.)

It was the following day at pay parade that I found out that the wing man was in fact the pay sergeant. Later the same day I met Mr Jones, who tried his best to get me to sign on as a regular, so I could play for the regiment. Knowing how nothing was guaranteed in the army, I had no intention whatsoever to sign on, so I declined.

I now realise that the very last scheme I did proved to me without a doubt that my usefulness as an OP operator had come to an end. We'd gone out and deployed as always, but this time I was told to report to the gun lines. The OP was some miles away, and the only way to get there was to walk. I got there maybe two hours later. I reported to TSM Watkins that I'd been sent from the OP as being surplus to requirements. After a short pause, he told me to get a Bren gun and go to one end of the gun line and make a Bren pit as if I were covering the flanks of the troop against an enemy attack. I stayed in this position for the rest of the scheme, only moving when grub was up. It seemed very strange that after being in the thick of everything I was now being sidelined as a nonentity. Still, I knew I'd done my little bit, no matter what, in the two years' service I'd given.

After dinner one day I was in the billet when I got duped into going outside on a false pretext. The reason for this was that I had an RHA cap badge; the distinguishing feature was that the wheel on the badge would spin round. I knew immediately I got outside it was a set-up. Like a shot I dashed back inside, only to find the badge missing; in its place was one that just slotted into the beret. It was a joint operation and any one of four people could have had the badge. From now on any spare kit I had did not go to anyone in the billet, nor did anything else of my kit. The gloves went to Sergeant Clay, and a very good set of brushes to a joiner who was working nearby. All the spare cutlery I had was given to others outside the hut.

I had only about a month to three weeks left to do when I next went on leave. I returned, only to find that Dennis had been sent on a pre-demob course of firefighting, somewhere up north, near Barnard Castle I think. Being near his home town he would be only too glad to go. This move meant that I would lose touch with him for some time. We have, however, been very good friends ever since. Some of the other lads had also been sent on pre-demob courses, so I was more or less just kicking my heels.

It would be some time before I could get in touch with Dennis again. Butch Gladwin would be another one I met up with after service. He came up from down south to take photographs of the three bridges at Widnes. Sorry to say, I lost his address when I moved house not long after.

In the final days I said farewell to most of my old buddies, and when the very last day came I went into the Q stores to say goodbye to the sergeant in there. He asked if this was my final day; when I said yes, I was dumbstruck when he asked me if I would mind the store while he went for a NAAFI break. I honestly didn't know how to take what he'd said; then I began to understand that he was giving me an opportunity to take whatever I would like from the stores. The only thing I took was a set of Don R gloves (dispatch riders' gloves). I later realise that I should have taken things that could become memorabilia in years to come, like cap badges, division signs, trade badges and the like – the list is endless.

The sergeant returned, wished me all the best, then, with my discharge papers in my hand, off I set for home. I think it can safely be said that nearly all national servicemen didn't like being in the army at all. The main theme when you listen to these lads reminisce is the waste of time it was and the stupid things you had to do just to survive. Some stories seem unbelievable. It's only another NS man who can confirm their truth and relate to them.

Demobbed and Discharge Papers

The demob papers were in fact a small green booklet. On the front it had the words 'Regular Army' followed by 'Certificate of National Service'. Inside it gave a brief description of the individual including when they started and finished.

0013605

A.B. 571

No.............

(See paragraph 4(b) on page 3.)

Army Number.......23426018

CHARGES PAYABLE BY:—OFFICER I/C ARMY PAY OFFICE, TRANSPORTATION ACCOUNT, ALDERSHOT.

TRAVELLING WARRANT—SECOND CLASS

(This Warrant forms part of the Reservist's Instruction Book and any person making improper use of it will be liable to prosecution.)

CALLING OUT OF RESERVISTS ON PERMANENT SERVICE

The Railways or Steamship Companies concerned are hereby requested to provide for the reservist (who will produce the book referred to above) conveyance by the recognised direct route to the destination station shown on the reservist's Notice of Recall (A.F. D 403) or Notice of Posting for Mobilization (A.F. D 7254).

This demand will be torn off and retained by the Booking Clerk issuing the through ticket as a warrant for the recovery of the fare by the Undertaking concerned.

Stamp of Officer i/c Records

R.A. RECORDS.
FOOTS CRAY, SIDCUP,
KENT.

The Railways and Steamship Companies in Great Britain and Ireland will issue, on this demand, a through SINGLE JOURNEY ticket—

(a) from a station or port in Great Britain, Northern Ireland, Channel Islands, or Isle of Man, or the Republic of Ireland.

(b) to the station or port in Great Britain, Northern Ireland, Channel Islands or Isle of Man being the destination station shown in the reservist's Notice of Recall (A.F. D 403) or Notice of Posting for Mobilization (A.F. D 7254).

TO BE FILLED IN BY UNDERTAKING CONCERNED

Name of Undertaking making claim*................................

Station or Port from which ticket Issued*................................

Destination Station*................................

Route*................................

Number of ticket issued*................................

Date issued*................................ Military Rate £ : s. d.

*To be filled in by the Booking Clerk

17

Printed for H.M. Stationery Office by Cheltenham Press Ltd., Cheltenham
(38421) Wt. 20603/5612 19,000 1/64 417

Army Book 571

ARMY GENERAL RESERVIST'S
INSTRUCTION BOOK

(ISSUED BY ORDER OF THE ARMY COUNCIL)

This book is issued for information and guidance to all men who, being members of the Army General Reserve by virtue of the Navy, Army and Air Force Reserves Acts, 1954 and 1959, have been selected by the competent military authority for IMMEDIATE recall to military service in the event of a NATIONAL EMERGENCY.

It should be read in conjunction with the Notice of Posting for Mobilization (Army Form D 7254).

(See ALSO the instructions on page 2.)

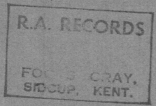

R.A. RECORDS

FO   RAY,
SIDCUP,   KENT.

Stamp of Issuing Office

Any person finding this book is requested to forward it in an unstamped envelope to:—

The Under Secretary of State,
The War Office (MP2),
London, S.W.1.

A 168263

REGULAR ARMY

CERTIFICATE

OF

NATIONAL SERVICE

Any person finding this book is requested to hand
it in to any Barracks, Post Office or Police Station,
for transmission to the Under-Secretary of State,
The War Office, London, S.W.1

Royal Artillery Records,
FOOTS CRAY Sidcup, Kent.

Tel: FOOTSCRAY 3361 EXTN: 38
REF: 3/AGR
DATE: 28 OCT 1965

Dear Sir,

You will of course know that you are liable on mobilizatio
to recall to Army service under the Navy, Army and Air Force
Reserves Acts, 1954 and 1964, but you have not, to date, been t
how and where to report if needed.

It has now been decided that in your own interests and tha
of speedy mobilization your reserve should be brought into line
with the other classes of reserves and be given this informatio

It must be stressed that this does NOT mean that you are
now more likely to be recalled than you were before, nor does
it in any way alter your legal liability to recall.   The
instructions issued with this letter will take effect only in
the gravest emergency necessitating general mobilization, when
the recall of reservists would be notified through the post or
may be given by special announcements over the radio, in the
Press or by other means.

Yours faithfully,

M. A. Runacres.
ED.
for Colonel
Officer-in-Charge,
Royal Artillery Records.
(M. A. RUNACRES)

Mr. A. Balmer

23426018

Military Conduct **VERY GOOD.**

NOTE.—The Range of Military Conduct Gradings possible is :—

  (1) Very Good ; (2) Good ; (3) Fair ; (4) Indifferent ; (5) Bad ; (6) Very Bad.

Page 10
Army
Book
111

Testimonial. *(To be completed with a view to civil employment and to be identical with that on page 9.)*

Gunner BALMER has been an efficient gunner, signaller and infantry soldier during his term with the regiment. He is adaptable and cheerful and proved a staunch soldier on active service in Cyprus. He is a particularly good athlete.

UNIT STAMP

(stamp: "LE CATEAU" FIELD BATTERY 25 FIELD REGT. R.A. DATE.................)

P. Lewis
Signature of CO

Date   6 Oct 59

A Balmer
Signature of Soldier

To be Completed by Unit sending Soldier on Terminal Leave

UNIT STAMP	TERMINAL LEAVE
(stamp: FIELD REGIMENT R.A. OCT 1959 HEADQUARTERS)	begins on 9 OCT 59
	and ends on 1 NOV 59 both dates inclusive.
	Signature of OC Unit
	Date ....

(43274) Wt. 46991—4977 200000 10/56 W.O.P.

On the last page of the booklet (opposite) was a reference to the soldier's service. Mine reads:

Conduct – Very good

Testimonial – Gunner Balmer has been an efficient gunner, signaller and infantry soldier during his term with the regiment.
    He is adaptable and cheerful and proved a staunch soldier on active service in Cyprus.
    He is a particularly good athlete.

I suppose most men received a good report from the officer who wrote them out, so that if their new employer asked about their last job this could always be shown. In my case, I got a job with Pilkington Bros. I'd finished the obligatory medical when the doctor asked what my last job was. When I said I'd just been demobbed, he replied in an exasperated voice, 'Why didn't you say so when you came in the room? Then I wouldn't have needed to give you an examination. The army wouldn't discharge you if you weren't A1.' I got a job even though I was still on a two-week discharge; this meant that if I received any recall I would have to report back to camp and forgo my employment.

I thought that I had completely finished with the army now, but I was very wrong. After a few weeks I remembered that I had not been informed about the polio jab I should have had, so I contacted my own GP and explained to him the problem. He asked for all my details of service and said he would chase up the necessary information. Within a week I was able to get the final jab. A second problem I encountered was from the local Social Security office, which was at Canal Street in St Helens. I received a letter from them informing me that I owed them two National Insurance stamps for a two-week period over Christmas 1958. I took the letter to the office and was confronted by a young girl. I explained that, at the time stated in the letter, I was in the forces in Cyprus serving in a combat zone. However, this fact did not seem to get through to her. The discussion began to get a little heated, to say the least.

She went away almost in tears, bringing back her superior. I went through all the same explaining as before, but still hit a brick wall. I then upset the apple cart altogether, when I asked if the supervisor too, was stupid, because I had been in the army, being paid by the government. She was in a government office asking for a payment that the government should have paid. Even if I had not been in the army, I would still be allowed to be two stamps short in any one-year period. She continued to demand the payment and would not be convinced.

I did not pay anything at all, but received no more letters on the subject, so the matter was dropped. This little snippet only goes to prove that even when serving as a national serviceman you still had to pay national insurance each week if your pay was over a certain amount. This is one huge thorn in the side of ex-service people who are pensioners today, but told they don't fit criteria for better payment.

Another problem I had was because I had a brother with the same initial A as I have. I have only one Christian name, but he had two, giving his initials as AW. Well, unbeknown to me, two letters from the MoD had arrived with the initial A on them. He had picked them up and thrown them on to the fire without opening them. On the third occasion I was standing in the lounge when my father offered the third letter to my brother. He took it and threw it on the fire again, but this time my father grabbed it quickly. Giving it him back to him, he told him to open it and see what it was all about. My brother opened it, read it, then handed it to me, sheepishly saying, 'Here, it's for you.' I took the letter and read that this was a third and final warning: if I did not reply to this letter I would be liable to a six-month jail sentence, or a £100 fine. To say I lost my temper was to put it mildly, but my brother insisted it was my own fault because it had the wrong initial on it. From then onwards any letter with an A on it I opened, no matter whether I was expecting a letter or not. This incident therefore caused problems between us.

I would still receive mail from the MoD up until 1965, telling me that I was now an army reservist and indicating where to report in the event of a further call-up.

The final one I have in my possession told me that in the event of a government announcement, whether by newspaper, poster or broadcast, I was instructed to report to 372 Field rest RA (TA), Kimnel Park Camp, Rhyl, Flintshire, for which the nearest railway station was Rhyl. It is dated: 28 Oct 1965.

Nothing came after this date.

Cyprus Postscript

Even though the peace agreement had been signed in March/April 1959 to end the conflict in Cyprus, some personnel still perished until late in the year, with an eventual total of about 400 killed during the four-year period of hostilities. The EOKA pamphlet shows that all parts of the population were at risk during this period, and that an accurate account of casualties does not exist.

Due to continued disagreement between Greeks and Turks on the island, an invasion by Turkish troops was made in 1974. The British troops on the island were not allowed to intervene and were just bystanders watching Turkish paratroops landing on the central plains, then engaging the Greek forces on the island. This action is the one most remembered in England, giving the false impression to the lay person, that EOKA was a Turkish organisation. It was in fact a Greek-Cypriot organisation, wanting unity with Greece. This left the British soldier in the unenviable position of trying to keep peace on the island while being piggy in the middle.

The Cyprus campaign was the last action outside the UK that national servicemen took part in alongside regular soldiers. On many Remembrance Day services, Cyprus seems to be the one conflict that is omitted, although all other small wars are mentioned where losses were incurred. If people try to play down the role of British forces here, why issue them with a GSM (General Service Medal)? Other troops who received GSMs still receive recognition for the part they had in their particular conflict. The answer may lie in the fact that Cyprus is still a divided island but a popular holiday destination for many thousands of English tourists. However, with Cyprus joining the European Union along with Turkey, recognition may well be on its way.

Glossary

10-Line Exchange	A device for connecting ten telephone lines
B/D	Bombardier (2 Stripes)
BC	Battery Captain
BHQ	Battery Headquarters
BSM	Battery Sergeant Major
Champ	Like a Land Rover but more rounded features with snorkel device fitted and engine encased
CO	Commanding Officer
CP	Command Post
Demob	Demobilisation
Dingo	Small open-top vehicle for scouting the terrain, sometimes known as a scout car
Div Sign	A patch on the arm of uniform depicting a division
Dobie	Washing, i.e. laundry
ETA	Estimated time of arrival
Flaggy	Regimental Signaller
GOC	General Officer Commanding
Gun Park	Area for vehicles when in camp
Gun	Twenty-five pounder gun
Infantry	Foot soldiers
L/B/D	Lance Bombardier (1 Stripe)
Lance Jack	Army Slang for Lance Corporal/Bombardier
Limber	Ammunition trailer
Mess Hall	Dining Hall

Met Rep	Weather report
NAAFI	Navy Army Air Force Institute (i.e. canteen)
OP	Observation Post
Open Order	Ranks step one step forward and or back (three ranks) to enable the officer to inspect
POL Point	Petrol and Oil Depot
Quad	Towing Vehicle of square features
RHQ	Regimental Headquarters
RSM	Regimental Sergeant Major
SGT	Sergeant (3 Stripes)
Small Arms	Rifle, pistol, Sten gun, Bren gun
Stag	A two-hour period of guard duty
TARA	Technical Assistant Royal Artillery
Tiddler	Message giving full information
TSM	Troop Sergeant Major
Wagon Lines	Area for vehicles when in battle

6743130R00155

Printed in Great Britain
by Amazon.co.uk, Ltd.,
Marston Gate.